HILLMEN

HILLMEN:
A History of football in Coquetdale

Jon Tait

Rough Badger Press

For Dad

First Printing: 2017

ISBN 978-1-326-85443-0

Rough Badger Press
Denton Holme
Carlisle, Cumbria.

www.lulu.com/spotlight/Jontait72

Many of the team photos including in this book were scanned from club pictures and newspapers. Mary Scott took a great number of the original images and is credited here for her outstanding contribution in saving teams for posterity. Thanks to Kevin Coe for kindly providing many of the cuttings and Tom Mac-Pherson for match reports from the 2009/10 season.

The Early Years

NOT MANY football teams can claim to have had members of the clergy removing their dog collars in the wooden hut of a dressing room and pulling on a heavy, hessian-like shirt that soaked up water during the game, cuffs hanging down over hands as the strip pulled out of shape in the rain and mud.

But Rothbury FC, deep in the hills of Northumberland, counted a number of the local Church officials in their ranks as founder members of one of the earliest Association clubs in the county. Two of the best players that ever ran out onto the green of the Brewery Field pitch in the village were the sons of the local vicar who went on to become highly-esteemed men of the cloth themselves.

An early captain of the Rothbury team in 1882, Francis Edward Ainger was the fourth son of the Reverend George Henry Ainger, D.D., Hon. Canon of Newcastle and Rural Dean of the Deanery in Rothbury from 1871, who lived at Whitton Tower.

Football was a popular pastime among the gentlemen of the clergy in the village, as the Reverend W.S. Wrenford, the Curate at All Saint's in Rothbury, also played in those early sides.

Francis was capped by Northumberland in 1884 when he played against Cleveland at Middlesbrough with players from the big early Tyneside teams Rangers and Tyne Association. He was also ordained in that year by the Bishop of St. Albans.

His elder brother Walter H. Ainger was another great player that shone in a Northumberland Association Challenge Cup (now the NFA Senior Cup) tie at Bedlington Burdon, which was reported as 'one of the hardest fought games ever witnessed in the district' at the time, so the Ainger brothers could mix it when the going got tough and you have to remember that injuries such as dislocated shoulders were commonplace in the rough and tough early days of Association Football.

Walter was an original member of Rothbury Football Club who went on to play for Cambridge University and Old Carthusians, and was an England amateur International inside-left.

The brothers were playing as possibles in a County Trials match at Bedlington in 1886 with players from the likes of Elswick Rangers and Shankhouse against the probables that had players like Oldham, Taylor and Aitken from West End and Beckett from East End – now known as Newcastle United.

The Reverend Francis E. Ainger appeared on a passenger list sailing to Tasmania that year and the great adventurer and footballer moved out of bonny Coquetdale when he became the Vicar of Sparsholt, Hants in 1893.

He was such a respected member of the establishment that his marriage at St. Paul's in Knightsbright in 1894 to Miss Mary Douglas, the third daughter of the late Right Reverend H.A. Douglas, D.D., Bishop of Bombay, from a respected Scottish family, took him into the Peerage.

His brother and old team-mate Rev. Walter, then the Curate of All Saints' in Newcastle-upon-Tyne, was one of the three officiating clergy. Walter had been educated at St. John's College, Cambridge, where he took his B.A. degree in 1888 and M.A. in 1893.

On the 14th January 1888, Walter Henry Ainger played – and scored the goal – for the South in a North v. South game organised by the FA at the Oval. The North won 3-1. In the return game at Newcastle Road, Sunderland a year later, he was again on target with the winner for the South as they won 2-1. The games were also known as gentlemen against player's games, or amateurs v. professionals, with players from the likes of Notts. County, Aston Villa, Nottingham Forest, Wolverhampton Wanderers, Stoke and Bolton Wanderers turning out for the North while the gentlemen lined up from the likes of Old Brightonians, Oxford University, Swifts, Old Westminsters and Ainger's side, Old Carthusians, who had won the FA Cup in 1881. He'd gone a long way from the navy blue and white stripes on Brewery Field.

Walter trained at Wells Theological College, and was ordained deacon in 1890 and priest in 1891. From 1890 to he was curate of Dereham, Norfolk, and from 1893 to 1898 was curate at All Saints', Newcastle. He then went to St. Augustin's, North Shields. In 1899 he went to St. Nicholas' Cathedral, Newcastle, being there until 1902 when he was appointed Vicar of Prudhoe, then went to All Saints', Gosforth, and in 1910 Haydon Bridge, from where he went to Eglingham in 1924. In October, 1939, he resigned the living at Eglingham on account of ill-health.

Their father, George Henry, who hailed from Saint Bees in Cumbria where his father William Ainger was first principal and was known as the great builder of the College and restorer of the Priory, died at Rothbury in 1886 and a memorial stained glass window was placed in the Church in 1899. The brass lectern in the Church was given by Mrs Ainger as a memorial in 1894.

Francis Edward Ainger returned to the Borders when he became the Rector at Jedburgh in Roxburghshire and he died on 30th October 1905. His eldest son Herbert Cecil Ainger was a Lieutenant in the Royal Flying Corps and the 3rd Battalion, Royal Scots Regiment. He died aged 22 in 1917 during the First World War.

Rothbury's earliest games were friendly fixtures against other local sides such as Alnwick, who were 4-0 victors in Coquetdale in February 1882 in one of the earliest recorded games.

Rothbury, whose official formation date is 1876 and they have a hundred year certificate from the Football Association confirming this, were reported in the Alnwick Mercury as showing some good play for a new club – which brings the date of the foundation somewhat into disrepute.

Rothbury lined up with Brown in goal, F. Worsnop and Caw-thorn, Rev. W, S. Wrenford and R. Donkin, junior, as half backs, A. Underwood, B. Burchell, T. Worsnop, J. Foggan, Green, and A. Benson (the captain and secretary) as forwards.

When the two sides met again two years later, Rothbury were much improved and held the visitors to a goalless draw in an evenly-contested encounter. Alnwick did, however, play with one man short.

Benson did well with some good tackling while Ainger and Green went close a couple of times at the other end but neither goalkeeper really had much to do in a match played with strong wind and showers of hail during the second half.

On this occasion Rothbury had Mitcheson in goal, Benson and Davy as backs; the half backs were Armstrong and Hogarth and the forwards Ainger, Billam, Clark, F Worsnop, Foggon, and Green. That year Newcastle B also played at Rothbury and won 3-1 in a fast and exciting game, where Benson, Davy and J. Worsnop were best for the hosts.

Rothbury also thrashed Bedlington, a newly formed team, in 1883 with A. Benson scoring twice from corners. W. Billam also scored two goals with F. Worsnop and Clive grabbing the others. Rothbury lined up as follows: C. Mitcheson (goal), F. Ainger (capt. and back), A. Benson and W. Armstrong (half backs), W. Billam, T. Worsnop, F. Worsnop, J. Clive, A. Underwood, J. Foggon and J. Green (forwards) and in 1884 they went down 2-0 at Tyne 2nds, with Charlton scoring twice.

With the game developing in popularity in Northumberland at the time, Rothbury travelled to Belsay in December 1886 to play the newly formed club there and came away with as comfortable 6-0 victors.

Each of the five forwards - Mackay, Davy, Worsnop, Ainger and Benson – got on the scoresheet and two more were disallowed. The captain, F. Worsnop was considered the best performer on the day, while John Worsnop refereed the game.

In February 1887, Rothbury sent a weakened side to play against Whittingham, a team composed mainly of young men working on the railway, and won by a solitary goal from their best player – F. Worsnop – while full back T. Tait and half back T. Mackay also received mentions for playing well. Whittingham put on a tea after the match and it was noted that 'a few pleasant moments were passed round the tea table.'

Rothbury won the return match 2-0, a well-placed corner by Benson being rushed home within five minutes and J. Mackay added the second with a 'well directed side shot.' Benson thought he'd chested in a third just before the end, but it was disallowed as time had been called. *Rothbury:* C. Mitcheson, J. Dobson, R. Tait, T. Mackay, T. Murray, G. Hay, J. Green, J. Mackay, F. Worsnop, A. Benson, R. Dobson.

By 1888, when Walter Ainger was starring at Old Carthusians and Francis was on the other side of the world, the Rothbury side had a humbler look with brothers Thomas and Robert Tait, a cartman and labourer respectively, appearing for the Coquetdalers alongside the likes of the Mackays, the Dobsons and the Grieves when John Green hit a hat-trick in a 6-2 win over Glanton at Rothbury. They could have had more, but Glanton's goalkeeper kept the scoreline down by fisting out a number of shots. He was under heavy pressure again in the return match at Glanton in April as Rothbury crashed in eight times without reply, four goals being scored in each half.

Rothbury's side was as follows - W. Curry, goal; R. Tait and R. Dobson, backs; J. Dobson, F. Grieves, and Davy, halfbacks; J. Clarke, A. Benson, F. Worsnop (captain), J. Mackay, T. Mackay, forwards. Umpire, W. Grieves.

Newcastle Wanderers visited the village in 1889, catching the 8.20 a.m. train, which was the only one available during the day. Unfortunately Sadler, who was one the best players on the team advertised, through misunderstanding about the time of starting, missed the train, but an excellent substitute was found in Mr. M. Robinson. The Wanderers occupied their time on arriving at the beautifully situated country town in various manners, such as visiting Cragside (through kind permission of Lord Armstrong), visiting friends, &c.

Having dined, the team changed their travelling garments at the house of Mrs. Robson, and at once made for the field of play. The game started shortly after 2.30, Rothbury kicking off against the wind and hill. In the first half the game was principally confined to the Rothbury half of the field, but the latter's line of forwards was strong, and played well together, though seldom dangerous in front of goal. Out of a rush up by the left wing, however, a good shot only grazed the bar and bounded past into play.

About a quarter of an hour after the start, Davy, of Rothbury, unfortunately sprained his knee in kicking the ball, and was obliged stop playing. Another player was allowed to take his place, and was a worthy successor. Though the Rothbury goal was fairly besieged at times, the backs and goalkeeper stuck to their work well, the latter only allowing two goals to pass him, though another was given off side.

On crossing over at half time, Newcastle held their opponents well in check, and after many attempts and rebuffs, scored again, the Rothbury men only once invading their opponents' backs, and scoring one goal amid great applause. There was a fair attendance of spectators present. The game was played in two thirty-fives. Afterwards, tea was provided by the home team, and due justice to it was paid by the visitors, who, however, had to hurry for the last train at 4.35 p.m. Teams:— *Rothbury*—Goal, Brand; backs, R. Tait and Mackay; half-backs, F. Grieves, W. Rawson, and F. Worsnop (capt); forwards, W. Grieves, J. Mackay (Right wing), A. Benson (centre), A. Richardson and J. Clarke (left wing). *Newcastle Wanderers*—Goal, H. Stowell; backs, J. C. Edminson and G. Urwin; half-backs. Lockey, R. Attridge, and M. Robinson; forwards, J. Grieveson, W. Davidson (right wing), J. G. Burn (centre), W. Greener, and F. Patterson (left wing). Umpires, Mr. Greene and Mr. Mason; referee, Rev. B. Smith.

The same year Rothbury were beaten 3-0 at Ashington, with the Recreation enclosure not in good condition. Rothbury won the toss and elected to play towards the north goal. Ashington kicked off, and some give and take play was the game for the first fifteen minutes, when Ashington began to play better, and the ball from Hunter on the wing was neatly passed to Weatherstone, who put through No. 1 for Ashington.

This seemed to encourage them, and they warmed to their work, and the ball was kept in the visitors' territory for the rest of the first half, and Wood had to save several good shots, but just before the whistle blew for the change, Weatherstone put through No. 2 for Ashington.

After the change, some hard play took place, but Rothbury were unable to wipe out the score, although they played well and hard, but Nelson was equal to everything sent to his goal, and fisted out several times. Some neat dribbling and passing was made by Hunter for Ashington, and Norris played well half back while Worsnop and Ransome played a good game for the visitors, and during the second half Weatherstone scored No. 3 for Ashington.

Teams :—*Ashington*—Nelson, goal; W. Davison and T. Nelson, backs: J. Jackson, J. Weatherstone, and J. Norris, half-backs; J. Rutter, Weatherstone, H. Thompson, G. Bell, and Geo. Hunter, forwards. M. Nelson, sen., umpire. *Rothbury*—J. Wood, goal; R. Tait and T. Mackay, backs: Scott, Benson, and Grieves, half backs; Worsnop, Mackay, Ransome, Dobson, and Clarke, forwards. T. Worsnop, umpire, and J. Waldock, referee.

In November 1891 Rothbury beat Broomhill 5-1 in a fast and exciting game but in February 1899, the Coquetdalers were beaten 3-0 in a match at local rivals Wallington and Blyth 2nds knocked them out of the Minor Cup 7-2 in front of a good crowd at Rothbury.

Later that year a newspaper report was enquiring into the health of Rothbury Football Club and they were pleased to note that they were to play against their old opponents Alnwick. In an interesting little side note that has been the bane of rural football sides ever since their formation, it seems, the writer said: 'Our poor little club has received several heavy blows since last winter, alas, it has always been so. Just when our young players have become skilled players and useful, the stern energies of seeking work have withdrawn them from our ranks and left us weak again.'

A good crowd turned out to see Rothbury beat Longframlington 5-0 in December 1894 with J. McKay (2), Tait, Dobson and Graham scoring the goals.

In the late 1890s there was a fall out between the Northumberland Football Association and the clubs outside of Newcastle, who saw the Association as Tyneside-centric and formed their own breakaway Northern Association.

Rothbury remained on the outside but an interested visitor who watched them beaten 3-1 by Ashington's second string in the village in April 1899 was hopeful that both Rothbury and Ashington would join the Northern 'instead of standing aloof' and 'receiving the cold shoulder from the Newcastle Association.' It was muted that Morpeth Harriers, one of the best sides in the North East at the time, would send a side to Rothbury for an exhibition game if they joined the Northern Association the following season.

'The objects of the Northern Association have always been to encourage and assist local clubs in the country, and all who become attached to it find themselves in a better and improved position. There is little doubt but that the Northern Association will be a power in the county next season, and that its strength is recognised cannot be ignored when we find the Northumberland Association attempting to form an amalgamation,' contin-ued the writer.

A League was formed by the Northern Football Association that year and was divided into four Divisions - the Southern division, the Wansbeck division, the Coquet division, and the Tweedside division. The clubs making up the Tweedside division were Belford, Horncliffe, Tweedmouth, Berwick and Spittal. The champion club of Tweedside were to play the champion of the Coquet division, with the winners being declared the champion of North Northumberland. They would then play the champion of the south for gold and silver medals presented by the Northern Association. The rebellion, however, was eventually quelled and the Northumberland clubs returned to the fold of the Northumberland FA.

In early December 1899 Rothbury suffered a heavy home defeat at the hands of Alnwick Working Men's Club, going down 8-1 in a game played in two halves of thirty minutes due to the late arrival of the visitors. Whinham put Alnwick ahead with a beautiful shot and Benson equalised from a corner – but it was all downhill from there. The hillmen reckoned after that two of the Alnwick players were Scottish professionals.

Mackay played well at the back and the half-backs played fairly well together, although Worsnop did not seem just up to his usual form, whilst Benson as centre was all there. Rothbury 'lacked the combination of the visitors, but with practice they will improve considerably.'

Rothbury: W. Green, goal; F. W. Ross, T. Mackay, backs; H, Storey, F. Worsnop (capt.), Isaac Scott, half-backs; Patton, Soulsby, right wing; A. Benson, centre; J. Mackay, G. Baston, left wing; umpire, J. Worsnop; Referee, Mr J. Sproat, Morpeth.

And Rothbury were left complaining on a very cold return game against Alnwick W.M. Club with the moors covered in snow and ice and a gale that whipped over the pitch – but it was the performance of the referee that gave them most cause for consternation. Although Rothbury were beaten, the reporter considered them the better side on the day and was upset by the 'deliberate fouls and trips of the Alnwick players.'

He was also enraged that they wouldn't stand 10 yards away at kick-off, yet 'claimed ten yards kick from goal on the other hand.' The goalkeeper was running six or seven with the ball, when the rule was to only take two steps, and when this was pointed out to the referee, he ignored it and the Rothbury men 'got disgusted at a lot of this one-sidedness.'

Ambrose Benson, who starred in these early games, was the man with the distinction of being Rothbury's first secretary and captain and was a schoolteacher from Leeds who lived on Bridge Street. The Reverend W.H. Ainger died aged 84 in 1948 – just as Rothbury were making the move to their new and current ground at Armstrong Park on the Cragside estate. The Ainger's and their contemporaries in those early Rothbury sides were true heroes and real gentlemen of the game who should be long remembered by Northumberland's football community for their part in kick-starting the game in Coquetdale.

There was a standing invitation for the two teams to have tea at the Rectory after games, recalled the North Northumberland League Chairman J. Whinham, who was a player in Alnwick's first team in 1879. He said: "Dr. Ainger's two sons and the curate waited upon the teams. It was always a great day going to Rothbury."

A boyhood photo of a young Walter Henry Ainger.

NORTHUMBERLAND ASSOCIATION CHALLENGE CUP
—BEDLINGTON (BURDON) v. ROTHBURY.—These two
clubs having been drawn together in the first round
of the Northumberland Challenge Cup competition,
played off their tie on the ground of the former at
Bedlington on Saturday. After one of the hardest
fought games ever witnessed in the district, the
match resulted in a win for the Bedlington (Burdon)
by one goal to nil, the goal being got from a kick
from the left wing forward (William English). It
would be impossible to pick one man out of the
Burdon team who did more to win than another, as
the whole of the eleven players did their best to gain
a victory. For the losing team W. Ainger showed
most prominently. Messrs. Benson, Billam, and F.
Ainger played in their usual style. Teams:—
Bedlington (Burdon): C. Patterson, goal; W.
Douglass and H. Walker, backs; J. Metcalf and E.
H. Metcalf, half backs; forwards, B. Berkley
(captain) and T. Richardson, right wing; Wm.
English and G. Hindmarch, left wing; R. Thomp-
son and Thos. Reed, centres; S. Davidson, umpire.
Rothbury: C. Hutchison, goal; F. Ainger, back;
A. Benson and J. Davy, half backs; forwards, J.
Green and J. Foggan, right wing; W. Ainger
(captain) and J. Wornop, left wing; J. Clark, F.
Wornop, and W. Billam, centres; J. Armstrong,
umpire; Wm. Wood (North-Eastern Football Club),
referee.

1883 – Rothbury in the Northumberland Challenge (now Senior) Cup.

ROTHBURY.

FOOTBALL—BEDLINGTON BURDON v. ROTHBURY.—
These teams having been drawn together in the first
round of the Northumberland Football Association
challenge cup competition, played their tie off at Rothbury on Saturday last, which resulted in a win for the
Burdon by one goal to nil. The Burdon captain, having
won the toss, decided to play with the wind in his
men's favour. Worsnop kicked off for Rothbury, but
the ball began to travel fast towards the Rothbury
goal. Owing to the strong wind, the shooting for goal
was very erratic. Time after time the ball was kicked
into the Rothbury goal-keeper's hands, who during the
game kept goal splendidly. It was not till thirty
minutes had been played that the Burdon men could
get a goal, and then only by their centre charging the
goal-keeper through when in the act of picking up the
ball. After the change of ends the Burdon men
showed better form, as the forwards made some magnificent runs against the wind the whole length of the
field, Thompson, Young, and Auld being conspicious;
but owing to the defence made by the Rothbury goalkeeper they were unable to score. For Rothbury,
Ainger and Mitcheson, as goal-keeper, played best; as
for Bedlington it would be unnecessary to mention
names, as the whole of the team worked hard with the
exception of Hindmarsh, who was only once called
upon to defend his goal. Teams:—Rothbury: C.
Mitcheson, goal; J. Hutchinson and L. Davy, backs;
C. Hogarth, J. Clark, and J. Dobson, half-backs; W.
Ainger, J. W. Firth, F. Worsnop, J. Green (captain),
and A. Benson, forwards; John Worsnop, umpire.
Bedlington: George Hindmarsh, goal; W. Dougbus
and H. Walker, backs; W. Leach, J. Metcalf, and E.
H. Metcalf, half backs; J. Burton, R. Thomson, (cap-
tain), G. Young, W. English, and J. Auld, forwards;
G. Reay, umpire; M. J. Eden, Newcastle, referee.

1885- Knocked out of the Challenge Cup by Bedlington - again.

ROTHBURY v. TYNE 2ND.—Played on the Tyne
ground, and resulted in a victory for the home team
by three goals to nil. The Tyne winning the toss,
elected to play down, with a strong wind in their
favour. After a good deal of loose play Charlton
scored the first goal from a pass off the left wing by
Pattinson. On ends being changed, the visitors
playing with determination, looked like equalising
matters; but the home backs, playing with judg-
ment, relieved their side, and McNab, with a long
screw, kicked goal No. 2. The ball being started
again, there were some long kicks by both sides,
and after some fast play, Charlton scored again.
The visitors were after this unable to pass the home
half backs, and no further score was made. Teams:—
Rothbury: Mitcheson, goal; Benson and McKay,
backs; Griebes, Firth, and Clark, half backs; T.
Worsnop, centre; Foxgon and Green (captain)
(left wing), and T. Worsnop and Hogarth (right
wing), forwards. Tyne 2nd: Jackson, gaol; Parker
and McCoull, backs; McNab and Maling half backs;
Morrison and Stanton, centres; Pattinson and N.
Bennett (left wing), and Charlton and J. W. Burnett (captain) (right wing), forwards.

Tyne Association was the oldest club in Newcastle, being
formed in 1877. Rothbury visited their Brandling Village ground
at Jesmond here in 1884.

Interestingly, when the Newcastle Scottish Association
formed a club to rival them in 1878, Lord Armstrong of Cragside,
then Sir William Armstrong, accepted the position of President.

FOOT-BALL AT ROTHBURY.—The annual foot-ball play took place betwixt the villages of Rothbury and Thropton, on Tuesday last, and resulted in favour of the former up to the time of the ball being taken up. The playing this year by both parties was of the most severe and determined nature ever witnessed. It has been the topic of conversation for the last six weeks, and the Thropton party did not fail to secure all the strength they could possibly obtain from the surrounding villages; but it was all of no avail, as the Rothbury party, even deficient of strength, easily made it up by their great activity and science in kicking the ball. It is well-known, and likewise admitted by the Thropton people, that the majority of players in Rothbury far exceed them in swiftness of running and science in kicking the ball. The play lasted about four hours, the ball coming to Rothbury about one and a-half miles from the "throw-up." The bailiffs took the ball, and asked if they were all still willing to play. The Rothbury party still determined; but the reply from the Thropton players was that the ball was not to be put down again. Consequently, the Rothbury party had the honour, as they have had for the last thirty-two years, of being proclaimed the winners. The number of

1862, The traditional Shrove football game as reported in the Newcastle Journal.

An original Rothbury 'baa, now held in the Bailiffgate museum in Alnwick.

Shrove Football

BEFORE THE Rothbury Association Football Club was formed in 1876 (or 1881), the village had long played an ancient Shrove Tuesday game of 'futbaa' which was started from a cairn on the hills above the village against neighbouring Thropton. The Rothbury goal, or hale, was the church porch, the Thropton men's the bridge over the Wreigh Burn, with the last married couple in the village providing the ball.

These ancient folk football games were originally contested between the married and unmarried men of the village above the age of 8-years-old, on pain of paying a shilling fine for non-attendance. It was later contested between Rothbury and the men of 'Tattie Toon.'

The Wintrips, Clarks, Robsons, Cairns, Mathers and Turnbulls generally made up a good portion of the old Thropton sides with the Watsons, Mavins, Kidds, Dixons, Burns, Cummings, Aynsleys, Shottons, Foggons and Soulsbys and all getting mentions for Rothbury.

The custom of playing the game had been observed for decades until 1867, when it was discontinued due to windows getting smashed and gardens trampled by over enthusiastic players. There were bitter disputes, too, such as the time the Thropton men were compelled to write in to the Newcastle Daily Journal newspaper complaining that instead of being placed on-top of the cairn, as was customary, a Rothbury man, a bailiff of the Duke of Northumberland, pitched the ball as far down the hillside towards Rothbury as he could to start the game. The Thropton lads also reckoned that they'd been outnumbered two-to-one and offered to play against the best of the Rothbury men with an equal number of their own for £10 a side – quite a considerable sum in 1862.

The Thropton writer – who signed himself 'Fairplay' - requested that 'the Rothbury party fix the day within a month hence, the ball to be placed on the top of the cairn, and the men standing at a radius of 50 yards, and to start by signal, given by a disinterested party, the ball to not less than 6 inches diameter. If the Rothbury men accept the challenge, let it be sent in writing to the Cross Keys, Thropton, as soon as may be; if not, let them from henceforth withhold their boasting ; the Thropton lads are willing to pay for their temerity.'

The newspaper report on the game seems to contradict the Thropton view, however, claiming that they had 83 players to Rothbury's 75 as they (Rothbury) took their 32nd consecutive victory after four hours, the ball travelling around a mile and a half from the 'throw-up.' The Rothbury men then kicked the ball back down into the village amid loud cheers in celebration. For the record, the Rothbury bailiff was Thomas Cummings and Thropton's was William Milburn.

But the traditional Baa' game can be dated even further back to the days of the Border Reivers, when the heidsmen of clans would call a game as a pretext to arranging a raid. The Coquetdale men also played a game against the men from neighbouring Redesdale at Alwinton every year. Before that, a match between Coquetdale and Redewater was played at Harehaugh on the boundaries of Rothbury and Elsdon Parishes, which 'often ended in blows or even bloodshed' as it stirred up the 'ill-blood that existed for centuries' and sparked old Border feuds – with four brothers named Potts keeping the peace.

When the game began to get organised into the modern Association sport, Leagues sprung up all over the county. The North Northumberland League was formed in the Nag's Head in Alnwick on a summer's evening back in 1898. That meeting was presided over by William Hogg of Amble and seven clubs comprised the first season's teams to compete for the League title. The North Northumberland league was to be an amateur competition and the committee wanted to keep it local so players could only be picked from within a three-mile radius of their club's headquarters, which then, as now, was most likely a pub. Broomhill, Alnwick Association Club, Amble Seconds, North Sunderland, Radcliffe, Bamburgh and Amble Blue Star were the founder members, with Broomhill winning the first title, but requiring a re-match on the first Saturday of the next season to confirm it as they had not completed a game against Alnwick during the season. The League was also unearthing local talent and had high hopes for the future of a Broomhill player called Snowball who had impressed in that debut season.

The first Secretary of the NNFL was John Carse, junior, of Amble and the first treasurer was A. Anderson of Broomhill, with W. Chism of North Sunderland taking on both of those roles the following season.

Other early clubs to compete in the first few years of the NNFL included clubs which are still going such as Alnmouth, Wooler, Shilbottle and Embleton Whinstone Rovers and others which are sadly missed like Percy Rovers. Sides such as Rennington, Alnwick St. James's A, Alnwick Caxtonians, Alnwick United and Warkworth were also early trailblazers for organised Association Football in the area.

At Berwick-upon-Tweed in 1901, the Border League was founded, with teams from both England and Scotland taking part in the competition. Eyemouth, Kelso, Coldstream and Duns represented the Scots contingent and Berwick Rangers and Tweedside Albion were the English sides. Albion were holders of the Shielfield Cup and they donated the trophy to the committee for the silverware to be played for. John Elder was the first Chairman with Mr Redburn elected Secretary and Mr Scott the treasurer. By 1904, Percy Rovers and Chirnside had been added to the ranks of the Border League.

In 1902, the Coquetdale League was formed by ten clubs in mid-Northumberland, with Rothbury being founder members along with Amble Black Watch, Amble Saint Cuthbert's, Amble Blue Star, Chevington United, Felton, Warkworth, Shilbottle, Newburgh United and Widdrington. Mr. R. Donaldson of Amble was the first Secretary of the League. By 1906, clubs such as Radcliffe Harriers, Radcliffe Temperance, Sheepwash Rovers and Ashington Excelsior were playing their football in the competition. The East Northumberland League, the Northern Combination and the West Tyne League were also in operation as the game really took hold in the area.

One of Rothbury's earliest League games, in October 1902, saw them travel to Widdrington where they were beaten 4-2 in front of a good number of spectators but they were praised for their performance. The top teams battling it out for the title, however, were the Amble sides Blue Star and St. Cuthbert's who met on Christmas Day in a clash that saw Blue Star run out 1-0 winners in a gale that left the players 'shivering in the blast and grinding their teeth in vexation,' while the ball kept getting blown off the field and far from the action which 'afforded a large amount of amusement for the onlookers' in the large crowd, who left the field at the end in 'anything but good humour, and the referee and the weather got a fair share abuse to finish with.' Some things never change.

In January 1903 Rothbury Football Club were holding their annual Dance in the Jubilee Hall, which was attended by 'upwards of forty-five couples.' The music was supplied by Messrs. Ross, of Harbottle while J. Hill and Ballantyne were the MCs.

It wasn't all fun and games however, and the serious physical nature of the game at the time was illustrated in the October of the next season when Rothbury back James Angus sustained several internal injuries in tackling a visiting Alnmouth forward and 'was conveyed to his apartments in Rothbury, where he is now lying in a critical condition.'

Mr. T. Hill of Rothbury was the referee for a Northumberland Minor Cup game between St. James's and Berwick Rangers in 1904 but was hammered for his nervous performance by both sides after, while Rothbury's first home game of 1907 saw them play North Northumberland League side Alnwick St. James's A and Jamieson cleverly netted for the hosts fifteen minutes into the second half, but it was disallowed. Cummings headed in a Smith corner to put them in front, but Alnwick equalised from a corner themselves. Rothbury also played Amble United in the Minor Cup that year, United beating the 'hillmen' 3-0 but claiming after that it had been 'one of their toughest matches of the season.'

Match details, however, are sketchy from around the time. The Coquetdale Association Football League put a wanted ad in the Morpeth Herald in 1904 requesting two or three good minor clubs to apply for membership and in 1906 and 1907 Rothbury weren't taking part in the League, which comprised the sides Bothal St Andrew's, Linton, Stobswood, Radcliffe Harriers, Amble 'A', Alnwick United, Chevington and Widdrington while the North Northumberland League at the time contained Stobswood, Radcliffe United, Amble West End, Alnwick Aydon Rovers, Felton, Alnmouth, Whittingham, Wooler and North Sunderland.

Rothbury crop up in the records again when they beat Morpeth Old Boys at Rothbury in 1905 and in November 1912 they played a friendly fixture at local rivals Longframlington, but tracking much more from the time has proved somewhat tricky with the horrors of the First World War having a devastating effect on local football.

Rothbury are reputed to have taken some part in the Border League (not to be confused with the Border League around Berwick), which was holding a meeting at Cambo Library in September 1911 for interested clubs. The League Secretary was Mr John Carr of Elsdon Schoolhouse, Otterburn. But finding details of the ill-fated League have proved very difficult and no evidence can be found for Rothbury's involvement; near neighbours Netherwitton had been playing in the Coquetdale League in 1907/08 with a record of played 22 matches, winning 16, drawing 2 and losing just four and were planning to enter the Northumberland Cup the following season.

In March 1903 Netherwitton were beaten 3-1 by Whalton in a friendly but in 1908 they had thumped Hirst Corinthians 6-2 in the Coquetdale with goals scored by J. Robson (2), J. Dunn (2), A. Robson and G. Robson. The Robsons made a great chunk of an early Netherwitton side that lined up: W. Temple, E. Dunn, G. Dunn, W. Robson, B. Gosling, W. Anderson, L. Robson, A. Robson, J. Robson, G. Robson and G. Robson for a game against Radcliffe Harriers in 1909, with the heavy ground for the Christmas Day fixture said to suit the Netherwitton 'heavyweights', suggesting that they had a powerful and tough-tackling team.

In July 1911, Mr J. Trevelyan was presenting the club with medals won in connection with the Border League when they'd topped the table and the local vicar, Rev B. Wilkinson, joked that it 'was good to see the progress in the civilisation of the Border inhabitants, contrasting the raiding of farms with peaceable and friendly football matches.'

The following season their derby rivals Wallington were establishing themselves as firm favourites to take the League title for a second time after two wins over Netherwitton in a week and a victory over Whitehouse. Cambo and Capheaton also had sides in the Border League, which vanished before 1914.

Netherwitton resigned from the Coquetdale League in July 1950.

Netherton Football Club in 1924. They may possibly have been beaten 2-1 by Alnwick in the 1921 Minor Cup, but details on the village side have proved fruitless in tracking down. Players above include Sam Kirkup and Jack and Jim Foggon. *Pic courtesy Ursula Murray.*

SATURDAY, FEBRUARY 4, 1882.

NT

FOOTBALL.

Alnwick
e above
n, Esq.
Linsley,
Watson

assessed
; East

ided by

ALNWICK *v.* ROTHBURY.—A match between the above Association clubs took place on Saturday last at Rothbury, resulting in a win for the visitors by four goals to *nil.* The home team showed some good play for a new club. Teams :—Rothbury: Brown, goal; F. Worsnop and Cawthorn, backs; Rev. W. S. Wrenford and R. Donkin, jun., half backs; A. Underwood, B. Burchell, T. Worsnop, J. Foggan, Green, and A. Benson (captain and secretary), forwards. Alnwick: A. Ross, goal; W. Slater and J. Duns, backs; W. Elliot and G. Tait, half backs; J. Clark, W. Sullivan, Stewart, W. Davis, O. Mackeny, and W. Appleby (captain), forwards.

FOOTBALL.

ALNWICK *v.* ROTHBURY. — A match between the above Association Clubs took place on Saturday last, in the Football Field, Waggon Ways. which resulted in a victory for the home team, by four goals to nil. Teams —Alnwick (goal), A. Ross; backs, W. Slater, J. Duns; half backs, W. Hacket, W Elliott; forwards, Clarke, Sullivan; stewards, W. Duns, G. Mackey; W. Appleby (Captain). Rothbury (goal), Brown; backs, Ainger, (captain), Davy; half backs, Rev W. Wrenford, Mason; forwards, Benson, Cawthorn, Burshell, Fogin, Green, and Worsnop.

1882. Rothbury's first and second games.

The North Northumberland League

BY THE 1920/21 season Rothbury were in the North Northumberland League playing against sides such as Alnwick United, East Chevington, Embleton, Lesbury, Ferney Beds, Felton, Broomhill, West Chevington, Belford, Amble and Alnmouth.

In October 1920 a Rothbury side that lined up Taylor, Aldcroft, Laidler, Hounam, Wood, Dignam, Gibbon, Snowdon, Gregory, Rutherford and Edmondson played up at Scremerston and several threatened to leave the field after a dubious penalty decision, Dignam having to persuade them to remain. They were trailing to a Moffat shot that beat Taylor and went in off the upright, when they had the chance to level from the spot. Gregory took it and scored, but the referee ordered a re-take as two of the Scremerston players had encroached into the box. Gregory's second was saved by Patterson and they went down 3-0, with Taylor, Wood, Gregory, Snowdon and Edmondson, formerly of Haggerston Athletic, the pick on the day. They had a decent side and Rothbury demolished Felton 8-2 in the League that December.

The following season (1921/22) Rothbury were 2-1 winners over Amble in November but with mostly just fixtures and results in the local press, further details are difficult to come by.

In 1922, Warkworth and Radcliffe Excelsior were added to the League and in 1922/23 the North Northumberland League was strong enough to continue with a North and South Division, with Rothbury competing against the likes of Amble in the South section while Belford, North Sunderland, Alnmouth, Embleton, Boulmer, Wooler, Spittal, Scremerston, Craster, Hedgeley, Lesbury and Howick were playing in the North.

The club suffered a tragedy in the 1923 close season when player Rowland Hill, the son of Mr. Hill, a gamekeeper at Bilsmoor, was drowned while bathing in a lake near Crag End, despite the attempts of a companion to save him.

That season Rothbury were playing against the teams above as well as the Duke's School Old Boys, as the League returned to one format due to the collapse of the Southern section – Ferney Beds and Ellington being forced to withdraw into the Ashington League by the NFA and Warkworth and Broomhill being unable to meet the costs of travelling to the far north of Northumberland.

Rothbury beat Spittal Rovers 1-0 in October 1924 despite being without their burly forward George Common, who was wrestling up at the Northumberland Shepherd's Show. Kick-off was delayed as Spittal arrived late and they were unlucky not to go ahead as Rothbury keeper Richards saved well from Purves, who soon after rattled the bar. Rothbury settled in the second half with Nichol backing up the forwards finely in attack, and Arkle and Steel were dangerous forwards. After the woodwork had been struck with Patterson beaten, Milligan got possession and his shot curled away from Patterson's outstretched arms into the net, giving Rothbury their first brace of points of 24/25. Rothbury's side was: Richards; Armstrong and Cairns, Robson, Nichol, and Sewell; Arkle, Gregory, Steel, Milligan and Laing.

But by February 1925, the team was languishing in ninth position out of twelve sides having won four, lost seven and drawn two of their games. Craster were top, followed by Amble, D.S. Old Boys, North Sunderland, Felton, Boulmer, Hedgeley and Embleton, with Spittal Rovers, Wooler and Alnmouth below the Coquetdalers. The following side was beaten 3-1 at Spittal in the April. *Rothbury*: E. Richards, E. Hounam, T. Armstrong, C. Major, R. Nichol, Edmondson, Milligan, G. Common, Y. Shields, A. Laing, J. Gregory. Nichol scored while champion wrestler Common, of

Harbottle, who was 'tekkin' hod' into his 70s, engaged in some 'heavyweight contests' with Rover's defence.

Rothbury weren't competing in the NNFL in the late 1920s but had returned to the League in the 1930s, being in 9th spot out of 11 teams near the end of season 1931/32, with Wooler and Craster below them – Rothbury having played 14 games, losing ten, winning three and drawing one and they again finished in 9th spot out of 11 sides in the NNFL First Division in 1932/33.

The Coquetdaler's team that were beaten 3-2 at Spittal Rovers in the North Northumberland League in February 1934 lined up as follows: H. Tait, E. Cairns, A. Mole, J. Laidler, S. Nichol, P. Fairgrieve, D. Davy, S. Robson, J. Swanston, G. Danby, W. Laidler. Robson netted twice, and although Harry Tait saved a penalty by punching it over the bar and pulled off a few more fine saves during the game, when Swanston was fouled in the box ten minutes from time Mole took the spot-kick at the other end but was denied by a left-handed save from Rovers' keeper Johnson.

Alndales, Rothbury's great rivals in the 1930s.

League Football at Wansbeck: A packed Portland Park for an Ashington game in Division 3 (North) during the 1920s. Below: The DLI trained for trench warfare at Rothbury in 1915/16. Here is the 6th Platoon football team in the village.

Rear: E Cairns, N Nichol, A Harris, J Laidler, T Wilson, S Nichol. Front: E Laidlaw,
D Davy, P Fairgrieve, W Laidler, R Laidler.

1935/36
Honours: Division One Champions

ROTHBURY CLAIMED their first ever silverware with a thrilling winning run-in after Easter to pip Spittal Rovers and Shilbottle to the North Northumberland League title.

In January 1935, the Coquetdale lads went down 3-2 at Spittal's Billendean ground. The conditions weren't great and Rovers went ahead after a few minutes as Demee fired in a low drive. Rovers were well on top and it came as no surprise when Winter netted a second following good play by Dumble. It looked all over when the Black and Whites added a third just before half time through Logie.

But Rothbury hit back after the break and poured forward with Thompson reducing the arrears on the hour. They were given further hope when Davy netted before the end, but Rovers held out to seal the win.

Rothbury's team that day was Harris, S. Nichol, Ballantyne, N. Nichol, J Laidler, Fairgrieve, Thompson, Laidlaw, Davy, W. Laidler, Murray. By the April, when Rothbury won 2-0 at Alndales, the Coquetdale side were in sixth place in the table, having played 17 games, winning six, losing ten and drawing one with 28 goals for and 51 against – Duke's School Old Boys topping the table with 13 wins and just two losses from their 15 games. But Rothbury were to stun local football circles when they lifted their first trophy the following season.

1935/36 started well with Rothbury demolishing Longhoughton 5-2 and in the November they surprised unbeaten League leaders Shilbottle on their own ground with a 1-0 win to shatter the Colliers 100% record. The newspapers claimed Shilbottle looked 'a good thing at home against Rothbury, but they dumbfounded their supporters by being defeated by the only goal of the game.'

Rothbury also missed a penalty. 'This is not the first time this season that the Coquetdale team has sprung a surprise, and Saturday's performance must rank as their best to date,' reported the Morpeth Herald.

Rothbury made the trip to top of the table Scremerston, who had been beaten them at home early in the season, and turned the tables to inflict a sixth straight defeat on the hosts in the January of 1936.

Scremerston hit the woodwork twice through Weddell but found themselves 2-0 thanks to goals from W. Laidler and Fairgrieve, who headed in from a corner. Although Weddell pulled on back, W. Laidler broke away to add a third. Scremerston drew level with strikes from J. Turnbull, and very soon after, G. Thomson, but Laidler, who had been very prominent on the wing for Rothbury, scored twice to put the issue beyond doubt. Two of his four goals were practically walked into the net, the Scremerston defenders claiming on one occasion that ball halt had been past the goal-line. The report noted that 'Scremerston's football was played much too close, and was of little avail against a heavy and strong kicking Rothbury side.' *Rothbury*: Harris; G. Nichol. T. Ballantyne, W. Nichol, J. Laidler, G. Maughan; D. Davy. A, Stephenson, P. Fairgrieve, R. Laidler, W. Laidler.

Rothbury followed up this success with 7-2 win in the return game at Ellingham as they started firing on all cylinders. A 3-1 win over Wooler in March took Rothbury up to second in the table, five points behind unbeaten leaders and favourites Spittal Rovers, but with a game in hand. An unprecedented three games in four days gave Rothbury an impressive six point haul - Good Friday saw Rothbury record a 2-1 success at Alnwick United before they really turned up the heat at the top by beating Spittal 5-2 at Rothbury the following day. A packed Easter fixture list was rounded off with a 5-1 drubbing of Alnwick on the Monday. The wins kept coming after Easter and Rothbury secured their first Championship with a record of played 22 games, of which they won 18, drew 1 and lost 3. Spittal Rovers had been six points clear at the top in April, having won 15 drawn 2 and lost 1 with 71 goals for and 29 against on 31 points. Rothbury were second having played two less, winning 12 drawing 3 and losing one while Shilbottle had six games in hand on the leaders, winning ten, drawing one and losing one. Spittal finished runners-up having won 17, drawn 3 and lost 2.

Captain Tommy Ballantyne received the trophy and medals at the North Northumberland League presentation evening at the Nag's Head in Alnwick, where an interesting discussion regarding the club took place.

The Chairman said that 'it was interesting to note that Rothbury was one the oldest teams the county. He had in his possession old fixture card for 1882-83—the only one in existence - in which Rothbury were then down for fixtures with Alnwick. The old saying "Everything comes to him who waits" was surely justified in this case as without doubt Rothbury had not won out of turn, and hoped now that they had broken the ice, would go from success to success.'

Tommy Ballantyne thanked the chairman for his remarks and said it 'was a pleasure for him to be there as the captain of the first Rothbury team to win any trophy. They all knew how long Rothbury had been playing football, and that it was not before time that they had won something.'

Near neighbours Harbottle applied to join the League for the following season at the meeting, along with Whittle Colliery Welfare, Longhoughton and Swarland.

THE DEFENDING Champions made a good to the new campaign in 36/37 and romped to a 4-0 success at North Sunderland. Pinder Fairgrieve should have given them the lead when he raced clear just before the break, but shot wide. He made amends with the first following the turnaround, when he gave keeper Pearson no chance with a shot just inside the upright. He added his second soon after when he capitalised on a misunderstanding in the home defence and completed his hat-trick a few minutes from time. Within sixty seconds he'd added his fourth after Bertram mis-kicked.

Rothbury: Harris, Ballantyne, Nichol, Underwood. Nichol, Laidler, N. Laidler, R. Laidler, Fairgrieve, Davy, Stevenson.

Rothbury suffered their first defeat in October when Scremerston took the points at Union Park with the outstanding J. Johnston shooting the visitors ahead after ten minutes. Hector Thompson doubled the advantage just before half time when a Dixon shot rebounded into his path

Rothbury 'played fast, robust football' and Fairgrieve, described as 'an Alnwick Town forward' pulled one back with a good goal when he went through the visitor's defence. The Scremerston keeper D. Patterson was 'frequently applauded for daring saves' and Scremerston secured the points when H. Thompson's shot flew over the keeper's hands into the far corner of the goal.

Fairgrieve was later embroiled in a rare tussle with Longhorsley defender Sam Ford in a dour, goal-less fourth round Minor Cup tie that Rothbury won in a replay before going out of the competition up at Scremerston in round five.

Rothbury were reckoned to be 'a smart lot and, if any, were individually cleverer than Scremerston, but they had not the same team spirit and the defence did not knit well together,' on the day. J. Johnston's fast shot gave Harris no chance for the first and while Rothbury looked like hitting back for a while with Laidler and Fairgrieve dangerous, G. Short added a second.

Scremerston centre forward W. Hope made it three from close range before half time with Rothbury pulling one back straight after the re-start as Fairgrieve went through to score. Scremerston withstood late pressure to advance, with Ballantyne, Nichol, G. Laidler, W. Laidler and Fairgrieve outstanding for Rothbury. The side was: A. Harris; T. Ballantyne, G. Nichol; J. W. Underwood, J. Laidler, A. Stephenson; T. Holliday, D. Davy, P. Fairgrieves, D. Hall, W. Laidler.

Rothbury reached the Final of the Alnwick Infirmary (Sanderson) Cup after a 4-0 blitz of Alndales – who went on to lift the NFA Minor Cup in May. Rothbury's defence 'played really outstanding football, noteworthy being Smith and Nichol.' Underwood shot home the opener and Stephenson beat Davidson from close range after a forward pass from Smith for the second. Nichol netted the third with a second-half penalty and Fairgrieve secured the fourth when he intercepted a pass from the left, got past Lough, and beat Davidson.

Rothbury were so close to winning a second title but finished the season as runners-up, just a point behind the Champions Spittal Rovers. Rothbury had played 18, won 13, lost 4 and drew 1 while the Billendean side won 13, lost 3 and drew 2.

Rothbury's 64 goal haul was 11 more than the Champions but they were misfiring in the Final as they stuttered to a goal-less draw with extra-time unable to separate them and Scremerston.

A number of the Rothbury team were away watching the FA Cup Final at Wembley and missed the game at St. James's Park, Alnwick. Rothbury lined up: H. Tait, E. Cairns, S. Nichol, B. Smith, E. Laidler, W. Underwood, D. Davy, A. Stephenson, P. Fairgrieves, H. Hall, N. Nichol.

Scremerston almost won it when Thompson rounded Harry 'Hack' Tait, deputising for Harris in the Rothbury goal, and drove towards the empty net, but Underwood appeared from nowhere to block a certain goal. Tait was also applauded for a couple of good saves to deny Johnson and Thompson. But the two sides couldn't be separated and the Final went to a replay in the September of the following season that Scremerston won comfortably 4-1 in front of a large attendance.

J. Turnbull, Scremerston's centre-half, ran onto a clearance from the Rothbury goalkeeper and drove the ball in with a low, hard shot to make it 1-0. Scremerston increased their lead when a shot from Hope struck the crossbar, the ball rebounding for Roughead to head in. Johnston's well-placed shot made it 3-0. Rothbury centre-forward Hall pulled one back but Thompson rounded things off with the fourth.

1937/38
Honours: Division One Champions

ROTHBURY CLAIMED a second Championship title in 1937/38. The Coquetdalers battled through an early Minor Cup tie at Wooler in October, making only one change with H. Tait replacing Harris in goal – and he pulled off a couple of fine saves to keep a clean sheet.

W. Laidler headed Rothbury in front with the wind at their backs in the second half and bustling centre-forward Moore added a late brace to send Rothbury through.

Rothbury: Tait; Stevenson, Nichol; Smith, Laidler, Underwood; Davy, Fairgrieve, Moore, Hall, Laidler.

Later that month Rothbury annihilated Wallington 10-0 on their own ground in the First Round of the Northumberland Amateur Cup. A 4-2 win at Duke's School Old Boys saw Stephenson fire in a long-range shot, Moore net a low drive and add his second before J. Laidler got the fourth from fully 40 yards.

In April, Rothbury beat Spittal Rovers 2-1 with both sides missing from the penalty spot and they went on to secure a second North Northumberland League Championship, winning 11 of their 18 games, losing three and drawing four to beat Alndales into second spot by two points. Rothbury crashed in 50 goals during the League season and conceded 29 with Pinder Fairgrieve writing himself into Coquetdale football folklore.

THE CHAMPIONS didn't make a great start to the new season in 1938/39, losing two and drawing one of their opening three fixtures to sit in ninth place in the table. Also competing in the North Northumberland League at the time were Felton, who led the early running, old rivals Scremerston and Spittal Rovers, Wooler, Radcliffe, Belford, Longhorsley, Alndales, Shilbottle and Acklington RAF. The likes of Swarland and Brinkburn had teams in the Second Division and an unfamiliar Rothbury side lined up- Murray, Stevenson, Nichol, Walker, Hall, Underwood, Phillips, Davy, Fairgrieve, O'Hare and Laidlaw in a 1-0 defeat at Spittal Rovers in September.

In January, on a frozen and frosty pitch, Hall struck twice with fast, powerful shots in a 2-2 draw with fancied visitors Radcliffe. Laidlaw picked him out unmarked with a centre for his first, and his shot was fired in with the left foot from Davy's centre. Radcliffe's wingers Young and the dangerous Handyside hit the replies.

Belford came away from Union Park with the points in March as they secured a 3-2 win in front of only a handful of spectators in heavy rain. A goal from Batey gave Belford the lead and although Laidler, switched from his normal left wing position to the right, was unlucky with a shot that cannoned off the woodwork, a defensive error let in Henderson to drive the visitors further ahead.

Nichol was pushed forward in an attempt to salvage something from the game and after beating Nair set up Davy to slam in a fast shot. Nichol himself grabbed the equaliser after the break with a rising shot that crashed off the bar and was deflected into the net for the equaliser. Batey grabbed what proved the winner when he headed in from a narrow angle. The Rothbury side for the game was: N. Temple; B. Smith, S. Nichol; W. Walker, J. Green. W. Underwood; W. Laidler, H. Hall, D. Davy, A. Stephenson, A. Mills.

After crashing 5-0 at Alndales in the Sanderson Cup – and losing 2-1 to them in the Amateur Cup - they suffered another heartache over the Easter weekend as Alndales came down to Union Park and thumped them 4-0 in front of a good crowd. Rothbury included new left winger Bell and Howey, who was only 15 years of age. 'Making his debut he showed some neat touches and ought to improve with experience,' the report noted. Rothbury's side was: Tait; Nichol, Smith; Walker, H. Hall, Underwood; Davy, Laidler, Stephenson, Howey, Bell.

Tait made a good double save though Armstrong returned the ball for Jefferson, whose cross shot was again saved by Tait, but Drysdale ran the loose ball in from close range. Jefferson drove the second home well out of the keeper's reach and the same player later headed in the third. Jefferson was brought down by Nichol, but Tait pulled off a spectacular save to parry J. Gray's resultant penalty wide.

Gray made amends later when he smashed in Armstrong's centre off the underside of the bar. The game ended in a melee as two of the Alndales forwards fouled Tait and Smith ended up being sent off three minutes from time.

The matter didn't end there – Smith was hauled in front of the NFA North and North East Disciplinary Committee at the Queens Head in Morpeth for an offence of 'dirty fouling.'

The referee, W F Lillico of Alnwick, said: "The player was cautioned for tackling an Alndales player when the ball was dead. About three minutes before the final whistle the Rothbury goalkeeper was fouled by an Alndales forward. I blew the whistle for the foul. This player ran up and put the penalised player on to the ground by charging him in his back. He anticipated what was going to do and he said; 'Go on...you can send me off the field.' and I did so.'" Smith replied that in the first incident he simply gave the winger what he would call a 'country charge.'

"The second incident happened when there were two of the Alndales players at our goalkeeper," he went on. "The whistle to my knowledge had never gone, and I rushed in and charged the man with my shoulder. As far as I am concerned the ball was not dead and the whistle had not gone. The referee ordered me off and I took my order straight away."

Mr J. Monaghan, secretary of the Rothbury club, spoke in support and the Rothbury linesman said the whistle was just as the two players met.

"There was no ill feeling in the game whatever," said the player. "I have nothing against the Alndales. They are a lot of fine fellows."

When Smith was told he would be suspended for seven days and fined, he said; "I have no intention of paying any fine. You can suspend my football career. I have a football career of nearly 20 years and I can come out of the game without a blemish."

The Chairman replied: "We will see that when the time comes. You will be suspended until the fine is paid."

With one game to play in May, Rothbury were languishing in seventh spot with 17 points from their 19 games – winning 7, losing 9 and drawing 3. Radcliffe – who also lifted the Sanderson Cup - had completed their fixtures and topped the table with 28 points and only Alndales, who trailed by a point with a game to play would be able to ruin their title celebrations.

But celebrations were the furthest thing from anyone's minds as events began to unfold in 1939 with many men from the village – including the majority of the football team – becoming embroiled in the Second World War and suffering unthinkable atrocities at the hands of the Japanese as Prisoners of War in the Far East.

NO DECISION IN RUNCIMAN CUP REPLAY

BRINKBURN (h), 1; CHRISTON BANK, 1.— That these teams are well-matched rivals was testified on Saturday, when they shared two goals in their replayed tie. Their first meeting in the competition took place on the visitors' ground four weeks previously, when a goalless draw was the outcome. Having the advantage of their own ground, it was expected that Brinkburn would account for the Bank. They might have succeeded but for brilliant play by the visitors' defenders, who effectively repulsed a series of determined onslaughts by the home attack in the closing stages.

Brisk play was served up by both sides during the opening phases, and Harris, the home custodian, distinguished himself by some fine goalkeeping. Gibson, the home centre-half, was showing his worth as a craftsman, and was instrumental in the launching of many inspired attacks, but the visitors' defence was in formidable mood, and held out under severe pressure. The first half had been evenly contested, the finishing of both sides leaving much to be desired.

The second half opened with the Bank pressing hard. Campbell had a terrific drive stopped by Harris. The exchanges now became very keen, and some really fast play was witnessed. The Bank took the lead about midway through the half, when LUKE converted a well-placed centre by Varnham. However, the visitors did not hold on to their lead very long, for it was only 10 minutes later that Brinkburn were awarded a penalty, through which they equalised, LAIDLER being the scorer. This success rallied the home side to greater efforts, and they forced several corners. The Bank defence was now undergoing a severe test, and it was largely through the fine goalkeeping of Murphy that it survived many furious onslaughts.

Taking the game on the whole, the result was a fair reflection of the play, the defenders carrying off the honours.

Brinkburn were best served by Harris, Tait, and Gibson, while Murphy, Bell, Cockburn, and Ford were prominent in the visitors' ranks.

Teams:—Brinkburn: Harris; Tait, Ferguson; Walker, Gibson, Stevenson; Redpath, Clark, Arkle, Robson, Laidler. Christon Bank: Murphy; Bell, Mattches; Ford, Maxwell, Cockburn; Campbell, Luke, Liddle, Hall, Varnham. Referee: Mr T. L. Murphy.

Local football was booming during the 1930s. There are some familiar names lining up in this Brinkburn F.C. side that was playing in the Second Division of the North Northumberland League in 1938 against the likes of Beadnell, Whittle Colliery, Swarland, Bamburgh and Craster Rovers.

Brinkburn were holding a whist drive in aid of the football club as early as 1919. They were beaten 14-0 by Alnwick United in the NNFL in 1920; on the same day Rothbury beat Warkworth 8-1.

Brinkburn player F. Moffatt was also in hot water with the Northumberland FA in March 1939 after he'd been reported by Referee G. Gerner for 'using filthy language and refusing leave the field.' The referee stated that about eight minutes from time he had occasion to award a free-kick in the game between Brinkburn and Ellingham in the Runciman Cup. On giving his decision, Moffatt made use of a filthy expression. He asked the other for his name and, being refused, told Moffatt that, 'he would give him two minutes to get off the field.' As the player did not go off within that time, he stopped the game.

Later he asked the Brinkburn captain for the name of the offending player and was told that the captain did not know the player's name. William Hardy, secretary for Brinkburn, stated that he considered that the referee had treated his players badly. He was running the line, but he never heard referee Gerner order Moffatt off, though it was correct that the latter refused his name when asked. The player Moffatt was ill. Moffatt was fined 5s., and suspended from playing football for one month dating from Monday, March, 27th, and ordered to pay the referee's expenses.

The Brinkburn side that were beaten 3-0 at Ellingham in the Cup tie lined up – Harris, Moffatt, Arkle, Tait, Laidler, Mole, Laidler, Millar, Laidler, Watson, J. Tait.

Brinkburn's NNFL Division Two opponents Craster Rovers pictured above and Ellingham below in 1937.

Rothbury FC Championship side 1935/36: Rear: Jack Monaghan (Secretary), Ernie Cairns, Norman Nichol, Albert Harris, Jim Laidler, Alfie Stephenson, Sam Nichol, Joe Maughan (Chairman). Front: Willie Laidler, Percy Fairgrieve, Tommy Ballantyne (Captain), Willie Underwood, Denis Davy. *Courtesy George Tait.*

LONGWITTON, ROTHLEY, AND DISTRICT HORTICULTURAL SOCIETY.

THE Eighteenth Annual EXHIBITION will be held in a Field at Longwitton (by the kind permission of Mr. T. Snowdon), on Saturday, 14th September, 1901. The following items will take place during the afternoon :—

A FOOTBALL MATCH between Netherwitton and Wallington Clubs. (Silver Medals to be presented to the Winning Team.)

Wallington's first trophy. They scored twice near the end to win 2-0.

After the War

THE COQUETDALE LEAGUE was re-organised in September 1946 and Rothbury joined up along with ten other teams - Felton, Meldon, Newton -on- the-Moor, Wallington, Morpeth St. Georges, Netherwitton, Thropton, RA.F. Morpeth Unit and Bothal Barns Rangers.

Rothbury drew 1-1 with Wooler in the Alnwick Infirmary Cup in January of 1947 and by the end of the new season they'd drawn with Felton in the Final of the Medal Competition, requiring a replay the following season to decide the winners which Felton won 3-2 – B. Smith with a penalty and Anderson the Rothbury scorers.

Felton won the re-formed League and Morpeth St. George's were runners-up, with Radcliffe Welfare winners of the Hospital Cup. The secretary, Mr. J. Noble, reported a successful season from both financial and a playing point of view. The season started with eleven teams, but Bothal Barns Rangers resigned in the middle of the term. There were 375 players registered during the season. Two new applicants for admission the league were accepted —Morpeth Villa and Ashington West End.

The Coquetdalers played in front of a bumper crowd of 700 as they were beaten 2-1 at Broomhill by Radcliffe on a Monday night in the first post-war Morpeth Cottage Hospital Cup competition. The game was played at a fast pace with Smith and McLennan doing well in the Rothbury defence.

Two goals in six second half minutes won it for Radcliffe – Handyside and Spears netting. Mills pulled one back in the 61st minute with a header following good work by former Morpeth Town player J. Gregory. Anderson almost equalized in the final minute, but his shot was turned over the bar by keeper Davis.

Rothbury came mighty close to lifting the title silverware the following season, 1947/48, having to play Ashington West End in a deciding game for the Championship and finishing as runners-up.

Things weren't all plain sailing, however, and in December 1947 Rothbury crashed out of the Minor Cup in the third round with a 9-1 hammering up at Wooler, but the report claimed that the scoreline didn't really reflect the way they'd played with Wooler snapping up their chances. Chisholm netted five times.

Rothbury beat derby rivals Thropton 4-2 the following month to go fourth in the table, two points ahead of Thropton in fifth. Felton were top, followed by Ashington West End and St. George's. Below the Coquetdale teams were Morpeth Villa, Widdrington, Longhorsley, RAF, Wallington, Meldon and Netherwitton propped up the League.

A couple of Rothbury players made the Coquetdale League representative team to take on the Bamburghshire League on the Easter Monday, with the squad comprising of R Jobson (Felton); J Quinn (Meldon), J Birkley (Felton); J Dawson (Morpeth St. George's), J Laidler (Rothbury), J Jester (Ashington W.E); R W Mullens (St. George's). W Holmes (Felton), S. Turner (Felton). J G Wilson (St. George's), G Winter (Thropton). Res: R Laidler (Rothbury), A Gordon (Longhorsley), N Clark (Wallington). The team's colours were maroon shirts and blue shorts.

Felton beat Rothbury 3-0 in the semi-finals of the Extra Medal competition in front of a large crowd at Longhorsley. Holmes hit the first from a good cross by Hall. A few minutes later Turner broke through to score Felton's second. Rothbury showed their fighting spirit to hit back and Felton keeper Jobson was kept busy for some time. A penalty was awarded for Rothbury, but Jobson scrambled the ball out. A melee in the goalmouth followed and the ball was forced into the net, but the referee awarded a foul. Felton's forwards played good football during the second half, Holmes in particular being top form. Atkinson, in the Rothbury goal, saved his side from heavier defeat, but had no chance to stop a hot shot from Hall. Mills and Butters were outstanding for the Rothbury side, and Gordon and Holmes put up a good show for Felton, who went on to beat Ashington West End with a late goal in the Final.

By the 30th of April both Rothbury and Ashington West End had completed their fixtures, giving both sides a two-point lead over Felton at the top and with the League not deciding things on goal average, a deciding game was arranged between the two teams with a six o'clock kick-off on the Saturday night at Felton.

In front of a large and excited crowd, Rothbury put the Ashington goal under pressure from the start and went close as Ramsey's shot was turned around the upright by Ashington keeper Slaughter. With West End deploying an offside trap, Rothbury were often frustrated and when they did get through, Slaughter showed a save pair of hands to deal with everything that came his way – but Rothbury did almost make the breakthrough when Laidler beat the stopper, but J. Robinson cleared off the line.

The low evening sun was causing Rothbury's defenders a few problems and Soulsby shot Ashington ahead following a mistake at the back caused by the dazzle. Johnson added a second with a powerful shot that keeper Atkinson didn't even see.

Gregory's long, dipping shot went just wide as Rothbury tried to get back in the game and Frazer cleared off the goal-line after Slaughter had fumbled a shot.

Ashington added a third through Lister when he followed up a sliced clearance and Alderson headed in a Richardson cross for the fourth. Mills and Butters were the outstanding Rothbury players in a side that lined up: Atkinson, Butters, Arkle, Ramsay, J. Laidler, Davison, Gregory, R. Laidler, Anderson, Mills, Swan.

1948/49
Honours: Coquetdale Challenge Cup Winners

Rothbury picked up some silverware in the shape of the Coquetdale Challenge Cup with a surprise win over Longhirst at Morpeth Sports Stadium.

A Saturday night visit to Ashington West End's Noble's Field saw them hit for six in the October of 1948. The newspaper report however noted that 'Rothbury were real sports and never played like a beaten team,' and Belford's German goalkeeper Delowski put in an inspired performance as the North Northumberland side knocked Rothbury out of the Amateur Cup 5-1.

By the January of 1949, Rothbury had turned things around and beat the League leaders St. George's 3-2 in a game that 'proved a battle of excellent defences opposed to poor forwards until ten minutes from the end when the position was entirely reversed and four more goals were added.'

Rothbury were ahead at half time but Morpeth turned things around with two late goals. A defensive slip let Rothbury's speedy centre forward in to equalise and, with just two minutes to go, the Rothbury 'left-winger put across a centre and, to his delight and astonishment, saw the ball curl into the far top corner of the net give Rothbury their third winning goal.' Outstanding for Rothbury were Old Barney (Smith) at fullback and Laidler the centre-half who kept Wilson quiet for most the game. The left-winger that netted the late winner was an unfortunately un-named schoolboy.

And Rothbury put a halt to Meldon's winning run in March as they held them to a 2-2 draw at North Side. Anderson shot over from a Winter cross, a defender cleared from Mills and Winter himself went close as Rothbury pushed on a heavily waterlogged pitch. Butters, Rothbury's left back, dribbled through from the halfway line towards the penalty area and was brought down by Dunn outside the box, but the resultant free-kick was cleared. Soon after, Winter, the Rothbury outside-left, collided with the home right back, Quinn, and had receive attention but resumed shortly after. Butters had a shot that looked a certain goal had it not struck Anderson on the head as he was in the act of rising from the ground and he was knocked out by the blow. It was end to end stuff and Wilson drilled in a low shot from 18 yards that beat Atkinson in the 57th minute to open the scoring.

Rothbury equalised in the 70th minute when Anderson's shot came back off an upright and Mills set up Winter to score from the rebound. They went ahead as Winter went away down the left, the winger beating Quinn on the run and scoring from a very acute angle. Rothbury were down to nine men through injury when Scott levelled two minutes from time, shooting in from just outside the penalty area. *Rothbury*: Atkinson, Aynsley, Butters, Ramsey, J. Laidler, Carruthers, Sheale, R.Laidler, Anderson, Mills, Winter.

Rothbury turned the tables and went into the semi-finals of the Challenge Cup by thrashing Meldon 9-2.

Anderson and Mills combined with the latter firing in a low ground shot for the first. Anderson was again instrumental as R. Laidler netted the second. Anderson added the third and Mill's notched the fourth with an overhead kick.

After the fifth went in, Anderson added his second for number six. Mills hit two more for seven and eight and Butters put away a penalty to complete the rout. The side lined up: Atkinson; Smith, Butters, Ramsey, J. Laidler, Carruthers, Aynsley, R. Laidler, Mills, Winter, Anderson.

They were back among the goals again in a 5-1 demolition job on Felton in March.

Anderson set up Mills to put Rothbury ahead and from a free-kick for a foul on Ballantyne, Aynsley centred for Anderson to score Rothbury's second minutes later. J. Laidler, son of Rothbury's veteran centre-half, was playing his first league game and was showing great promise. 'Playing at left-half he was holding Felton's right wing and finding time set his own left wing going.' From one of his passes, Mills received the ball about the centre line and beat all opposition only for Anderson given offside. Ternant pulled one back in the 40th minute but at the other end Anderson just missed with an overhead kick. Rothbury increased their advantage in the 55th minute as good play between Winter and Mills ended the latter potting in a fast ground shot which went off the post. Mills then put through Winter and his cross was converted by Anderson four minutes later. Mills headed Rothbury's fifth goal after 75 minutes from a corner. The team was: Atkinson; Smith, Butters; Ramsay, Carruthers, Laidler; Aynsley, Ballantyne, Anderson, Mills, Winter.

A fortnight later and Rothbury beat Longhorsley 4-0, with four of Longhorsley's players failing to turn up. Mills put Rothbury in front after ten minutes. Anderson added the second ten minutes later from a R. Laidler centre. The third came when Mills' centre was headed into the goalmouth for Anderson score from close range. R. Laidler had a hand in the fourth two minutes after half time as Anderson took his cross and put Mills through to score.

Rothbury left it late in their 2-0 Coquetdale Challenge Cup semi-final win over Netherwitton at Felton on Easter Monday. With full time fast approaching in what appeared to be heading for a stalemate, Mills went through on his own and was pulled down, Butters making no mistake from the penalty spot and Mills himself added a second just before the end to seal the victory. *Rothbury*: Atkinson: Smith, Butters; Caruthers. J. Laidler, Aynsley; Winter, Mills, Anderson, R. Laidler, Ramsay.

Rothbury then took on Wallington in the Coquetdale League and blooded four young players that had been playing well in the reserve side.

'The experiment proved highly successful and though the home team went down 3-2, the experience gained by these young players should stand them in good stead later on,' the report stated.

Ballantyne had cleared a Kell shot off the goal-line before Anderson shot Rothbury in front in the 35th minute with a low drive. Kell beat Butters and netted the equaliser for Wallington after 46 minutes play and in the 55th minute Wallington took the lead when a loose ball deceived Butters who expected it to cross the goal-line. Atkinson ran out to clear, but Parker secured possession and immediately centred for Kell to shoot into an empty net. Kell completed his hat-trick with the third on the hour following a goalmouth scramble from a corner.

R. Laidler pulled one back with ten minutes to go as he got the ball and went on to beat Telfer. With two minutes to go Rothbury almost equalised; a cross from M. Tait on the left was pulled down by Anderson and from a very difficult angle he shot against the crossbar with the 'keeper well beaten. The two sides were as follows. *Rothbury*: Atkinson; Aynsley, J. Laidler, jun.; Ramsey, Butters, Ballantyne; A. Tait, R. Laidler. Anderson, Mills, M. Tait.

Wallington: Telfer; Storey. Stamp; Batey, Johnson, Moffit; Grey, Simpson, Kell, Kennedy, Parker.

Although Rothbury had started the season not too well and suffered a number of set-backs before Christmas, they found their feet in the heavy going of February and March. Although their title chances had faded by then, 'their aspirations for the Challenge Cup were no secret among the other clubs in the league. After carrying everything before them in the preliminary rounds, Netherwitton gave them hard game in the first semi-final, and when it became known that had mastered Morpeth St. George's in extra time in the second semi-final, it was freely predicted that the final would he a battle royal.' This did not really materialise, but Rothbury lifted the Challenge Cup with a 1-0 win over Longhirst at Morpeth Sports Stadium.

In the first half, just after Longhirst had missed a good opportunity, Aynsley dribbled down the wing and crossed for Mills to head in the winner and although they had to withstand some pressure after the break, Rothbury held on for the win. The Red and Whites had a reputation as one of the most consistent teams in the Coquetdale League, while just missing out on honours, and their reputation in the Cups was the same. Winter's cross was met by Laidler, who rattled the bar as Rothbury almost increased their advantage. Aynsley was doing well on the right wing and it often took the combined efforts of Tully and Learmouth to keep him quiet – though he did fire in a cross that dropped onto the bar and ran along the woodwork before dropping out of play to great excitement on the sidelines.

Longhirst almost levelled when Turnbull and Bell got the better of Carruthers, but old Barney Smith battled his way through to block with his body. At the other end, Laidler span fired in a snap-shot with Longhirst keeper Hogg making one of the saves of the game to turn it around the foot of the post. Rothbury stood firm to take the Cup.

In handing over the trophy to Rothbury captain Anderson, Mr. G. Gordon, chairman of the League, complimented both teams upon a very fine game. He had been associated with the League since 1925 and it was very pleasing to find that two of the oldest clubs in the tournament had qualified for the final and had put up such a clean and interesting game. They had both tried to carry out the traditions of the Coquetdale League, and though he had seen many a classical game in higher spheres, he had never seen a cleaner one nor one which had held the interest until the last minute. In recent years Rothbury had been very unfortunate in just missing honours, but this year they had won the Challenge Cup and Longhirst had given them a really good game for it.

After the Rothbury captain had accepted the trophy, the chairman of the Rothbury club remarked that the winning of the cup would give the club, players and supporters every encouragement to go forward with their plans to encourage football in the district, and he warmly congratulated the Longhirst team for the clean game they had played and hoped that they might be the winners next time.

The Longhirst defence looks on in horror as Mills' header finds the back of the net to win the trophy.

Jimmy Anderson, the Rothbury captain, receives the Coquetdale League Challenge Cup from Mr. G. Gordon, the league chairman.

1949/50

Rothbury Football Club were busy preparing their new playing field at Cragside Park in April 1949 and it was expected to be ready for the beginning of the new season. The scheme, which cost in the region of £500, included the removal of the turf, levelling the ground and replacing the turf. Thanks to volunteers the grass was rolled and lifted at the week-ends and during the evenings. A pavilion was also erected for the use of the home and visiting teams.

Tommy Ballantyne was very instrumental in raising funds for the new pitch by running whist drives every Thursday night for around four years, which brought in hundreds of pounds to the club kitty and together with donations for £100 being received, the total cost was almost assured. Tyneside giants Newcastle United donated £25.

The newspaper reports reckoned that when it was finished it would be one of the finest local football grounds in Northumberland with its natural grandstand on two sides, also being very accessible, on the main Rothbury to Morpeth bus route.

Jack Monaghan's 27 years' service as Secretary to Rothbury Football Club was officially recognised at the Northumberland Football Association's annual dinner that year in Newcastle. Mr. Monaghan was presented with a suitably inscribed plaque, in appreciation of his long service to football. Before taking over the duties of secretary, Mr Monaghan was a member the Rothbury A.F.C. committee for many years. During the Second World War when football was almost extinct he arranged friendlies with Army teams stationed in the locality. While Mr. Monaghan never played football himself, all the hard work he had put in was solely the pleasure of others, except that he got great thrill out of being a spectator. He was also a key mover on the new pitch, while the club also commemorated the occasion with Vice-President Mr. Jack Tait presenting a clock.

Rothbury began the season in the First Division of the Coquetdale League competing against Longhirst, Ashington West End, Wallington, Netherwitton, St. George's, Widdrington, Thropton, Ellington Village, Longframlington, Felton and Morpeth Villa with a reserve side in the Second Division, comprised completely of reserve teams.

The first League game on the new pitch at Armstrong Park saw the Challenge Cup holders take on the League Champions, Morpeth St. George's, in an exciting game that saw the visitors win 4-2.

There was a large crowd in attendance and they weren't disappointed by the quality of the football on show, Rothbury twice fighting back before St. George's won it with two late goals.

Rothbury were worthy winners when they beat Morpeth Villa at the Sports Stadium in Morpeth with a disputed penalty reckoned to be the turning point in the game in the November.

Villa chalked up the first goal after five minutes when Townsend beat Atkinson from a pass by Davidson. The hosts increased their lead when Hope added a second.

But Rothbury hit back and when they were awarded a spot-kick, left full back L. Butters made no mistake. A strong wind was swirling around the pitch which affected both teams, who struggled to judge the true flight of the ball.

Rothbury found top gear after half time, however, and Mills scored the best goal of the match to equalise. The third came from the right when a cross was swung over and Villa keeper Williams had the mortification seeing it curve into the net. Near the end of the game a defensive misunderstanding allowed Anderson to seize his opportunity to flash the ball past Williams to register Rothbury's fourth goal.

Anderson put away a hat-trick as Rothbury romped to a 7-2 win at Felton. The skipper set up Dick Laidler for the first and soon after, Dick Laidler's shot stopped in a pool of water and Mills had the simple task of tapping it in. A Butters penalty was splendidly saved by home keeper Brooks but Anderson added the third with a long range shot that the keeper misjudged.

He added his second with a cross shot from ten yards and Mills made it five after a neat interchange of passes.

R. Laidler followed up to score after the keeper parried a shot and Anderson completed his treble before Clough had to pick the ball out of the net following a penalty taken by Kitchen.

By January 1950, Rothbury were eighth in the 14 team League having played 12, won 4, lost 6 and drawn 2 with 35 goals for and 36 against. Local rivals Thropton were in 12th, having won 2 lost 10 and drawn 3, with 18 goals for and 34 against. Wallington were languishing below them, having won 3, lost 11 and drawn 1 with 19 goals for and 44 against.

Two goals in three minutes gave Rothbury a narrow 2-1 success over Longframlington as they came from behind to take the points. J. Halliday shot 'Fram in front but Rothbury got back on terms when Aynsley headed out to Tait, whose centre was met by Anderson, who banged the ball into the net well out of keeper Hedley's reach. Soon after, Mills collected a pass from D. Laidler and ran on to put away the winner.

The Rothbury side that romped to a 6-0 win over Felton in February 1950 lined up as follows: Clough, Smith, Butters, Aynsley, J. Laidler, R. Laidler, Arkle, D. Laidler, Anderson, Mills, Tait. Anderson gave Rothbury the lead at the interval and they piled on the pressure following the turnaround, with Mills adding two more, R. Laidler striking and Anderson going on to complete another hat-trick.

Rothbury played host to St. George's again in a Challenge Cup tie that was reckoned to have been one of the best games seen all season in the Coquetdale League.

Both teams were on form and played all-out for the entire game and Rothbury were a little unfortunate not to force a draw, but St. George's had that extra luck which makes all the difference between win and lose in cup football. The pitch itself provided contrast as one side was marshy while the other bone dry and it was a tribute to the fitness of all the players that the pace never slackened during 90 minutes under the conditions.

S. Relph shot St George's ahead in the first half but Rothbury, the holders of the Cup, came more into the picture in the second half and play went from goal to goal with many near misses and much excitement on the part of the spectators.

St. George's increased their lead after 10 minutes when Trewick, the right winger, nodded pass from Dymond down to his feet and made no mistake from 15 yards. This spurred Rothbury and after a period of sustained pressure a goal came from their left winger, Winter, after good work by Anderson and Mills.

Soon after this the St. George's left half Neil was knocked out and had to be carried off after heading a hefty kick from veteran Barney Smith. This left St. George's with only ten men

for the last 25 minutes but they were not downhearted and pro-
ceeded add another goal when Dymond 'sent in whizzbang shot
which the 'keeper held, but could not stop and both the ball and
he went into the net.' With the heavy leather balls that soaked
up water at the time, it wasn't an unusual occurrence.

Rothbury went all out reduce the deficit and succeeded in
doing so when they were awarded a penalty. Anderson took the
kick and gave Spurgeon no chance. During this period St.
George's owed a lot to the brilliance of Spurgeon, who put up a
display 'which would not shame a First Division team.'

In March the League leaders Ellington came to the village
and left with two points in a clear-cut victory. The newspaper
report did note, however, that 'although Ellington were the superior side, Rothbury might easily have made a draw of it for
they had what appeared to be a good goal in the net but it was
ruled offside, and a visitors' defender appeared to handle in the
penalty box, but the referee was unsighted.'

J. Laidler, senior, playing alongside his son, 'was laid out by
a fast shot from Thompson which looked a winner all the way' –
those heavy balls again!

Ellington went ahead after 20 minutes when they took advantage of a defensive error and W. Thompson went through to
score. A Rothbury free kick was collected by Mills, who beat all
opposition and centred. The cross was met by R. Laidler near the
penalty spot, who netted, but the referee ruled it offside. Blain
then got caught in possession and was robbed by J. Thompson,
the winger running on and firing in a cross-shot to increase the
Ellington advantage.

Rothbury almost replied in the second half when Mills made
a brilliant solo effort and finally passed out to Blain, who, unmarked, found himself with the goalkeeper to beat but he ran on
too far and shot into the goalkeeper's hands. After J. Laidler had
saved a certainty for a corner, Aynsley cleared with a powerful
kick. Anderson got possession but his final shot just skimmed

the bar. Then Tait had a good opening but shot hopelessly wide. Peary tried a long shot which was well on the target but Gregory saved and cleared easily. *Rothbury:* Gregory: J. Laidler, jun., Aynsley, Ramsay, J. Laidler, sen., D. Laidler; Blain, R Laidler, Anderson, Mills, Tait.

In May a bumper crowd of 400 turned up at Armstrong Park to see champions Ellington beat Longframlington 3-0 in the Coquetdale League Challenge Cup Final to seal the Double and the growing interest in local football was shown by a large attendance at Rothbury's annual meeting in June. The chairman, Mr R. Storer, who presided, was again elected for the coming season, and the secretary, Mr J Monaghan, gave a detailed report of the club's activities during the past season.

The new pitch at Armstrong Park had proved a great boon to the spectators as well as the players, and gates were better due to the easy access to the park. The club had run two teams in the Coquetdale League. They had not gained any honours, but had enjoyed a grand playing season.

The treasurer, Mr J. Swanson, read the financial statement, which showed the club to be in a very sound position, with probably the best-ever credit balance in the long history the club. The question of draining the pitch was fully considered but it was thought that the price quoted for the work was too high and other means would be looked into by the committee to save expense.

It was agreed that the club should enter only one of the N.F.A. Cup competitions the following season, the Amateur Cup, as, with increased numbers in the league, the team would have a full fixture list.

Goalkeeper Clough was signed by Blyth Spartans reserves with Len Gregory taking over between the sticks in a 3-2 win over Longhirst at Armstrong Park in October 1950, and making some brilliant saves, while the retired J. Laidler was proving difficult to replace at centre half.

Rothbury centre forward Winter hit a fine hat-trick in a win over Wallington at Armstrong Park in November of 1950/51. His first came after just five minutes and was almost a gift. Telfer's weak bye-kick went straight to him just outside the penalty area, and he made no mistake with a quick return into the back of the net.

Wallington levelled three minutes later when Aynsley made his only mistake, a miss-kick which sent the ball to Crozier who banged the ball home from close in.

In the 20th minute Ramsay checked a visitors' raid and sent the ball just front of Winter, who ran on and beat Telfer with a fast shot. Rothbury's third goal was the best of the match. Aynsley made the first move to send Winter away, and after beating Storey he found himself about a yard off the bye-line. Nevertheless he took aim from this difficult angle and beat Telfer with a shot into the far corner the net. The visitors reduced their arrears with a simple goal after defensive error by Rothbury.

The side continued to show improved form later that month when they beat Pegswood 3-0 in a Coquetdale League game. The home forwards combined well and looked like getting goals in every attack, while the defence was sound in every department. Mills powered a shot against the bar and at the other end Gregory, in goal, was able deal with all Pegswood's scoring efforts. Anderson tried a shot which hit the post before play moved to the home goal after a good passing move between A. Lee and W. Oliver. The inside-left shot accurately and Gregory did well to save the foot of the upright.

After 20 minutes Rothbury took the lead, following a combined effort by Butters and Mills, the latter finally beating McDonald to shoot hard into the net. Rothbury went further ahead when, after cleverly beating two men, Mills centred for Winter head smartly into the net. The visitors staged a revival and only good tackling by Aynsley prevented their progress.

Reid made a good solo effort and after beating L. Butters he centred perfectly for Oliver to skim the bar with a header. This was a lucky escape for the home goal and the only time that Gregory appeared to be beaten. After the interval Pegswood were first to make progress, a powerful cross shot by Lee nearly scored, Gregory making a flying leap to turn the ball round the post for a corner.

Ramsay gave Anderson a good opening and after centring well, Winter headed into the goalkeeper's hands. After 30 minutes Rothbury completed the scoring following a brilliant solo effort by Mills, who placed the ball through for Anderson to complete the move with a well-placed shot. Near the end R. Laidler tried a long dropping shot which Oliver did well to save. *Rothbury*: Gregory; Carruthers, L. Butters; Ramsay, Aynsley, D. Laidler; Anderson, R. Laidler, Winter, Mills, N. Butters.

Mills was then the star of the show with a hat-trick in a 4-3 win at Morpeth Villa. He headed Rothbury in front inside six minutes and added his second just minutes later. Sanders pulled one back reduced the arrears for the home side and straight after the re-start they were level as Davison scored a clever equaliser. It looked like Rothbury had blown it when Slaughter put the Villa ahead, but the lead was short lived -Winter, Rothbury's centre forward, netting to level things up. Mills headed in the winner with ten minutes to go to secure the two points.

Into the New Year and Rothbury won a fast and entertaining game at Felton's Alnwick ground 5-3 in a game that 'deserved a bigger crowd of spectators than the average one that assembled.'

R. Laidler headed a corner past Felton's Dunn to open the score. Shortly after L. Butters put a stop a good run by Foggin; his clearance sent his forwards off and from a centre from Anderson, Mills scored the second goal.

A number of Felton forwards had good attempts stopped by Gregory and against the run of the play Rothbury got number three through D. Laidler, who headed past Dunn. Kitchen had a good effort saved Gregory and Foggin's shot was also stopped at the foot the post by the 'keeper. Within two minutes after half-time Rothbury got two more goals, Anderson and Mills being the scorers. Felton were not put off their game when five goals down and, playing good football, they often had the Rothbury defenders hard pressed. This pressure continued and last Gregory was well beaten by Jeffreys. Some good passing ended with Foggin scoring Felton's second goal. Within a few minutes the same player gave Oliver a pass which he took on the run to score Felton's third goal. Felton looked like making a fight it and with luck they might at least have got a point. It was L. Butters, Carruthers and Gregory who were the means of stopping them.

Fred Carruthers was a player of some repute who had played for the Northern Alliance teams Bedlington United, Morpeth Town, Amble and Alnwick before the War. He was a Sergeant Major in the Army Physical Corps during the conflict and played for Yorkshire Amateurs before returning to Rothbury school in November 1945 and turning out for the local side. He had an interest in all sports, such as boxing, road walking, cross-country and basketball, but his first and last love was Association football.

At the end of the season a Coquetdale League XI took on a North Tyne League XI at Armstrong Park in a match to celebrate the Festival of Britain. Coquetdale lined up: Hogg (St. George's), Hedley (Longframlington), Warwick (Widdrington), Riddell (Widdrington), Appleby (Longhorsley), Kitchen (capt. Felton), Elliott (Longhirst), R. Laidler (Rothbury), Turner (Felton), W. Mills (Rothbury), Halliday (Longframlington). Res: Tully (Thropton), Foggerty (St. George's), Thompson (Longhorsley).

The North Tyne side was: Cherryman (Wark), Newton (Kielder Hearts), Wilson (Elsdon), Stewart (Elsdon), Anderson (Elsdon), Glendinning (Barrasford), Thompson (Bellingham), Familton (Elsdon) and Wylie (Wark).

Coquetdale Football League

The final table of the above league for the season 1950-51 is as follows:—

DIVISION A

	P	W	L	D	F	A	Pt
Widdrington .	28	24	4	0	108	36	48
Longhirst	28	18	3	7	118	66	43
Rothbury	28	19	7	2	101	58	40
Longframl'gton.	28	16	5	7	96	47	39
Morpeth Villa .	28	14	10	4	76	72	32
Felton	28	10	11	7	61	63	27
R.A.F.	28	10	12	6	56	62	26
Ellington V. ...	28	11	14	3	84	79	25
Wallington ...	28	10	13	5	50	61	25
Chop'ngton H.P	28	9	14	5	58	72	23
Pegswood W. A	28	9	16	3	43	78	21
St. George's	28	7	15	6	49	72	20
Stannington ...	28	8	15	5	64	82	19
Thropton Utd. .	28	6	21	1	43	92	13
Longhorsley......	28	5	18	5	38	107	13

SECTION B

	P	W	L	D	F	A	Pt
Chop'ngton R. ...	20	12	3	5	61	29	29
Longhirst R.	20	13	5	2	79	40	28
Belsay S.C.	20	12	5	3	72	44	27
Ellington R.	20	11	7	2	76	39	24
Felton R.	20	10	7	3	44	46	23
Morpeth R.	20	6	8	6	36	31	18
Rothbury R.	20	8	10	2	36	35	18
Longf'ml'gton R .	20	7	9	4	44	50	18
Netherwitton ...	20	8	10	2	32	47	18
Thropton R.	20	4	10	6	28	70	14
Wallington R. ...	20	2	16	2	19	60	6

Rothbury raced into an early seventh minute lead at Morpeth Villa in their second game of 1951/52 season but were undone by a fine performance from the host's centre half Elliott.

Inside right Mills shot Rothbury ahead at Stobhill with the Villa keeper Miller getting a touch but being unable to keep it out. Elliott headed in the equaliser in the 35th minute and he was at it again with another as he fired in from close range ten minutes after half time.

McDonald added a third and centre-forward Hannah rounded things off with a header centred for the Villa leader to nod
past the Rothbury 'keeper. Jimmy Anderson played well with the
report noting that 'the fleetness of Rothbury inside left Anderson could never be ignored by the home defence.'

In November 1951 Rothbury were 7-1 winners at home to Ellington but the 19-year-old Robin Emery, from Pegswood, then
had 'the Rothbury defence rocking on their heels with amaze-
ment' with his ball control as the Villa drew the return game 3-3
at Armstrong Park in terrible wintery conditions.

Brown – Rothbury's centre-forward - scored the first but
Hill levelled five minutes later with a forty-five yard drive. Good
work by Emery was now showing and it was a worthy solo effort
of his which brought him his first goal. Collecting the ball, he
raced down the field, beat two men with superb ball control, and
flashed the ball into the net. A few seconds later Emery scored
his second goal when again received the ball, beat three men
and shot past the astounded goalkeeper.

At the restart, Rothbury attacked and Robinson scored their
second goal with a beautiful shot from the left wing. This proved
the turning point and Morpeth were turned completely on the
defensive. Emery was trying gamely to pull the game out of the
fire but ten minutes from time Rothbury got the equaliser when
Robinson scored again, this time it was a fifteen yards drive.
This proved the last goal of the match but it was by no means
the end of good football for Rothbury were swinging the ball
about and playing open football. The Villa mistake was over in-
dividualism. Emery tried hard but he could not find the co-
operation of his fellow forwards. Morpeth therefore had to fight
gamely for one point after leading at half time.

In January, 1952 the following Rothbury side – Gregory,
Ramsay, Butters L., Ballantyne, Aynsley, Butters F., Blain,
Laidlaw, Robson, Mills and Tait – were beaten 5-3 at Felton with
Gregory tipping a penalty over the bar but Rothbury were four

down before R. Laidlaw pulled one back with a deflected shot. Blain hit the second with a shot that flashed in from the wing and Aynsley got Rothbury right back in the game with a powerful low free kick from just outside the box before a late fifth killed them off, a clearance hitting a Felton forward in the face and bouncing into the net.

Neighbours Thropton had some familiar names in their line up when they were beaten 7-2 at the Villa in the February, with Gregory, W. Bland, Foggin, Bucknall, Tully, Laidler, T. Bland, G. Green, R. Green, Tailford and Davison turning out for the village side. The difference in class was also evident when Rothbury were trounced 9-1 at Seaton Delaval Amateurs in the NFA Amateur Cup that same month and they also went down 5-0 at Widdrington in the League.

Thropton, however, only went down 2-1 at defending Champions Widdrington on the Easter Monday, with the *Tattie Tooners* unlucky not to force a draw – a stunning performance by 16-year-old goalkeeper Smith earning all the plaudits.

Thropton: Smith; Ashford, Foggin; Green, Gregory, Hunter; Bucknall, Tailford, Green (R), Green (Ron.), Davison. In the fifth minute, Smith dived full length to push header from Grainger round the post for a comer. Widdrington were creating all the chances and Tweddle had opportunities galore. He shot over from 20 yards with only the goalkeeper to beat. Jeffrey then took the ball through, but shot across the goalmouth. Grainger had an opportunity from 12 yards, but shot over. Smith pulled down a hard shot from Grainger. Tweddle had two shots stopped by defenders.

At the other end Bucknall also joined the list of near misses when lifted the ball over from eight yards. But the hosts took the lead with 'one of the most amazing free-kicks ever which was taken by Bolton from 30 yards. The Thropton defence, instead standing in front of their goals, stood well away to the sides of the goal and all Bolton had do was to shoot the ball into the corner of the net.'

After half time, Jeffrey shot past the upright from close range following a right wing centre. A minute later he shot over the bar from 20 yards. Widdrington failed to increase their lead when they were awarded a penalty in the 55th minute, after a Thropton defender fisted shot from Black over the bar. Hawgood took the spot kick, but shot a few inches wide of the upright. Bolton took the ball through, but shot past when within six yards of the goal. In the 65th minute Widdrington went further ahead through Kelly, who scored from close range with a shot into the top comer of the net. Kelly's left foot 15 yards drive skimmed the crossbar. Smith saved a hard shot from winger Grainger. Foggin shot from 40 yards but Weddell pushed over the bar, his great height enabling him to do this with ease. It was in the last 15 minutes that Thropton really got going. Their forwards combined well and gave the home defence many close shaves. Thropton scored in the 80th minute when Tailford headed in a Hunter centre. The holiday crowd which attended applauded the young Thropton goalkeeper, Smith, for the saves which he made, some of them 'on the verge of brilliancy.'

The Coquetdale League representative side that played the R.A.F. at Longframlington's ground in May 1952 lined up: Gregory (Rothbury); Lumsden (Choppington), Scott (St. George's); Tully (Thropton), Aynsley (Rothbury), Kitchen (Felton); Robinson (Choppington), Jordan (St. George's), Wood (Choppington), Mills (Rothbury), Brown (Felton).

The 1952/53 season started with a defeat at Morpeth Villa and it didn't get much better as Rothbury began to struggle somewhat against the strong pitman's teams from the south east of Northumberland.

They weren't helped by two goalkeeping errors that led to the Villa goals at the Stobhill ground. Villa striker Hannay netted both but he had J. Davison to thank for creating them – the first coming after Rothbury's keeper had saved a shot but collided when a defender and dropped the ball at Hannay's feet, the second when the stopper fumbled under heavy pressure and Davison teed him up for the second. Rothbury's inside right pulled one back late on.

In the December Rothbury were thumped 7-1 at Linton and in April they crashed 5-1 at Longhirst, but the side still had a couple of players included in the Coquetdale Inter-League match with North Tyne League, which was played on the Bellingham ground on the Easter Monday. *Coquetdale League:* Laidler (Pegswood); Underwood (Felton) capt., Jobson (St. George's); Bolton (Felton), Aynsley (Rothbury), O'Hare (Morpeth V.); Elliott (Longhirst, Cunningham (St. George's), Turner (Felton), Dodds (Swarland), Morton (Widdrington). Res: Hall (Felton), Laidler (Rothbury).

Coquetdale Football League

Division "A"

	P	W	L	D	F	A	Pt
Longhirst ...	23	15	4	4	99	56	31
Felton	23	15	5	3	96	41	33
Choppington .	21	15	3	3	92	42	33
Widdr'gton .	19	15	3	1	92	27	31
St. George's ..	23	14	6	3	102	56	31
Morpeth V. ...	24	9	10	5	74	66	23
Swarland ...	19	7	11	2	41	60	16
Pegswood ...	20	7	11	2	41	60	16
Linton W. ...	20	6	12	2	52	56	14
Rothbury ...	20	5	12	3	41	72	13
Wallington .	22	5	15	2	36	79	12
Thropton ...	22	5	16	1	44	116	11
Ellington ...	22	3	16	3	34	94	9

April 1953

The Coquetdalers' side had an unfamiliar look with a number of new faces coming into the team during season 1953/54 but they continued a decent run with a 2-1 win over Choppington in the first round of the Coquetdale Challenge Cup in the December.

Rothbury: Atkinson; Tate, Tully; H. Smith, Aynsley, Davison; A. Smith, Mills, Robinson, Armstrong, Tait.

The match was played in atrocious conditions with both teams having trouble controlling a slippery ball, which in the later stages was often difficult to see.

It took Choppington just ten minutes to net the opener, a quick throw-in on the left catching out the home defenders and inside-right Owen ran through to score with well-placed shot.

But Rothbury hit back and levelled when left winger Tait smashed a hard drive in from an acute angle giving the visitor's keeper Ross no chance.

Choppington hit the crossbar but Rothbury won it with a controversial penalty just five minutes from the end.

During a breakaway, centre-forward John Robinson was fouled in the area when he looked certain to score. Aynsley stepped up and drove the resultant spot-kick wide, but the referee signalled an infringement and ordered it re-taken amid a storm of protest. Aynsley kept his cool and made no mistake with the retake, drilling it home.

Rothbury beat Thropton 8-2 to inflict a 10th straight defeat on their rock-bottom neighbours on New Year's Day 1954, maintaining third spot behind Longhirst and Pegswood, and away from the bread and butter of the local League there was great excitement at Armstrong Park in the April of 1954 as the black and white striped shirts of Newcastle United appeared at Rothbury for the very first time.

The Magpies played in a benefit match on a pleasant Wednesday evening in front of a good crowd of spectators and won 4-2 against a team chosen from the Coquetdale League.

The match raised the sum of £33 10s 0d for the Coquetdale League and was arranged by Mr. J. Noble, secretary of the league. Mr. Lorne Campbell-Robson, vice president of Rothbury Football Club, was present to watch the match between the local players and the notable visitors, most of whom were members of United's Northern Alliance 'A' side.

Goals were scored for Newcastle by Tulip, Keen (2) and McKechnie. The local lads who scored for Coquetdale were J. S. Scott and J. W. Kelly. The weather was bright and fair throughout the game, with only a slightly chill breeze and a very dry ground which made the ball lively. Afterwards, the visitors were entertained at the Turk's Head Hotel. Mr. J. Monaghan, secretary of Rothbury Football Club, was one of the officials who assisted in organising the benefit match.

When Rothbury Football Club was re-formed after the War in 1949, they'd received a donation of £25 from Newcastle United, and a friendly association between the two clubs was to continue throughout the decade.

Newcastle United's 1955 FA Cup winning squad – the Magpies kindly brought the trophy with them on what became their annual visit to Armstrong Park to play a Coquetdale League XI.

Rothbury FC at the Armstrong Park opening in 1949. L to R - front kneeling - Fred Carruthers, Michael Aynsley, Les Butters, Capt Jimmy Anderson, Alec Mills, Dickie Laidler. - back row (all standing) L to R - Jackie Monaghan, Dr Armstrong, Ronnie Ramsey, Sid Atkinson, Barney Smith, Geordie Winters, Jimmy Laidler, Eddie Thompson, Harry Murray, George Fletcher, Mr Storer, Mrs Storer. *Courtesy Robin Murray.*

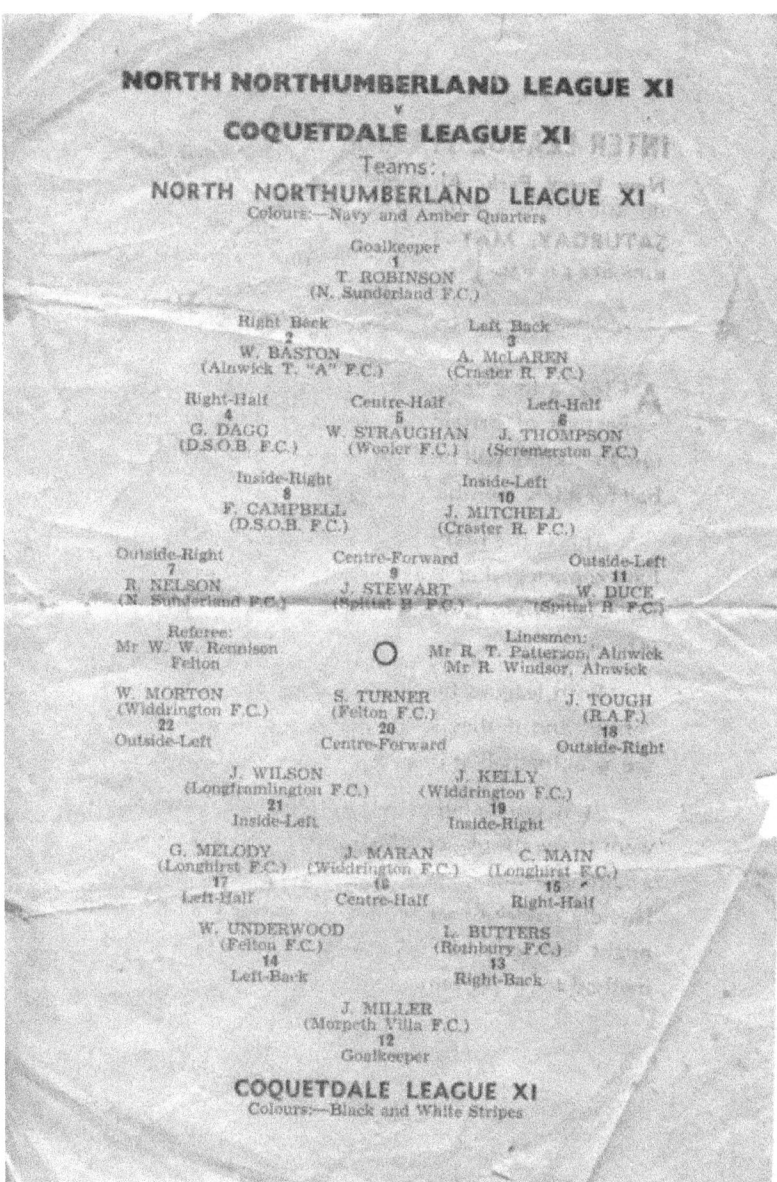

NORTH NORTHUMBERLAND LEAGUE XI

v

COQUETDALE LEAGUE XI

Teams:

NORTH NORTHUMBERLAND LEAGUE XI

Colours:—Navy and Amber Quarters

Goalkeeper
1
T. ROBINSON
(N. Sunderland F.C.)

Right Back
2
W. BASTON
(Alnwick T. "A" F.C.)

Left Back
3
A. McLAREN
(Craster R. F.C.)

Right-Half
4
G. DAGG
(D.S.O.B. F.C.)

Centre-Half
5
W. STRAUGHAN
(Wooler F.C.)

Left-Half
6
J. THOMPSON
(Scremerston F.C.)

Inside-Right
8
F. CAMPBELL
(D.S.O.B. F.C.)

Inside-Left
10
J. MITCHELL
(Craster R. F.C.)

Outside-Right
7
R. NELSON
(N. Sunderland F.C.)

Centre-Forward
9
J. STEWART
(Spittal R. F.C.)

Outside-Left
11
W. DUCE
(Spittal R. F.C.)

Referee:
Mr W. W. Rennison
Felton

O

Linesmen:
Mr R. T. Patterson, Alnwick
Mr R. Windsor, Alnwick

W. MORTON
(Widdrington F.C.)
22
Outside-Left

S. TURNER
(Felton F.C.)
20
Centre-Forward

J. TOUGH
(R.A.F.)
18
Outside-Right

J. WILSON
(Longframlington F.C.)
21
Inside-Left

J. KELLY
(Widdrington F.C.)
19
Inside-Right

G. MELODY
(Longhirst F.C.)
17
Left-Half

J. MARAN
(Widdrington F.C.)
16
Centre-Half

C. MAIN
(Longhirst F.C.)
15
Right-Half

W. UNDERWOOD
(Felton F.C.)
14
Left-Back

L. BUTTERS
(Rothbury F.C.)
13
Right-Back

J. MILLER
(Morpeth Villa F.C.)
12
Goalkeeper

COQUETDALE LEAGUE XI

Colours:—Black and White Stripes

1951. Courtesy Alan Tailford.

COQUETDALE LEAGUE XI

v.

NORTH TYNE LEAGUE XI

Teams:

COQUETDALE LEAGUE XI
Colours:—Black and White Stripes

Goalkeeper
1
J. HOGG
(St. George's)

Right Back | Left Back
2 | 3
F. HEDLEY | **W. WARWICK**
(Longframlington) | (Widdrington)

Right-Half | Centre-Half | Left-Half
4 | 5 | 6
J. RIDDELL | **W. APPLEBY** | **F. KITCHEN**
(Widdrington) | (Longhorsley) | (Felton), Capt.

Inside-Right | Inside-Left
8 | 10
R. LAIDLER | **W. MILLS**
(Rothbury) | (Rothbury)

Outside-Right | Centre-Forward | Outside-Left
7 | 9 | 11
K. ELLIOTT | **S. TURNER** | **F. HALLIDAY**
(Longhirst) | (Felton) | (Longframlington)

Referee: | | Linesmen:
Mr. E. H. COLLIS | | One from each
Pegswood | | League

●

D. WYLIE | **R. THOMPSON** | **J. ANDERSON**
(Wark) | (Bellingham) | (Elsdon)
22 | 20 | 18
Outside-Left | Centre-Forward | Outside-Right

J. FAMILTON | **A. GLENDENNING**
(Elsdon) | (Barrasford)
21 | 19
Inside-Left | Inside-Right

A. STEWART | **J. CLARK** | **G. PRINGLE**
(Wark) | (Kielder), Capt. | (West Woodburn)
17 | 16 | 15
Left-Half | Centre-Half | Right-Half

D. WILSON | **W. NEWTON**
(Elsdon) | (Kielder Hearts)
14 | 13
Left Back | Right Back

V. CHERRYMAN
(Wark)
12
Goalkeeper

NORTH TYNE LEAGUE XI
Colours:—Red Jerseys with Black Collars and Cuffs

1951. Courtesy Alan Tailford.

Morpeth Villa, before they met and defeated Pegswood in the semifinal of the Coquetdale League Challenge Cup at the Stobhill ground, Morpeth, on Saturday. Douglas, second from left in front row, was carried off the field fifteen minutes after this photograph was taken. He was conveyed to the Cottage Hospital with a broken collar-bone. [Photo.: A. B. Arthur, Morpeth.]

Pegswood, who were defeated in the semi-final of the Coquetdale League Challenge Cup by Morpeth Villa at the Stobhill ground, Morpeth, on Saturday. [Photo.: A. B. Arthur, Morpeth.]

1952

Widdrington, who fought their way to the final of the Coquetdale League Challenge Cup with a 3—1
win over Morpeth St. George's at the Sports Stadium, Morpeth, on Saturday.
[Photo.: A. B. Arthur, Morpeth.]

Morpeth St. George's, before they took the field in their Coquetdale League Challenge Cup semi-final tie
against Widdrington. St. George's were beaten 3—1. [Photo.: A. B. Arthur, Morpeth.]

1952

Neighbours Longframlington, Challenge Cup winners in 1951.

The Widdrington team captain being congratulated by his opposite number of Morpeth Villa after the presentation of the cup by Capt. G. Tate, of Warkworth (centre) following the Coquetdale League Cup final at Morpeth last Saturday. [Photo.: A. B. Arthur, Morpeth.]

1952

A couple of Thropton F.C. teams in the 1950s.

Derby Days

EDDIE TULLY JOINED ROTHBURY from Thropton over the summer and went into the Coquetdale League select XI along with 'Goody' Armstrong and Aynsley to play Champions Widdrington in the 1954-55 season opener.

Rothbury were beaten 5-1 at Ellington and thumped 9-3 at home by Longhirst to sit tenth in the thirteen-team League after three games. Their opponents in the Coquetdale at the time were Widdrington, Longhirst, Choppington, Ellington, Felton, Morpeth Villa, Belsay, Pegswood, Thropton, St. George's, Wallington and Longhorsley.

Thropton were narrowly edged out of a Coquetdale League Challenge Cup tie at Felton in November, W. Brown netting a superb header to draw Thropton level after a spot-on pass from Corbett and Corbett was on target himself with a second as United were unlucky to go out 3-2, with Rothbury losing 4-1 at Longhirst in the League on the same day.

A 2-0 win over basement side Longhorsley at Armstrong Park saw them up to ninth in November with three wins and four defeats from their seven games, 20 goals being scored and 29 conceded. Thropton were up to sixth, having played eight games, winning four, losing three and drawing one.

A former vice-president of Rothbury FC – and the vice president of Morpeth Town – died in the December aged 88. Ex-Hearts and Hibs player James Smith, from Ratho near Edinburgh, was the manager of Ewesley quarry for 40 years and ran the Whitehouse team. He'd played in an early Rothbury side against Seghill before WW1 and had also turned out for Morpeth Harriers against Newcastle reserves.

The big derby game at Thropton took place on Christmas Day 1954, the two sides generally meeting in front of big crowds over the festive period.

Three years earlier, the Thropton United club was in a good shape, with £73 funds in the bank. At the annual meeting of the club in the Reading Room, Thropton in July 1950 it was decided that the club should enter for the Northumberland Amateur Cup and also continue as members of the first and second divisions of the Coquetdale League. Mr D. Davy agreed to again let his field to the club at a nominal rent of one shilling for the season, and the officials expressed their appreciation at this gesture. A request was made by Mr Davy to be relieved of the captaincy for the coming year and Mr A. Wood was elected in his place, Mr Davy being elected vice-captain. Mr Stanger Leathes was re-elected president and the following were elected vice-presidents: Messrs A. Straughan, W. Brown, W. Smith, W. Pye, T. Hedley, W. J. Bland, W. Morton, F. Whitton, Dr. McCracken. Messrs Hewitt, S. B. Hewitt, Chrisp, K. Green. Alexander, B. Reid, F. Scott and C. Robinson. Other officials elected were: - Mr G. Davy (chairman), Mr J. Foggon and Father Corrigan (vice-chairmen), Mr T. Proudlock (secretary and treasurer) and Mr R. Proudlock (assistant secretary and treasurer).

The club had been formed in 1946 as local football started to get back on its feet and they applied to join the Coquetdale League along with the other North Northumbrian sides Rothbury, Wallington, Netherwitton, Meldon, Morpeth St. George's, Newton-on-the-Moor, Felton and Warkworth, with the North Northumberland League claiming that losing Rothbury would be 'disastrous.'

An early side that was beaten 7-1 at leaders Felton in January 1947 lined up as follows - *Thropton*: Harris; Tait, Ramsay; Green, A. Wood, Storey; J. Wood, Stewart, Winter, Dunn, Murray.

Rothbury and Thropton drew 2-2 at Thropton in December 1949 with the return game taking place the following week and

Rothbury 'winning handsomely' - 5-1 - in the first clash between the two teams on Armstrong Park. Rothbury recorded the same scoreline over their neighbours on New Year's Day 1952.

The FA Cup in the Turk's Head, Rothbury, 1955. *Courtesy Hilary Woodburn.*

However, by 1957/58 Thropton were struggling and received congratulations from the League's Secretary, J. Noble, for their 'splendid sportsmanship in carrying out their fixtures to the end of the season.'

Longhirst were the champions that season, Widdrington won the Challenge Cup and Pegswood took the Subsidiary while Newcastle United were at Armstrong Park again in the match to aid League funds and sent another strong side to represent them.

A Rothbury side in the late 1950s - L to R (Back row) J. Tait, J. Monaghan, W. Miller, J. Cairns, S. Howden, J. Laidler, M. Aynsley, D. Blain. (Front row) T. Milligan, G. Heron, R. Cairns, T. Muir, B. Cairns. *Courtesy Margaret Hammond.*

But the following season, Thropton had bounced back and a side that lined up: Rogerson, Laidler, Stewart, Proudlock, Ashford, Foggon, Richardson, Cummings, Gutherson, Cairns and Heron beat Widdrington for the first time in the Coquetdale League, Gutherson's shot being deflected into his own net by King for the winner.

The League winners in 1959/60 were Longhirst and the runners-up Ellington. Swinney Bros. lifted the Challenge Cup in their first season with a 2-1 win over Widdrington in the Final and Longhirst completed a double by beating Red Row Welfare 3-2 after extra time in the Subsidiary Cup. Newcastle United sent another strong team up to Rothbury to take on the Coquetdale League XI at Armstrong Park, with the Magpies running out 6-2 winners.

Rothbury were thumped 10-0 at Red Row – who finished runners-up – in 1960/61 but were praised for the sporting manner in which they took the defeat then beat Northgate 2-1 as they got back on the rails. But reports and tables from the time have proved hard to track down in the local sporting press, with the North Northumberland and Miners Welfare Leagues receiving better coverage at the time.

In April 1961, Thropton booked themselves a spot in the Challenge Cup Final against Wallington as they demolished Longhorsley 7-0 at Armstrong Park. Longhorsley were outclassed as Swailes struck four times, Dodd twice and Dixon netted the other. The Oakford Park side lifted the silverware as they embarked on an amazing run and Rothbury could only watch on as their near neighbours from over the back of the Simonside hills won a treble in 1962/63, lifting the Coquetdale League Championship and Challenge Cup, then beat Blyth YMCA in a replay to win the Northumberland FA Amateur Cup.

The Green's striker Andy Turnbull is reckoned to have scored 105 goals in 42 games that season, with his brothers Sid and Ted, and the Cowan brothers John, George and Andy making up half of manager Inkie Fairgreave's team.

But the campaign was very hit-and-miss, with hardly a ball being kicked from the back end of November up until late February and the annual fixture between the Coquetdale League and Newcastle United at Armstrong Park did not take place due to a congested fixture list for both United and the League's teams.

Rothbury were 12th in the 15 team League in November, having played nine, won two and lost seven with 25 goals for and 43 against. Thropton were two places ahead, having played ten, won two, drawn two and lost six with 13 goals for and 41 against. Widdrington topped the table having won nine out of ten and they would take the Greens right to the wire. It wasn't all doom and gloom as Rothbury were 5-0 victors over Choppington in the first round of the Challenge Cup and beat Bebside 5-2 at Armstrong Park in the League to keep clear of the bottom.

The following campaign Wallington went all season unbeaten as they completed the double again in 1963/64 by taking the Coquetdale League title and Challenge Cup. And things went from bad to worse at Rothbury as they were thrashed 11-0 at Morpeth Police Boys Club for their eighth straight defeat of the season in the January. An acrobatic display from goalkeeper Darling and a decent showing from left winger Laidler meant they were the only two to come out of the battering with much credit. *Rothbury*: Darling, Foggin, Snowdon, Coe, Hunter, Carlyle, T. Bainbridge, F. Bainbridge, Miller, Croyle, Laidler. The offside trap ploy was Rothbury's main downfall as it was sprung time and time again.

The following month Rothbury were still stuck in the basement with ten losses from ten games, scoring just ten times and conceding 58. A 7-0 drubbing at Northgate didn't help matters and by April Rothbury were still rooted at the foot of the table having played 19, winning three and losing sixteen, with 28 goals for and 87 against. Things were so dire that the club withdrew from the Coquetdale League at the end of the season and did not compete in 1964/65 when Wallington were double winners for the third successive season in their most successful spell ever – also lifting the Amateur Cup with a win over Percy Main - earning them a move up into the Northern Football Alliance at the end of the season.

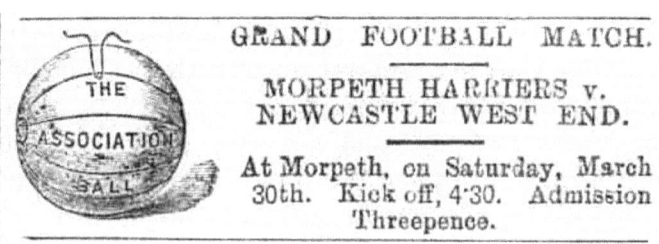

GRAND FOOTBALL MATCH.

MORPETH HARRIERS v.
NEWCASTLE WEST END.

At Morpeth, on Saturday, March 30th. Kick off, 4·30. Admission Threepence.

1889

1965/66

THE NEWLY REFORMED Rothbury FC were handed a home game against local rivals Thropton to welcome them back into the Coquetdale League, but things didn't go well as the *Tattie Tooners* went home happy with the points in a 5-1 success.

Billy Miller went through but drove wide with just the keeper to beat then Rothbury's Ken Tait was knocked out following a clash of heads with R. Brown. He carried on but looked very groggy and had to go off with ten minutes to go.

D. Wilkinson lobbed in Thropton's first and drove in number two from 20 yards but Bainbridge embarked on an 85-yard run and produced a finish at the end of it to reduce the arrears. Hedley fired against the Rothbury post and Proudlock managed to drill the rebound through a crowd of bodies for the third before half time. Hedley raced clear to make it 4-1 and the same player flicked the fifth over the keeper's head to complete the demolition job.

Rothbury: Darling, Hay, Tait, Cairns, Snowdon, Robson, Winter, Arkle, Miller, Laidler, Bainbridge.

Thropton: Gregory, Appleby, Cummings, Brown, Clark, Gutherson R., Stewart, Proudlock, Wilkinson, Hedley, Gutherson N.

An 8-1 defeat followed at Longhorsley in the Minor Cup with Rothbury making a last minute change to the team sheet, Michael Arkle coming in to replace Alan Arkle. Rothbury left half Berheley went off with a damaged leg during the game and as they were reduced to ten men, John Angus dropped back into the defence. Laidler scored with a dipping shot from the edge of the box with Miller Rothbury's most dangerous forward and Hay being described as 'easily Rothbury's best man' as he put in a good shift in the defence.

Rothbury started to find their feet again and won 3-2 at Swinney's with Angus firing in off a post and Laidler scoring direct from a corner.

Miller scored the third with an unstoppable shot that was so powerful that Swinney's keeper Hawkes hurt his fingers attempting to save and had to switch positions with the left back. Rothbury's keeper Aitchison was also injured and had to be replaced by Ray Cairns. Hay, Robert Cairns, Miller, Angus and Laidler all played well in the victory.

The Coquetdalers then produced their best display of the season but went down 5-3 at home to St. Mary's Stannington. Laidler pulled it back to 2-1 then Ray Cairns flicked the second into the top corner at 4-1. Miller put away the third from the penalty spot with Hay, Snowdon, Robt Cairns, Ray Cairns, Angus and Laidler all playing well.

Billy Miller took just two minutes to shoot Rothbury ahead at Stannington in the Subsidiary Cup and Raymond Cairns hit a quick-fire hat-trick as Rothbury ran riot. Angus put away the rebound after Laidler's shot came back off the post for the fifth.

In the second half Ray Cairns added his fourth when he chased a long through ball and outwitted Blacklock to net from ten yards, then Laidler again struck the woodwork before he got on the scoresheet with a free kick.

Rothbury: Aitchison, Hay, Bainbridge, Thompson, Robson, Robt. Cairns, Miller, Angus, Ray Cairns, Hunter, Laidler.

But Rothbury were heavily beaten, 7-2 at home by Longhorsley, in the next round with Laidler netting from the penalty spot and Ray Cairns netting the rebound after Miller's shot was parried.

And they went out of the Challenge Cup at St. Mary's 2-0, with the hosts the better side. Rothbury lined up: Aitchison, Hay, Bainbridge, Robson, Snowdon, Robt. Cairns, Miller, Angus, Ray Cairns, Thompson, Laidler.

The second leg of the Subsidiary Cup tie against Longhorsley didn't get any better, with Rothbury going down 4-1 though they'd had to make several late changes to the team. The red and whites were 2-0 down at the break and although Miller pulled one back soon after the restart when he fired in from the edge of the area following a goalmouth scramble, two further goals from the hosts saw Rothbury out 11-3 on aggregate. Miller, Snowdon and Hay were outstanding in the defeat with Rothbury's side being Aitchison, Hay, Thompson, Robson, Snowdon, Cairns, Miller, Angus, Bainbridge, A. Arkle, M. Arkle.

Alan Arkle was the star of the show as Rothbury got back into League action with a 4-1 win over Netherton T.S., with the team wearing their new black and white striped shirts for the first time.

Michael Arkle deputised for Robson at inside right in a late change with Cairns moving to half back and Alan Arkle beat the full back to blaze in the opener. He cut in from the left to drill home the second and although Clark pulled one back for the visitors, Bainbridge was unlucky not to stretch Rothbury's lead on several occasions before he finally got the third. Alan Arkle completed his hat-trick from close range, tucking away a Johnson cross.

Neighbours Thropton went down 1-0 at home to Longhorsley with full back Nelson Cummings netting an unlucky own goal but they bounced back to claim their second win over Rothbury in the season with a 5-1 Subsidiary Cup mauling.

Starling lobbed Thropton ahead in the 17th min but Laidler fired in a free-kick to level things up. Nick Gutherson was unlucky when his shot hit the inside of the post and was smothered on the goal line by Aitchison, but goals from Smith and Nick Gutherson put Thropton 3-1 up at half time. Starling went past Sutton and Snowdon and set up Proudlock to blaze in for 4-1 and when Nick Gutherson went to roll a ball into the empty net with his side-foot, Thompson's attempted clearance cannoned off Billy Snowdon into the net to complete the scoring.

Thropton: Rogerson, Cummings, Hedley, Ferguson, Brown, R. Gutherson, Stewart, Proudlock, Smith, Starling, N. Gutherson.

Rothbury: Aitchison, Hay, Thompson, Robson, Snowdon, Sutton, Miller, Robt. Cairns, Ray Cairns, Angus, Laidler.

Stannington Village then raced into a two-goal lead at Armstrong Park but Billy Miller completed a good solo run with a 20-yard drive to pull one back and Tait then played in Miller for the leveller. The second half was an ill-tempered, scrappy affair but Miller completed his hat-trick and Ray Cairns grabbed the leveller from a corner as it finished 4-4. Rothbury lined up: Foggon, Bainbridge, Thompson, Hunter, Snowdon, Robt Cairns, Miller, Hay, Ray Cairns, Tait, Arkle.

Rothbury missed a number of chances as they went down 2-0 away to St. Mary's, with Miller drilling a penalty straight at keeper Jordan, and the side were hit with injuries as they went down 2-0 at Stannington. Captain Robert Cairns was forced off injured and Alan Arkle bruised his ankle with the side again showing changes and lining up: Johnson, Watson, Hunter, Robson, Snowdon, Angus, Miller, Arkle, Bainbridge, Cairns, Tait.

Bainbridge and Tait were dropped and Hunter was unavailable as Rothbury went down 3-1 at home to Longhorsley with May, Thompson and Foggon coming into the starting line-up, but it took a good performance from keeper Johnson to keep the scoreline down. Although Miller hit the post early on and both himself and Arkle went close, Miller's 78th minute penalty was the only bright spot.

He then slammed in a hat-trick as Rothbury bounced back with a 5-2 victory over Stannington Village, glancing one in off the back post in the tenth minute and adding his second seven minutes later. John Angus fired in from 10 yards to make it 3-0 and Billy Miller completed his treble ten minutes before half time. Foggon made it 5-0 with a powerful 20-yarder shortly after the turnaround with Douglas and Russell pulling back goals late on.

With Cairns, Angus and Tait unavailable for the trip to Bebside Gordons, the team was again changed for the 2-0 defeat and lined up – Johnson, Hay, Thompson, Robson, Snowdon, Watson, Blythe, Arkle, Foggon, Laidler, Bainbridge. Bebside were at Armstrong Park a week later and again secured the two points with a 4-1 success. Arkle sent Miller away to open the scoring against the run of play in the 15th minute but tempers again flared in the second half with Miller and Rider squaring up as the play got scrappy. Bainbridge and Snowdon were the Coquetdaler's best performers.

Rothbury created numerous chances in a storming start against Stobhill Rangers with Laidler going close, Miller having one cleared off the line and Robson mis-kicking with the goal at his mercy from 8 yards. Cairns then fired just wide as the sides went in goalless at half time. At 1-0 down, Miller hit the bar and Tait fired the rebound wide and three late Rangers goals sealed it.

Alan Arkle hit a hat-trick as Rothbury again bounced back and crashed six past Swinney's Welfare, who netted three in reply and took an early lead.

G. Hawkes turned a Miller cross into his own net for the leveller and Arkle added the second when the goalkeeper's clearance fell to him and he drilled it first-time back into the net. Tait fired in the third from a narrow angle following a Cairns' free kick and Miller squared to Arkle to tap in number four. Laidler slammed one in from 25 yards before Arkle added his third. Stephen Davison impressed with some good tackling at the back and Snowdon made an important goal-line clearance in the game.

Rothbury: Bainbridge, Hay, Davison, Cairns, Snowdon, Laidler, Miller, Jobling, A. Arkle, Robson, Tait.

Rothbury were sitting in seventh spot in the ten team Co-quetdale League in May with just one game remaining, having played 17, won 5, drew 1 and lost 11, scoring 36 and conceding 52 for 11 points with Thropton a place ahead of them playing 16, winning 5, drawing 3 and losing six. Thropton had scored 32 and conceded 37, with 13 points on the board.

1966/67

ROTHBURY HAD A NUMBER of new faces in the side as they went down 6-3 at Choppington on the opening day of the new season, but the game would be best remembered for a bizarre incident.

A Billy Miller shot was cleared off the goal-line by a supporter, with John Angus blazing the loose ball back into the net. Amid all the confusion and protests, the referee amazingly awarded a goal-kick to Choppington.

Miller had slammed one in in the 48th minute and Laidler set him up for his second. Miller turned provider to create the opening for Jobling to score the third just before the end, with Rothbury lining up: Ewart, Snaith, Bainbridge, Angus, Snowdon, Laidler, Tait, Arkle, Miller, MacCauley, Jobling.

The team had another new look as they crashed 8-1 at St. Mary's in the Coquetdale Challenge Cup, with keeper Oliphant saving a penalty, Snowdon and Bell never giving up trying and Laidler scoring the only goal after good work by Miller.

Rothbury: Oliphant, Davison, Glendinning, Angus, Snowdon, Bell, MacCauley, Bowman, Miller, Laidler, Tait.

Rothbury looked to have turned a corner when they led Swinney's Welfare 5-2 at Armstrong Park with just 20 minutes to go – but crashed to their fifth consecutive defeat as Swinney's thumped in five times late on.

Angus played in MacCauley, who centred for Arkle to net from 12 yards and Angus himself intercepted a back pass to make it two. Swinney's hit back to draw level with two goals in quick succession, but Tait crossed for Miller to restore the advantage before half time.

Angus made it 4-2 with his second shortly after the restart and Miller completed his own double with the fifth 12 minutes later. Rothbury lost their grip on the game and tired as they collapsed from the 70th minute onwards.

It was a similar story the next weekend as they led 1-0 at Bebside Gordons, Miller grabbing the goal after his first shot was blocked on the line but following up to force the ball into the net a few minutes before half time. But once again the legs went after the 70th minute, with Bebside crashing in three times. Rothbury boss Geordie Winter had made five changes for the fixture, with Aitchison replacing Ewart, Snaith and Bainbridge being recalled, Cairns coming in at right back and Oliphant replacing the injured Arkle.

The horror run continued with a 7-0 mauling at home by Stobhill Rangers and another heavy defeat – 6-2 at Longhorsley. John Angus was the best player on the day, crashing one in off the underside of the bar and beating Durey to fire a great shot past Cuthbert for his second.

But after losing nine straight games, Rothbury shocked leaders Bebside Gordons at Armstrong Park as they ran out 3-1 winners. Laidler lobbed in the opener after 25 minutes and Miller almost made it two, heading a perfect Tait cross just wide at the back post. Laidler then shot just over following a strong run but Bebside started to get back into the game and had three chances cleared off the line and a penalty saved by Aitchison.

Laidler robbed a defender and cut in to fire in the second from a narrow angle and although a shot was deflected past Aitchison in the 77th minute, Angus killed them off with a superb shot that beat the keeper all the way.

But the old problems of 'a weak defence and shot-shy forward line' returned as Rothbury crashed to a heavy 5-0 defeat at Welwyn SC before a disappointing draw with Thropton in the festive period. Rothbury's linesman wasn't available and a supporter had to run the line, while Thropton's linesman was 'flag-happy' and the players 'appeared to lose interest' as a string of decisions went against them.

Laidler fired a penalty over the bar in the 15th minute and then had two goals disallowed – one with the referee saying the ball had crossed the bye-line for a goal-kick in the build-up, the other a dubious offside call.

Nick Gutherson shot Thropton ahead from 20 yards in the 55th minute and then beat four men to add his second soon after. Laidler headed in a Miller cross to reduce the arrears and Rothbury levelled from the penalty spot when their captain Miller made no mistake. Snowdon, Tait and Miller were best for Rothbury while Clark, Stewart and Nick Gutherson stood out for the visitors.

Rothbury: Aitchison, Hay, Bainbridge, Ewart, Snowdon, Coe, Miller, MacCauley, Laidler, Angus, Tait.

Thropton: T. Tait, Whitfield, Appleby, Arkle, Clark, R. Gutherson, Stewart, Proudlock, N. Gutherson, Brown, Wharton.

Rothbury followed the result up with a 1-0 success at Felton, John Tait scoring with a hard shot from a narrow angle after Angus had hit the bar and Laidler worked the loose ball out to the left winger.

Davie Hay broke his ankle after 40 minutes as Rothbury raced into a 4-0 lead against Stannington Village – with the ten men just hanging on to win it 4-3. Robert Laidler struck twice, Billy Miller headed home and was later involved in a scuffle with Douglas, and Tait got the other, the two wingers being the pick of the side.

A 4-2 win over Stannington Village put Rothbury into the semi-finals of the Subsidiary Cup; and they had to do it the hard way, coming from 2-0 down mid-way through the second half. Angus coolly side-footed in a penalty to get Rothbury back in the game and Laidler drew the sides level. John Tait tapped in following a defensive mix-up and Miller sealed the win when he shot home from five yards in the 85th minute. Bell, Coe, Mac-Cauley and Angus were the star performers.

Angus struck twice – one being a superb left-foot volley that left keeper Rogerson helpless – as Rothbury drew 3-3 at Stannington Village back in the Coquetdale League. Laidler hit the other from 30 yards, the hosts equalising in the 86th minute courtesy of a header by Glass.

Rothbury's seven game unbeaten run was halted by Choppington at Armstrong Park, however. Angus had a half-hit shot sliced into his own net by a defender and Tait added a second with two minutes to go, but the visitors netted five times, then Angus and Miller both scored headers in a narrow 3-2 defeat at Stobhill Rangers.

Swinney's Welfare crushed Rothbury 6-2, Glendinning scoring with a speculative long-range shot that slipped past the keeper and Bell adding the second with a fine shot from 20 yards, so few gave them hope when the two sides met again a week later in the Subsidiary Cup semi-final.

Rothbury, however, turned the tables and John Angus was the hero with a hat-trick as the Coquetdalers stunned the visitors. Laidler was also on target with a penalty in the 4-2 success.

John Angus equalised at the third attempt after a couple of near misses as Rothbury drew 1-1 with St. Mary's in their final League game before they looked to put a disappointing season behind them as they met the same team in the Subsidiary Cup Final at the Bedlington Welfare Ground on a Friday night but went down 2-0, with only great defensive displays from Snowdon and Bell saving Rothbury from a heavier defeat. St. Mary's had beaten Thropton in the semi-final.

1967/68

A NUMBER OF PLAYERS made their Rothbury debuts in the first game of 1967/68 with goalkeeper Terry Tait, Appleby, Amory and Hedley all starting in a disappointing 2-0 defeat by a young and inexperienced Longhorsley side at Armstrong Park.

Rothbury: T. Tait, Bainbridge, Appleby, Amory, Cairns, Laidler, Miller, Hedley, Angus, Rogerson, J. Tait.

But Rothbury were firing on all-cylinders when they handed out an 8-0 thrashing to an under-strength Thropton side in a replayed Northumberland Minor Cup tie soon after. Laidler hit the post from 30 yards before Miller opened up when put through by Angus. John Tait headed in the second and Laidler blazed in from 25 yards for 3-0. Angus and Miller stretched the advantage before the break and Cairns crossed for Miller to head in his hat-trick goal from 12 yards. Angus also completed his hat-trick as Rothbury ran riot, with Cairns and Miller outstanding.

Rothbury: T. Tait, Bainbridge, Appleby, Cairns, Snowdon, D. Rogerson, Hedley, Angus, Miller, Laidler, J. Tait.

Thropton: I. Rogerson, Oliphant, Robinson, M. Wood, Cummings, Wharton, Gregory, Ferguson, Mendum, Proudlock, A. Wood.

The black and whites were, however, dumped out 7-1 at Northern Alliance Wallington in the next round.

The good Cup form continued with a 6-0 thrashing of Fairmile United in the Northumberland Amateur Cup, John Tait's curling centre floating over the keeper's head for the first and Angus pulled back for the long-haired winger to tuck away number two.

Angus himself, Miller and Laidler (2) all got on the scoresheet while Angus's hot form continued as he hit a hat-trick in a 3-1 success at Swinney's in the League and Rothbury hit top gear with a 9-3 demolition of Felton; Robert Laidler sensationally netting five times, John Tait hitting a hat-trick and 15-year-old outside right Hedley being handed the ball and putting away a penalty.

But the smiles turned to frowns the following week as Rothbury drew 4-4 in a game at Welwyn SC that turned into a fiasco as the appointed referee didn't turn up and the Welwyn secretary took the whistle. Following a string of controversial decisions against them, three of the Rothbury team walked off the pitch and had to be persuaded back on by club officials, while youngster Hedley was punched in the face by an opponent.

Miller had shot Rothbury ahead and when John Angus pulled back into his path, he added his second to make it 2-1. Angus belted in from an Appleby free kick to make it 3-2, then it all kicked off. Angus also scored the fourth in what became a heated end to a farcical encounter.

Thropton had been annihilated 13-1 at Stobhill Rangers the week before, so it came as a shock defeat for Rothbury when they were beaten 3-2 at Davy's Field.

Appleby blocked a shot on the goal-line but Turnbull smashed in the rebound and then Arkle's pass released Glendinning, who crossed for Stewart to turn in the second.

Stewart made it 3-0 before a shot deflected off Gutherson and Angus was on hand to put away the rebound in the 35th minute. Rothbury pressed after the break but Robert Laidler's 63rd minute strike, direct from a free-kick, was all they could muster in reply.

Thropton: I. Rogerson, Ferguson, Hunter, Wood, Cummings, Gutherson, Stewart, Turnbull, Arkle, Cooper, Glendinning.

Rothbury: T. Tait, Hay, Appleby, Cairns, Snowdon, D. Ferguson, Hedley, Angus, Miller, Laidler, J. Tait.

A 5-2 defeat by Stobhill Rangers followed and the final competitive game between Rothbury and Thropton took place in the

Coquetdale League at Armstrong Park on the 23rd December 1967 with Rothbury taking the honours and local bragging rights with a 3-1 win. Rothbury made a number of changes to their team and this largely contributed to their festive derby victory. However, the visitors at times almost threw Rothbury out of their stride with their constant running and challenges. Two penalties were tucked away for Rothbury by Robert Laidler and John Tait. Thropton made one change with Snaith replacing Ferguson at full-back. Hay, Appleby and Rogerson all returned to the Rothbury defence and Mendum played his first game since his transfer from Thropton, Laidler moving into the attack.

Rothbury began strongly with a steady attack on the Thropton goal but it was not until 20 minutes had passed that they forged ahead with two penalties in five minutes. Thropton pulled a goal back when Cooper prodded home from close range. In the second half Thropton continued to come back into the game but all the near misses were up at their end. John Tait shot just wide and Billy Miller hit the side netting with Gutherson and Hunter blocking shots on the line. Near the end Rothbury did manage to score the goal that had eluded them for most of the second half when Hedley slung over a long centre and John Tait was on hand to slam the ball home.

Mendum was outstanding for Rothbury and Hay and Appleby defended well. Thropton's Wood had a good game with wing-half Stewart a constant threat to the Rothbury defence. The teams lined up: *Rothbury*: T. Tait, Hay, Appleby, Mendum, Snowdon, Rogerson, Miller, Angus, Hedley, Laidler, J. Tait.

Thropton: I. Rogerson, Snaith, Hunter, Wood, Cummings, Gutherson, Stewart, Turnbull, Arkle, Cooper, Glendinning.

Stephen Davison came into the side at full back and Moore at right half as Rothbury took a point in a 1-1 draw at Longhorsley with a late equaliser on a frozen ground.

Watson pulled back for Blakey to shoot past Terry Tait for the opener and Rothbury went close as Snowdon headed John Tait's perfect cross against the crossbar before Tait embarked on a mazy dribble down the field with ten minutes to go and was chopped in the box, Robert Laidler firing in from the penalty spot.

Rothbury went behind at Stannington in the 11th minute of the next game as Thompson beat T. Tait with a hard shot, but after that it was all Rothbury. Laidler struck twice to edge them in front then John Angus must have been having trouble with his studs on a hard pitch, left the field and returned wearing baseball boots. It did the trick as he went on to score a hat-trick! He coolly rolled in his fourth and Miller beat three men and hit number seven from 18 yards. J. Tait completed the scoring with two minutes to go as he fired in after being set-up by Laidler.

A long-running Challenge Cup saga with Longhorsley followed, with Rothbury needing two replays to go through.

Kidd shot Longhorsley ahead at their ground but Angus slipped in J. Tait to level from 12 yards. Kidd grabbed his second but Miller headed the equaliser just before half time. J. Tait then dribbled down the left and crossed for Miller to score easily and put Rothbury ahead for the first time. Brownlee made it 3-3, but Laidler latched onto a poor clearance to restore Rothbury's lead. Blakey grabbed the equaliser, shooting past Terry Tait, who was the game's outstanding player.

The replay at Armstrong Park went to extra time as the sides couldn't be separated again. Laidler ran through to level after Rothbury had gone behind, but there were some protests from the visitors who felt he'd controlled with his hand on the half way line before racing clear. Longhorsley went back in front then Miller and Hedley both saw efforts cannon out off the woodwork and Angus had his head in his hands after heading over an open goal from five yards. Laidler grabbed the equaliser with just six minutes left and a clearance rebounded off Miller to give Rothbury the advantage in extra time. Kidd completed his hat-trick to peg the Coquetdalers back.

Rothbury went through 6-2 at the third attempt, Nichol and Hedley both bagging braces with Miller and Laidler notching the others.

Rothbury's first leg of the Coquetdale League Cup semi-final at Armstrong Park against Stobhill Rangers turned into a bit of a farce as the referee – a substitute – ordered Stobhill's Dixon off but he refused to go and after a bit delay, the game continued. There were three own goals in the game which was marred by 'extremely rough play' towards the end and Rangers ran out 8-5 winners.

Rothbury were 3-0 down when a Dixon own goal gave them hope and 4-1 down when another own goal went in. Laidler reduced arrears further and when he made it 4-4 from a disputed penalty, Rangers lost their heads. Laidler completed his hat-trick, but the game had become a kicking match by then.

Davison, Rogerson and Arkle all came into the Rothbury side and John Tait missed his first match of the season, being replaced by Nichol, as Rothbury went ahead at Choppington when Laidler smashed home from 20 yards but the hosts hit back four times as they took the Coquetdale League title in March.

Rothbury keeper Terry Tait played on the wing in the final home game of the season and scored twice in the 5-3 success over Swinney's. Davey Hay went in nets for the first half and Stephen Davison took the gloves for the second. Dixon's snap-shot put Swinney's ahead in the 17th minute but five minutes later Terry Tait raced down the wing and his cross sailed into the net to draw Rothbury level. Arkle's hard shot from close range put Rothbury in front and Miller made it 3-1.

In the second period Logan's shot rebounded in off keeper Davison but Terry Tait scored his second at the other end. Buckley made it 4-3 but Neville Appleby hit a fine shot from 25 yards to round things off, with Arkle superb for the Rothbury side that lined up: Hay, Appleby, Davison, Arkle, Snowdon, Rogerson, Hedley, Miller, Angus, J. Tait, T. Tait.

Rothbury had a mountain to climb in the second leg of the Challenge Cup semi-final against Stobhill and it got harder when Mendum and Nichol suffered a misunderstanding which gave the 'Gers a corner from which McLevy shot home after the ball had come back off the bar. When the keeper dropped the ball at the other end, Laidler was on hand to level, but Rothbury went out 9-6 on aggregate.

With all of their games played, Rothbury finished the season with a friendly against Longhorsley Celtic and were beaten 6-2, Hay scrambling home after Miller's shot was partially saved and Laidler adding the second. Ballantyne hit a hat-trick for the visitors.

But the Coquetdale League ceased to exist in the summer as it was folded and neighbours Thropton sadly disappeared along with the competition, with a few of their players moving down the Coquet to Armstrong Park. So, after thirty years away, Rothbury applied to re-join the North Northumberland League.

1968/69
Honours: Division Two Champions and Tate Cup Winners

ROTHBURY'S MAIN OPPOSITION in their first season in the Second Division of the North Northumberland League were Fairmile United, who hailed from the Berwick shipyard. Rothbury played their inaugural season in the League in their Black and White striped shirts, which had been chosen following a vote on the colour of the new strips.

They were denied a win in their opening league fixture away to Lowick as two late goals condemned them to a 4-3 defeat. John Stewart put Rothbury in front in the 17th minute with a left foot strike after good work by Alan Arkle and Billy Miller. Lowick levelled eight minutes later when, following a corner, Jackson rushed in, crashed a shot against the post and fired the rebound into the net. But two quick goals from Stewart and sub Michael Arkle put Rothbury 3-1 up at the break.

Davey Hay was pushed up front in the second half as Lowick came back strongly, but wingers Miller, nicknamed Pierre the Frenchman after the Roy of the Rovers cartoon character with his dark good looks and quick running, and Stewart continued to cause problems on the break. Lowick pulled one back and levelled just four minutes from time as Riley cracked in a low 18-yard shot. In the dying seconds J. Patterson beat Alan Arkle and hit the winner.

Rothbury crashed out of the Northumberland FA Minor Cup as they went down to their second defeat a week later at Rochester - but they felt a bit aggrieved after the official referee failed to arrive and the game was controlled by a spectator, which led to some ill feeling on both sides. With Rothbury clearly unsettled by the events, Dodd put Rochester in front in the opening minute. But John Angus levelled when he picked up a long clearance and took the ball to the edge of the box, side-stepped the advancing home keeper and scored easily. Rothbury were under severe pressure but held out with keeper Terry Tait make some top class saves. After a number of niggling fouls that went unpunished by the referee, Nick Gutherson raced down the field and flicked the ball over keeper Binovec's head to put Rothbury 2-1 up in the 56th minute. Ten minutes later Rochester equalised and then Murray crossed and, with the Rothbury defence appealing in vain for offside, Curry tapped the winner into the net.

But Rothbury stormed to a deserved win when they visited Belford Reserves and came away with the 2 points with a 4-2 win for their first in their return to the North Northumberland League.

Shanks headed Belford one-up in the 34th minute but Rothbury made it 1-1 just 60 seconds later when Cummings netted after two shots had been blocked.

Belford had a shot cleared off the line and hit the bar before Rothbury went in front when sub Robert Laidler sent a high cross into the area that sailed over the keeper's head and dropped in.

Miller then crossed for Alan Arkle to add a third. A mix-up between Sim and Murray allowed John Stewart to nip in and add the fourth in the 73rd minute. Patterson got a late consolation with a headed goal.

Wark reserves were next to go down as Rothbury recorded a 2-0 win at Armstrong Park in a drab game. Bill Snowdon and Terry Tait were solid at the back and goals from Moore, with a 4-yard header, and Robert Laidler secured the points.

If that meeting had been uneventful, the next week Rothbury won a thriller in the return fixture at Wark with an amazing 8-6 success. Laidler scored four times, including one from the penalty spot when John Tait was brought down, Gutherson hit a hat-trick and John Stewart added the other.

Unbeaten League leaders Eyemouth United then suffered an upset at Armstrong Park as Rothbury began to display their title credentials with a 4-1 win. Alan Arkle sent John Tait clear and he beat keeper Sinclair with a hard 15-yard shot to put Rothbury in front. Four minutes later, Laidler doubled the advantage from the penalty spot. Gibson pulled one back at the start of the second half but an own-goal by Grieve put Rothbury 3-1 up. Winger John Tait grabbed his second to make it four with a powerful drive. Davey Hay, Bill Snowdon and John Angus performed well in the surprise win.

But the club's form dipped the following week as they were held to a 2-2 draw away to Fairmile United, where they missed a number of chances to win the game. Murray put the Berwick men in front but Rothbury levelled five minutes before the break. Laidler hammered a penalty against the woodwork but Gutherson headed back into the danger area where Laidler's second shot deflected off Gilly, onto Lugget and into the net.

Rothbury were on top after the break and Nick Gutherson gave them the lead with a 15-yard shot. Lugget levelled in the 83rd minute.

Nick Gutherson plundered another hat-trick as a poor Glanton team was thumped 7-0 at Armstrong Park. Stewart and Laidler added two more before John Angus dribbled through to score and Alan Arkle rounded off the scoring with a tremendous shot from the edge of the box.

Rothbury were up among the Division Two leaders the following week as Embleton went down 5-1 at Armstrong Park in game with enough chances to have seen both sides wrack up double figures. The visitors took the lead when a long pass was dummied by Richardson for Turnbull to run on and score. Robert Laidler made it one-all and Alan Arkle put Rothbury ahead with a fine 12-yard header. Armstrong sliced into his own goal for 3-1, and Gutherson added a double to complete the rout.

But Rothbury crashed to their first home defeat as two late goals against the run of play gave Wooler a 5-2 win. Wooler were 3-0 up after only 14 minutes with 'Rocky' Hood (2) and Davidson on target.

John Stewart pulled one back in the 37th minute when he beat his marker and fired in from an acute angle. Five minutes later Alan Arkle blazed a penalty over the bar, but Rothbury got back to 3-2 in the 63rd minute as Nick Gutherson rippled the net. Terry Tait saved a Davidson penalty two minutes later and, with Rothbury pressing for an equaliser and peppering the woodwork and seeing Cassidy pull off some great saves, Davidson and Moffat struck in the last ten minutes to seal an exciting game in the first clash between the two clubs for many years.

Rothbury put the set-back behind them and trounced rivals Fairmile 5-2 at Armstrong Park the following week. John Angus scored from a Robert Laidler cross after just three minutes as Rothbury got off to a flyer and he then returned the compliment and set up Laidler for the second. Anderson pulled one back and Jefferson levelled right on half time. Arkle sent an inch-perfect 50-yard path into Nick Gutherson who evaded a tackle and slip the ball over the advancing goalkeeper Gillie's head to restore Rothbury's advantage and Laidler struck again to make it 4-2. He completed his hat-trick in the 75th minute after good work by John Stewart. The game was the final one for defender Davey Hay, whose consistency throughout the two previous seasons had contributed greatly to Rothbury's success.

In the first leg of the Tate Cup second round, Rothbury built up an insurmountable lead with a 9-4 drubbing of fancied Lowick. Phillip Bathgate took just 45 seconds to shoot them in front and after Gutherson had scored, he added his second. Gutherson went on to add three further goals and Stewart, John Tait and Laidler were also on target.

Goal-hero Gutherson plundered another hat-trick- his third in a row - in the second leg as Rothbury stormed to a 6-3 win to take the tie by a massive 15-7 on aggregate and ease into the semi-final of the competition.

He beautifully headed in a left wing corner for his first, smashed in from 25-yards for his second and slipped past Johnson to thump in his third. A right wing corner wasn't cleared and John Tait shot through a crowd of players to make it 2-2 just before the interval. Tricky winger Tait thought he'd added a second but the flag was raised and a goal from Laidler and a John Stewart lob completed the massacre.

A five-week lay-off due to bad weather followed a it was a ring-rusty Rothbury who drew 4-4 with lowly Alnmouth at Armstrong Park in the New Year.

Thompson put the visitors in front and the Seasiders added a second when Terry Tait missed a clearance, allowing Thompson his double. Gutherson headed in a Stewart cross to reduce the arrears and John Tait sent Robert Laidler clear to lob keeper Mason and equalise.

Laidler then blasted home a penalty to put Rothbury 3-2 up at half time. Thompson got his hat-trick in the 75th minute when he cracked in as the ball bounced loose from a corner.

Gutherson restored Rothbury's lead from the kick-off and Laidler then missed two open goals before Douglas levelled late on.

And the troubles continued as they went down 3-1 at Glanton, who they had hammered 7-0 at home in November. Rothbury took the lead in the 8th minute when Gutherson headed on a corner and Phillip Bathgate slipped the ball home from close range. But that proved the only bright spot in a surprise defeat.

The season got back on track when League leaders Lowick were beaten 2-1 at Armstrong Park in a game played in a snowstorm. John Angus was out injured with Stephen Davison coming in at left-back for his first game of the season.

John Stewart crossed from the right for Gutherson to steer the opener wide of Cossar in the 4th minute. Lowick equalised following a goalmouth scramble as a shot was blocked by Terry Tait but M. Patterson followed up to score. Lowick then struck the bar and the post and Rothbury had a Gutherson strike disallowed for offside. The winner came in the 70th minute when John Tait put Laidler through on the left and he turned the ball back from the bye-line for Gutherson to score easily.

And the club's first visit to Seahouses in over 30 years paid dividends when North Sunderland reserves were swamped 5-1 to put Rothbury on top of the Second Division.

Good work by Bill Snowdon, Stephen Davison and Neville Appleby meant the Rothbury goal was never in danger and Gutherson shrugged off three tackles and fired past Day to open the scoring. Bathgate then set up Stewart to score in off the post from 12 yards two minutes later. The third came when Angus swept a pass out to the left and Laidler slipped past Thompson and drilled past the advancing goalkeeper.

Laidler set up Stewart for the fourth a minute later. Gutherson completed the scoring when he stroked a Laidler centre into the corner of the net.

Rothbury took full revenge on Wooler with a 6-2 mauling at Armstrong Park in the first leg of the Tate Cup semi-final with a brilliant display. Only an excellent performance by Wooler keeper Cassidy kept it down to six. John Tait hit a post and Robert Laidler rattled the crossbar before Tait shot Rothbury in front in the 38th minute, cutting inside Taylorson and leaving Cassidy stranded with an 18-yard shot.

Two minutes later John Angus's deflected shot made it 2-0. Gutherson fired in a Laidler cross and Angus followed up to score from 12 yards for the fourth. Alan Arkle received the ball 30 yards from goal, advanced five yards and skilfully lobbed Cassidy for 5-1.

Another deep, high cross saw Gutherson head in the sixth, despite being accidentally punched by Cassidy as the keeper struggled to clear.

Wooler beat Rothbury 2-0 in the second leg up at Glendale, but the Coquetdale side went into the final with a 6-4 aggregate victory. Rothbury were missing centre half and captain Bill Snowdon, Robert Laidler and John Tait but had the game's outstanding player in Alan Arkle. Amazingly, It was the first game since September 1967 in which Rothbury had failed to score.

Rothbury went into the semi-final of the Runciman Cup with a hard -fought 2-1 win at Fairmile United where the defence took a pounding - but held out. Rothbury went in front mid-way through the first half when Alan Arkle headed in a John Tait corner. They went two up in 63 minutes when a long shot from Laidler bounced badly for Gilly and in a scramble Nick Gutherson forced the ball over the line.

Renton stroked in a dubious penalty to set up a nail biting final 15 minutes for Rothbury.

On the Monday evening, Rothbury lifted their first silverware of the season as they beat Embleton 3-1 at St. James Park, Alnwick in the Tate Cup final. Alan Arkle fired a tremendous shot against the Embleton bar before Laidler fired in a long-range shot that Turnbull turned onto the post, with Gutherson following up to cross for John Angus to put Rothbury 1-0 up in the 20th minute.

Just two minutes later G. Turnbull put through his own goal following an indirect free-kick to increase Rothbury's lead. Embleton were on top for the first 15 minutes of the second half but never looked like scoring until Davison was adjudged to have handled in the penalty area and Sample netted from the spot.

John Tait made it 3-1 in the 70th minute when Stewart's centre evaded everybody, but the left winger was first to the ball and somehow screwed a shot past the surprised goalkeeper and in from near the bye-line, Turnbull hoofing the ball into the roof of his own net in attempting to clear.

An unimpressive 2-1 win over North Sunderland reserves at Armstrong Park kept Rothbury on course for the title and promotion, Alan Arkle thumping in a loose ball in the 44th minute and John Stewart firing in a low cross-shot off the foot of the post for the second.

John Angus opened the scoring as the march towards the title continued with an 8-2 win at Alnmouth. John Tait bent in a left wing corner direct for the second and he sent Gutherson clear to place his shot wide of the keeper for the third. Another in swinging Tait corner had Alnmouth in trouble as Angus added his second by shooting through a ruck of players for the fourth. Gutherson added number five, and Angus completed his hat-trick when Arkle sent him through. Rothbury's seventh was a fine exhibition of ball control, coolness and shooting power by Tait and Angus pounced for his fourth after the keeper had spilled a cross by Stewart.

The Second Division title was secured with a 3-3 draw at Embleton seeing Rothbury lift the trophy with 33 points from 22 games, having won 15, drawn 3 and lost four of their fixtures. Fairmile United finished in second on 32 points. Embleton themselves were in with a shout, for if they had won they would have finished joint-top with Fairmile. Embleton went in front but Rothbury hit back when John Tait dribbled past two defenders and crossed for Nick Gutherson to head home.

Rothbury went in front with a penalty after the break. Stewart's corner was headed on to Angus by Gutherson, but his net-bound shot was punched over the bar by defender E. Dunn. Alan Arkle kept his cool to smash the spot-kick into the roof of the net. Laidler then sent Gutherson clear and the hot-shot lobbed the ball over the advancing keeper for 3-1. Embleton hit back strongly and a mistake by Terry Tait saw Paxton pull one back. Embleton equalised in the 81st minute with a controversial goal. The unmarked Sample shot into the corner from just inside the area, with the referee choosing to ignore the linesman's raised flag for offside. Despite Embleton's desperate pressure, they could not find a winner and Rothbury held out to claim the Double and promotion in their first season back in the North Northumberland League.

1969/70

ROTHBURY PLAYED their fellow promoted side Fairmile United in their opening fixture in the top flight of the North Northumberland League, and came away with a 4-3 win. Last season's leading scorer Gutherson shot Rothbury ahead but five minutes later Fairmile equalised. In the second half Rothbury were well on top and Bathgate netted a good effort for 2-1, Gutherson added a second for 3-1 and Stewart put Rothbury in the comfort zone at 4-1. But Fairmile staged a late rally and came close to snatching a point after pulling two goals back.

The following week Rothbury nosedived out of the Northumberland FA Minor Cup in the first round after a 9-0 drubbing at Burnside.

Rothbury were finding it tougher going in Division One and were beaten 5-4 by Belford in an exciting match at Armstrong Park. Belford took the lead after fifteen minutes but Anderson hit a high ball for Robert Laidler to tap in the equaliser. Three minutes before the break a G. Patterson 20 yard drive flashed past Bainbridge for 1-2. Bathgate sent Laidler clear and his miss-hit shot bobbled under the keeper for a soft goal for 2-2. Belford regained the advantage but Laidler put away a penalty for his hat-trick. Carr scored for the visitors and Patterson completed his hat-trick for 3-5 with Stewart pulling one back when he shot home from a narrow angle in the last seconds.

Rothbury progressed in the NFA Amateur Cup with an 8-3 win at North Sunderland. Stewart scored two, as did Gutherson, with Laidler hitting a hat-trick for the second week running. John Tait went off with a stomach complaint and was replaced by Stephen Davison, who netted a penalty for number eight.

Laidler was again on target from the penalty spot as Rothbury went down 2-1 at home to Burnside in a hard-fought, well-balanced match and the points were shared in an amazing 5-5 draw at Percy Rovers.

Rothbury gained some revenge on Rovers the following week as they were beaten 4-2 at Armstrong Park in the NFA Amateur Cup to see Rothbury advance into the third round.

Rothbury then beat Aydon Forest 3-2 at home with Laidler crossing for Gutherson to tap in the first. Gutherson added a second when he beat two men and fired into the corner of the net. It was one-way traffic towards the Rothbury goal after that with the defence taking a tremendous pounding. Thompson pulled one back with a hard shot past Terry Tait and ten minutes later Forest were level when T. Cook's deflected shot wrong-footed the keeper. Laidler hit the winner in the last minute with an unstoppable shot that crashed in from 18 yards

Rothbury were then far from outplayed but went down 3-0 at the Champions and unbeaten league leaders Highfields United and shared the points in a 4-4 draw with Longhorsely in the first meeting between the two clubs since the Coquetdale League became defunct.

Rothbury were unlucky to go out of the Northumberland FA Amateur Cup 2-1 at Rochester, with a penalty goal five minutes from time knocking them out. Laidler scored for Rothbury with a shot in off the post.

Rothbury then thrashed Duns 6-1 in a game affected by pools of water and goal areas that saw the goalkeeper's ankle deep in mud. Nick Gutherson headed in a Bathgate cross before a comedy goal put Rothbury two-up. Stewart's cross stopped in a pool of water and with the defence all at sea he nipped in to poke home number two. Stewart added a second with a hard shot that gave the keeper no chance before Bathgate set up Davison who left keeper Turnbull helpless for 4-0. Bathgate added a fifth and Stewart completed his hat-trick for the sixth.

Rothbury were 4-2 down at Spittal with 15 minutes to go - but turned it around to emerge 5-4 victors. Laidler scored another 'carry-on' special when his shot rolled across the face of goal and into the corner of the net with the keeper kicking fresh air in his attempt to clear. Stewart then claimed a second when his shot crashed down off the underside of the bar and was adjudged to have crossed the line. A Laidler penalty got it back to 4-3 and then Arkle let fly with a 30-yard drive that stuck in a pool of water, Laidler rushing in to nick his hat-trick goal. Gutherson blasted in the winner which was hotly disputed by Spittal who claimed that Arkle had blocked off the goalkeeper.

Rothbury beat Wark 2-1 in the Anderson Cup first round but then went down 3-2 at ten-man Burnside in the league with a terrible display in their first game of 1970. John Angus, Alan Arkle and John Tait were unavailable but it was no excuse as they were beaten by a late winner.

And it was snowing heavily as Rothbury kicked off for a 3-2 home defeat at the hands of Percy Rovers. Appleby headed a shot off the line but Shanks fired in the rebound to give Percy the advantage. On the half hour Balmbra crossed and Shanks powerfully headed down his second into the net despite the desperate attempts of a sliding Appleby and Terry Tait to keep it out. Bathgate played in Stewart down the right and his cut-back was fumbled at the near post for Laidler to pounce and pull one back. Gutherson also took advantage of a goalkeeping error when he scored despite the attentions of two defenders. At the other end Angus cleared off the line but Balmbra shot home the winner to the jubilation of Rovers.

Rothbury then threw away a 4-2 lead at Wark and missed a penalty as the home team fought back to draw 4-4. A Laidler lob put Rothbury in front and Gutherson dribbled around the advancing keeper for 2-0. An Arkle 25-yard half volley streaked into the top corner for the third before Davison was unlucky to have a goal chalked off for offside. Gutherson headed in the fourth before Laidler crashed a penalty against the bar. Gutherson had the ball in the net in the final minute but the referee judged that the ball had gone out of play during the build-up.

Longhorsley maintained their unbeaten home record as Rothbury went down 4-2, then, amazingly, Rothbury again drew 4-4 with Wark in the return fixture at Armstrong Park. Rothbury were three-nil up after 15 minutes with goals from Bathgate, Stewart and Gutherson putting them in control. But Wark fought back to take a 4-3 lead and Rothbury breathed a sigh of relief as they levelled in the 85th minute. A long ball from Arkle found Laidler unmarked and he shot wide of the advancing keeper.

Rothbury were awarded a Sanderson Cup tie against Fairmile United after the third time they had tried to play the fixture and the visitors failed to show, much to the annoyance of the club officials and Rothbury's largest crowd of the season.

The club went down 4-0 at Aydon Forest, but three of the goals, all scored before half time, were controversial as Rothbury waited for offside decisions that never came.

Nick Gutherson scored a hat-trick as North Sunderland were routed 5-0 at the coast. Gutherson grabbed his first in the opening minute and John Stewart added number two. Gutherson then shot home low for 3-0 and Angus sent Laidler down the wing to cross for Gutherson to send a header rippling into the roof of the net for his treble. Alan Arkle added the fifth with a low header from a corner.

Title-chasing Belford thrashed Rothbury 6-0 before a point was gained with a 1-1 draw at Hedgeley. Angus put Rothbury in front when he scored from close range but Hedgeley equalised in the 80th minute when Robinson headed goalwards and as Terry Tait and Curry went up for it, the ball span off the keeper's gloves and dropped into the net.

Rothbury were dumped out of the Anderson Cup with a poor show at home to Burnside seeing them go down 2-0. But they bounced back with a 10-2 caning of Duns for the first double of the season. Gutherson hit another hat-trick with Laidler, Wood, Angus (2), Ballantyne (2) and Stewart all chipping in.

Rothbury dispatched Hedgeley 3-0 at home with Laidler shooting them in front from the penalty spot in the 55th minute before adding another. In the 85th minute Gutherson lobbed the keeper for 3-0. And Rothbury completed the season with a 3-0 win over Fairmile United, Laidler shooting home the opener after 35 minutes, Wood netting from close range for 2-0 and then adding his second from close range after the defence had misjudged an Arkle free kick in the 83rd minute. Rothbury finished eighth in the table with 19 points, Highfields claiming the title with 31.

1970/71

ALAN ARKLE and Philip Bathgate signed for Wallington in pre-season with Michael Arkle, Rex Ballantyne and Harrison signing for Rothbury. They went down 5-3 to an Aydon Forest side that had lost Miller to Berwick Rangers and Straughan to Alnwick Town on the opening day of the season. Nick Gutherson scored at the second attempt from a poor back pass to make it 1-1 and when a Gutherson shot was parried John Stewart tapped in the rebound to put Rothbury in front, but Rothbury found themselves 4-2 down at half time. Ballantyne headed in a Gutherson centre for a full debut goal but Aydon killed the game with a fifth in the 80th minute.

Rothbury went out of the Northumberland FA Minor Cup in the first round with a 4-3 defeat at Lowick. The home side were 2-0 up in 15 minutes but Laidler pulled one back. It was 3-1 just before half time then Stewart pulled another back as he beat Cossar with a low shot. Later, a Stewart in swinging corner came back off the bar and Harrison netted the third.

Alan Arkle returned to Armstrong Park but the club sank to another defeat as Burnside won 5-3 in Coquetdale. Laidler put Rothbury in front in the fifth minute when his shot beat the keeper and was helped into the net by a defender.

Armstrong levelled but 20 seconds later a Stewart cross was pushed out by the visitor's keeper and Gutherson picked his spot to score. After the break Armstrong headed in from a free kick and a Douglas shot deceived Terry Tait to put Burnside in front. Tait then pushed a Douglas cross into his own net and his nightmare continued when his bad clearance was picked up by Lambert, with John Angus bringing him down for a penalty. Jobson scored from the spot. Laidler scored to make it 3-5.

Two late goals secured the club's first win the following week at Eyemouth. Rothbury went behind when Gibson pulled the ball back for White to score but an Arkle free kick dropped between Grieve and keeper Budge with Stewart nipping in to head the equaliser. Gutherson then chipped in Laidler who went around the keeper and slipped into the net for 2-1 and from a Gutherson centre Stewart whacked in a close range shot that spun into the net off Budge's shoulder. The win was secured when Laidler's low shot beat Budge and Gutherson followed up to make sure as Young attempted to clear off the line.

And Rothbury were firing on all cylinders as visitors Wark were hit for six in the next fixture. Gutherson opened when he received a Stewart throw in the box and span to fire in from a narrow angle. Stewart then got on the score sheet with a clever overhead kick before adding a second for 3-0. A Laidler cross caused panic in the Wark defence and Stewart pounced to grab his hat-trick before the break. Mick Arkle scored an own goal in attempting to turn the ball back to Tait but Laidler crossed for Ballantyne to net a well-placed header at the other end. Gutherson got his second from a Ballantyne cross at the second attempt after Wark keeper Turnbull had again been left exposed.

Rothbury then travelled to Longhoughton and beat bogey side Burnside 3-1. They were forced to make changes with Moore and debutant Winter coming in for the unfit Alan Arkle and Harrison. Winter almost had an immediate impact when he fired just over from a Ballantyne corner. Burnside took the lead in the 56th minute through Brown but Gutherson got on the end of a Ballantyne free-kick to make it 1-1. Five minutes later Gutherson crossed for Laidler to thump in a near post header and Moore settled it on the break in the 75th minute as Burnside poured forward in search of a leveller and left themselves ex-posed at the back.

A 5-3 defeat at Highfields United saw the club go out of the Anderson Cup in the first round where they were one down af-ter only five minutes. Alan Arkle headed in from a corner to equalise but shortly after Rothbury were behind again. Nick Gutherson was then knocked out after colliding with the keeper. He continued after treatment but looked badly shaken and could only look on in horror as Highfields added a third. Alan Arkle struck again from a corner, smashing in off the underside of the bar at the near post but United struck twice more before Laidler hit a consolation

An entertaining game in the NFA Amateur Cup saw Roth-bury advance as they held out in a hectic finish to beat Rochester 4-3 at Armstrong Park. The game kicked off at 4.45 pm due to Rochester player Alan Dodds' wedding (he didn't play!) and the largest crowd of the season turned out.

Snowdon played in Laidler to cross for Gutherson to score in off the foot of the post and Alan Arkle's mis-hit shot from a cor-ner crept in for number two. Corbett headed in off the post to pull one back and the same player shot against the woodwork before the interval. A McDonald penalty restored parity but Gutherson shot through the keeper's legs for 3-2. Then Laidler's miss-hit shot was controlled by Gutherson who turned and fired in his hat-trick goal. McDonald side footed in at the other end but Rothbury held out in a nervous finish.

Newly-promoted Embleton then rocked Rothbury in the League with a 6-3 win at Armstrong Park, Ballantyne and Gutherson (2) on target and Aydon Forest also won 2-0 at Rothbury.

Rothbury were well on top but struggled to a 4-2 win over Eyemouth United in the first round of the Sanderson Cup. The visitors went in front in the 43rd minute when Grieve headed in a corner. Rothbury equalised almost instantly when Harding turned Ballantyne's downward header into his own goal with the United players complaining that the ball hadn't crossed the line. A Laidler penalty put Rothbury in front then Laidler flicked over Grieve and Gutherson ran in to beat Budge for 3-1. Young pulled one back but Stewart played a one-two with Gutherson and fired in the fourth.

And the good Cup form continued with a 5-2 win over Belford in the Third Round of the Northumberland FA Amateur Cup. Rothbury found themselves 2-0 down but Gutherson hit a post and fired in the rebound to make it 1-2. In the second half Laidler lobbed in off the post to level and a superb Alan Arkle header from a Laidler corner put Rothbury ahead. Gutherson headed in a Laidler cross for 4-2 and a Laidler penalty completed the scoring.

A 2-1 defeat at Percy Rovers with Gutherson again on target saw the club in mid-table and Gutherson hit two more as the club went down 5-2 at Belford to leave them trailing the leaders Aydon Forest by ten points.

Newbiggin CW sent Rothbury spinning out of the Amateur Cup with a 6-0 thumping but the result was less painful than it looked with a combination of bad finishing, bad luck and some brilliant saves by keeper Hindhaugh contributing to the downfall.

Rothbury got back on track as Eyemouth United were cut to ribbons with a 7-0 mauling at Armstrong Park. Ballantyne opened the scoring with a superb 25-yard drive and Alan Arkle headed in a corner for number two. Harrison set up Laidler to make it 3-0 at the break. Alan Arkle rammed in a Laidler corner to make it four and Stewart added the fifth. A Michael Arkle penalty was parried away by Budge but his ball sent Gutherson through for six. From another set-piece Ballantyne headed in to put Rothbury in seventh heaven.

It took an equaliser just four minutes from time to earn a point at Wark in the next fixture. Rothbury were 1-0 down but a Gutherson header hit the underside of the bar and crashed in off the diving keeper to level. Young fired into an open goal to put Wark back in front and late on Gutherson rounded Sim and pulled back for a jubilant Ballantyne to net.

A good crowd turned out for a local derby against Longhorsley at Armstrong Park and they went away happy after a 4-2 win. Gutherson shot into the net from Laidler's quick throw but E. Cromer levelled. Gutherson intercepted a pass to slip his second past the keeper and Alan Arkle shot home from a corner to make it 3-1. Gutherson completed his hat-trick after a mistake in the visitor's defence and Christie pulled one back in the final minute.

But Rothbury then slumped to an embarrassing defeat at Powburn as they were thrashed 11-3 by bottom-of-the-table Hedgeley for their heaviest hammering in years. There was a covering of snow but the pitch was playable and the only bright spot was Nick Gutherson's double which saw him chalk up his 100th goal for the club. W. Laidler hit the other.

Rothbury then went out of the Sanderson Cup 3-1 at Belford, Laidler latching onto a back pass to slide home the only goal.

A 3-1 victory over Spittal Rovers sparked a revival but they were 1-0 down to a W. Wood 25-yarder for a long period. It was late in the game when Appleby headed in a Laidler corner at the back post and another corner was headed on by Alan Arkle for Ballantyne to slot home. This was followed by a 9-2 thrashing of North Sunderland as Rothbury hit six in the last half hour. Laidler hit four, with Gutherson and Stewart two each. All-action midfielder Rex Ballantyne added the other, created three and had his name taken for a dangerous tackle.

Highfields were then 3-0 up before Laidler shook off two tackles and crossed for Gutherson to head in but the Berwick side added another before the end as the cub's away form was in stark contrast to the performances at Armstrong Park. This was again displayed as Percy Rovers were crushed 7-3 with goal-king Gutherson netting FIVE times and Stewart adding two more.

Rothbury were trailing 4-0 at North Sunderland before Gutherson again found the net and Alan Arkle hit a double. North Sunderland made it 5-3 before the final whistle. The slump continued as Rothbury went one up in the 15th minute against Highfields United as Gutherson flicked on and Mick Arkle drilled a low 15-yard shot past Chappell but United hit four at the other end.

Revenge was gained with a 6-4 win over Hedgeley at Armstrong Park that saw Gutherson shoot through Brewis's legs to make it 1-0 in the 15th minute. Hope headed in for 1-1 but after Stewart had hit the post, Alan Arkle again shot through the keeper's legs to put Rothbury in front. I. Dodds hit the post at the other end and Maiden tapped in to equalise. Gutherson fired in from 12 yards then John Angus, who had been Rothbury's top scorer four seasons earlier, hit his first goal of the season when he scooped in. Gutherson completed a hat-trick for 5-2 but Maiden pounced again for 5-3. A Laidler penalty gave Rothbury breathing space and M. Tait's goal for Hedgeley in the 88th minute was just a consolation.

Rothbury got over their travel sickness with a 7-0 win at Spittal Rovers with new boy Michael Anderson making his debut. An own goal put Rothbury in front and a Laidler penalty stretched the lead. Gutherson scored three and four before Stewart flicked a neat shot over the keeper's head from an acute angle for the fifth. Ballantyne raced through to score the sixth and Laidler's chip completed the rout.

A 3-0 defeat at Longhorsley saw the home team pull clear of danger with Rothbury looking like the relegation candidates and the club then crashed to their worst home defeat for a long time as Belford hit eight at Armstrong Park. Laidler curled in direct from a corner and Alan Arkle and Gutherson also struck in reply as the club finished lower mid-table.

The Glory Years

1971/72
Honours: Anderson Cup Winners

ROTHBURY WERE wearing new all-white shirts to replace the black and white stripes they had been wearing and they celebrated a 4-3 victory over Longhorsley in a game switched to Armstrong Park to open the season as they held out against almost incessant second half pressure. In the 22nd minute a deflected Michael Anderson shot flew in off the underside of the bar and four minutes later John Stewart's low shot squeezed into the corner of the net to make it 2-0. Gutherson made it 3-1 after Welsh had pulled one back and Longhorsley's Anderson added a second before Stewart's shot was parried and Rex Ballantyne followed up to complete the scoring in a thrilling first half. Terry Tait in the Rothbury goal made some terrific saves as Longhorsley poured forward after the interval but they could only add one more to their tally as Rothbury claimed the two points.

Full-back John Angus the struck twice, as did Robert Laidler, with Gutherson and Ballantyne adding the others in a great 6-1 win at Percy Rovers.

And the goal-glut went on with a 9-1 win at RAF Boulmer in the first round of the NFA Minor Cup that saw the whites cruising at 6-0 at half time. Both Ballantyne and Gutherson hit hat-tricks with Stewart (2) and Laidler getting the others. Wark were then trounced 6-3 on their own turf.

Rothbury gave as good as they got but went down to their first defeat of the season 4-2 at home to Champions Aydon Forest. Laidler and Stewart scored and Rothbury had a couple of penalty appeals waved away.

The club squeezed into the 3rd round of the NFA Minor Cup with a narrow 4-3 win over Belford. Ballantyne beat Allan and placed the ball wide of keeper Anderson as he advanced, he then touched a free kick to Laidler whose deflected shot flew in for number two and Michael Anderson made it 3-1 after the break. Laidler scored the fourth but then could only look on in agony as he had a penalty saved by Anderson.

Belford got their revenge a week later as they beat Rothbury 6-1 to send them out of the NFA Amateur Cup in the first round.

A Sanderson Cup tie against Spittal Rovers exploded in the last five minutes at Billendean Park as three players were booked following a general fracas in the Spittal area during a 3-3 draw. Laidler stabbed the opener into the net but Rothbury were 2-1 down when they brought on the influential Rex Ballantyne, who had been a surprise sub, and they started dominating the game. Stewart made it 2-2 with Rothbury now well on top and Gutherson raced through to put Rothbury in front. In the 80th minute Patterson rose unchallenged to head in the equaliser and take the tie to a replay. Ballantyne was shown yellow in the melee as he lost his temper.

And a goalkeeping dilemma didn't help as Rothbury were beaten 6-5 at home in the replay. With Terry Tait at a wedding and reserve keeper Davidson unavailable, Mick Wood went in goals, Mick Arkle took over at half time and the match ended with Alan Arkle between the posts. Encouraged by this, Belford were 3-0 up in fifteen minutes before Robert Laidler hit four, including one direct from a corner, and John Stewart made the visitors sweat for the win.

In-form winger Stewart hit two more, a chip and a header, as Rothbury went out of the NFA Minor Cup in the third round 3-2 at Chirton SC.

Back in the league, with Angus and Alan Arkle unfit, Corrish came in and John Tait returned with Stewart and Gutherson scoring in a 3-2 defeat at Burnside. Bathgate had returned from Wallington, came on as a sub for Tait, and was unlucky as he sliced the winner into his own goal from a corner.

League leaders Highfields United then left Armstrong Park with the two points after a 5-2 win. With a number of senior players missing, Fiddes and Gibson came in for their first starts. Stewart headed in in great style and Alan Arkle added the other before the side began to settle with Lowick being beaten 5-2 at Armstrong Park the following Saturday.

Rothbury hit five again the following week at Longhorsley for another good win. Stewart put Rothbury in front but they were trailing 2-1 at half time. Laidler put away a penalty for the equaliser and Stewart's high cross deceived the keeper and dropped in to put Rothbury 3-2 up. John Tait sent Laidler clear and his low cross was turned into his own net by a defender before John Stewart headed in his hat-trick to seal the win.

Rothbury were outplayed for long periods at North Sunderland but grabbed a last minute equaliser to secure a point. Trotter shot the Fishermen in front after Terry Tait had parried a drive but the in-form Stewart crashed in low to level. In an action-packed encounter Fiddes fired a clearance against his own post before Hogg hit what looked to be the winner. But Rothbury had other ideas and in the dying seconds Gutherson evaded Day's tackle and went on to shoot right-footed past keeper Hogg.

The club then pulled of a shock 4-3 victory at the Pier Field over League leaders Highfields United. The half-fit Alan Arkle replaced Fiddes who was unavailable and Ballantyne returned to the attack in place of John Tait. Nick Gutherson struck all four, latching onto a pass from man of the match Philip Bathgate to shoot home before firing in another from a breakaway. He completed his hat-trick in the 83rd minute when Bathgate's perfect cross left keeper Simpson stranded at the near post as Gutherson headed in at the back. In the 89th minute Laidler's swerving centre was spilled by the keeper and Gutherson pounced to poke in the winner.

He hit four more as North Sunderland were sent crashing out of the Anderson Cup 7-1 at Armstrong Park. Bathgate, Stewart and Angus scored the others as Rothbury hit six in the second half.

And Rothbury should have had more than the four they hit against Eyemouth without reply in the League the following week but they were let down by poor finishing. Gutherson and Stewart both struck twice.

But they re-found their shooting boots as Rex Ballantyne inspired Rothbury to a 7-2 demolition of Lowick on their home soil as he was the game's outstanding player, scoring two and creating three more. Robert Laidler also hit two with Anderson, Bathgate and Gutherson also stretching the net.

Ballantyne hit another double and Gutherson a hat-trick as they scored seven for the third time in a month with a 7-1 crushing of Glanton at Armstrong Park. Bathgate and Stewart were also on target and it could have been more as they had two shots cleared off the line and twice rattled the woodwork.

Third-placed Spittal were then dumped 6-3 up in Berwick as Rothbury kept on smashing in the goals. The Billendean pitch was a quagmire with the goalmouths deep in mud and pools of water but it couldn't put Rothbury out of their stride. Wilson shot past Tait to give Rovers the lead but a Ballantyne free kick flew in off Mole's head with the Spittal defenders watching danger man Gutherson. Wilson struck again for the home team before Bathgate let fly from 25-yards to level again. Stewart headed in a Laidler cross to put Rothbury in front for the first time before Laidler was unlucky as his shot hit the post. He was celebrating not long after, though, as he drilled in a free-kick from the edge of the box for 2-4. Ballantyne beat two men and sent Gutherson through to give keeper Scott no chance for the fifth and, after both Bathgate and Laidler had seen shots crash out off the underside of the bar, Laidler added number six. Wilson grabbed his hat-trick for Rovers late on but they had been well beaten.

Rothbury were then given a mighty fright by bottom-of-the-table Percy Rovers at Armstrong Park but still emerged 2-1 victors. Rothbury had been under pressure when a Ballantyne corner found Alan Arkle who had time and space to pick his spot and drill in. Gutherson increased the lead when an Alan Arkle free kick sent him through. Hope turned a Rowell cross past Terry Tait to give the visitors hope, but Rothbury held out to continue their winning sequence.

Rothbury looked to have given themselves a mountain to climb with two first half own goals from Alan Arkle and Bathgate but they fought back from 4-2 down to win 6-4 at Eyemouth. Laidler hit two and Stewart, Ballantyne, Gutherson and Alan Arkle the others for another two points.

A trip to the coast saw Embleton dispatched with ease 3-1. Gutherson headed in a Stewart cross for 1-0 in the 20th minute and Stewart then drew the keeper and shot in for 2-0. When a Laidler cross was cleverly allowed to run on by Bathgate, Gutherson was again on hand to smash in the third from six yards. G. Turnbull headed in a consolation from a corner and the fiery Ballantyne was again booked for retaliation on the half way line.

Title-chasing Rothbury racked up their tenth successive win and put paid to Spittal's own Championship hopes with a 4-2 win at Armstrong Park as they came back from one down with Gutherson hitting another hat-trick and setting up Bathgate for the fourth. Rothbury could also afford the luxury of a penalty miss by Laidler.

Hot-shot Gutherson found himself closely shackled by Burnside centre half Glass as the winning run was halted by Burnside at Armstrong Park in a hard, even game that ended 1-1. Rothbury's forwards were restricted as Burnside played a tight defensive line but in the 35th minute good interplay by Bathgate and Laidler saw Gutherson run through, dribble around keeper Stewart and slot his 40th goal of the season into the empty net. Brown equalised for the visitors deep into the second half.

But the whites went into the final of the Anderson Cup with a stunning 8-4 win over Championship favourites Highfields United. Rothbury were 5-2 up at half time with pacy winger John Stewart hitting four. Gutherson netted twice and Ballantyne and Alan Arkle were also among the goals.

Gutherson added yet another hat-trick in a 4-0 win at Glanton, with Stewart getting the other, and he was again the hat-trick hero in a 5-0 win over North Sunderland. The visitors half-back McKay was being watched by a Burnley scout and he twice cleared off the line, but the Fishermen had no answer to Gutherson. Stewart and Laidler hit the others in the rout.

Robinson and Tom Dixon made their Rothbury debuts at a very muddy Armstrong Park as Wark Castle were seen off 5-1 with the two points moving Rothbury into joint second, level on points with Highfields, Aydon Forest leading the pack by just a solitary point. Dixon had a dream start, his cross being headed on by Gutherson for Ballantyne to shoot first time past the keeper giving him no chance.

In the second half Anderson, Laidler and a Sim own goal added to the tally before Laidler scored from a penalty but the referee had spotted the goalkeeper move off his line and ordered a retake. This time Laidler blazed yards over the bar. Young pulled one back before Gutherson cracked in the fifth after Ballantyne had mis- kicked.

But Rothbury suffered a horrendous run in that cost them the NNFL First Division title as they crashed 4-0 at Aydon Forest and then slumped to a 7-2 drubbing at Belford that saw them slide to fourth in the table behind Champions Aydon Forest, Belford and Highfields. Belford also won 4-0 at Armstrong Park on the final day of the season.

But Rothbury took full revenge on Belford as they won the Anderson Cup final at St. James Park, Alnwick. Rothbury were 3-0 up at half time, allowed Belford to pull level with three goals in fifteen minutes after the break before John Stewart popped up with the winner in a pulsating game.

Rothbury played a man-marking system with Philip Bathgate picking up and shadowing danger man Johnny Duncan. It worked, and when Bathgate himself found a couple of yards space, his low shot was deflected past the keeper by a defender to put Rothbury 1-0 up. The second was well worked; Alan Arkle cleared down the left to Laidler who sent Stewart clear. He played in Gutherson who rounded the keeper and gleefully fired home. Gutherson turned provider when he side-stepped Hall's tackle and drilled across the face of goal for Stewart to score from close range and Rothbury were cruising.

Then came the second half collapse that saw battling Belford pull it back to 3-3 but a Ballantyne defence-splitting pass put Stewart clear down the right and the winger advanced into the penalty area before slipping the winner under keeper Anderson to claim the silverware.

ALNWICK ASSOCIATION FOOTBALL CLUB.		
1882.	CLUB	GROUND.
October 14,	Derwent Rovers,	at Burnopfield.
October 21,	North Eastern,	at Alnwick.
October 28,	Newcastle,	at Alnwick.
Nov. 4,	Tyne,	at Newcastle.
Nov. 18,	Rothbury,	at Alnwick.
Dec. 9,	Derwent Rovers,	at Alnwick.
Dec. 30,	Rangers,	at Newcastle.
1883.		
January 13,	Rothbury,	- at Rothbury.
Feb. 3,	Rangers,	at Alnwick.
Feb. 17,	Newcastle,	at Newcastle.
Feb. 24,	North Eastern,	at Newcastle.
March 10,	Tyne,	at Alnwick.
March 24,	Final Challenge Cup Tie.	

1972/73
Honours: Sanderson Cup Winners

ROTHBURY GOT their campaign off to a flying start with a 5-3 win at Eyemouth United. Rothbury were 2-0 down at half time but a storming second half display saw them take the points. Mick Wigmore, Derek Stow and K. Wood came into the side that took time to settle before goals from Gutherson (2), Straughan, Ballantyne and Laidler secured the points.

And Rothbury coasted into the second Round of the Northumberland FA Minor Cup with a 5-0 win at Wooler.

After crashing to a shock 3-2 home defeat to Embleton in mid-week, where they played the first 25 minutes with just ten men, Rothbury also hit five in the first round of the Northumberland Amateur Cup as Bamburgh were seen off 5-2 at Armstrong Park. Stewart beat keeper Steele from close range, Alan Arkle's powerful shot into the corner gave the keeper no chance and Gutherson flicked on a Terry Tait clearance for Stewart to beat the keeper as Rothbury romped into a three goal lead. Thirty seconds into the second half Bamburgh pulled one back but Gutherson beat two men and drilled in a left foot shot for the fourth. Alan Arkle headed down a corner for Stewart to make it 5-2 after Bamburgh had struck again.

Longhorsley then left Coquetdale happy with a point after a 1-1 draw. Mick Arkle and Ballantyne fashioned the opening for Bathgate to put Rothbury ahead but Harbottle volleyed the equaliser.

Rex Ballantyne and Mick Arkle were outstanding in midfield and Nick Gutherson scored twice but Rothbury were undone by Herron as they went out of the NFA Minor Cup 4-2 at Bomarsund Welfare.

Gutherson was again on target with a superb chip and the home side netted an own goal, but Rothbury also went out of the Amateur Cup in the second round with a 7-2 defeat at MERA.

Glanton went in front at home to Rothbury but the visitors completely dominated the second half to take the points with a 3-1 win. Stewart soon levelled and then added his second in the 75th minute with a back-header into the top corner from a Mick Arkle free kick. In the last minute a Laidler free kick was deflected into the net by Robinson as he attempted to clear.

And Highfields then lost their unbeaten League record as they were well-beaten 4-1 at Armstrong Park. Michael Arkle had to play as an emergency goalkeeper after Terry Tait was injured with Cummings coming on as a sub on the wing.

Stewart fired Rothbury into the lead and a Laidler shot made it 2-0. Laidler struck again from 20 yards for the third and after the leaders had pulled one back, Gutherson rounded two men and fired into the empty net to complete the scoring. Rothbury had also been forced to re-organise after Mick Arkle had to go off after taking a kick in the ribs.

But lowly Belford then pulled off a shock 3-2 win at Armstrong before Pilot were thrashed 7-0 at the Pier Field, Berwick as a runaway win got them back on track. Angus (2), Ballantyne, Laidler, Straughan, Gutherson and Alan Arkle all finding the net. And Rothbury were even more impressive the next week as North Sunderland were routed 10-2 in Coquetdale.

In the first round of the Anderson Cup holders Rothbury looked to be on their way out but two goals in the last fifteen minutes secured a 2-1 win at Aydon Forest. Billy Thompson headed Forest in front in the 25th minute of an entertaining match and Cook sliced into his own net under pressure from Stewart to make it level in the 75th. With five minutes to go Gutherson netted a superb header from Arkle's long ball to put Rothbury into the next round

The club had their shooting boots on as they hit TEN for the second time in a fortnight, thrashing Bamburgh 10-1 in front of the imposing red sandstone castle at the coast. Gutherson hit four, Laidler two (one from the penalty spot), Straughan (2), Ballantyne and Stewart one apiece.

The great run continued with a 3-0 win over Burnside with two goals in the last ten minutes securing a hard-earned win. Arkle headed the first in off the post before Gutherson and Ballantyne added to the tally late on. And Rothbury were given an early Christmas present with rivals Aydon Forest gifting them four goals as the Alnwick side were again sent tumbling out of a Cup, this time 5-3 in the second round of the Sanderson.

Rothbury nearly threw away the two points as they were leading 4-0 early in the second half at Longhorsley but just scraped a 5-4 win. The result halted Longhorsley's impressive run of ten straight wins. Stewart avoided a tackle and slipped the ball past Pile for the opener before heading in a Michael Arkle centre for the second. Ballantyne started a move in his own penalty area and ended it by netting from 12 yards at the other end to put Rothbury three up. Stewart threaded a ball through to Michael Arkle who beat the keeper with a low drive. But Rothbury played the ball around too much at 4-0 up and cruising and Longhorsley pulled two back with twenty minutes to go. A swerving Straughan 25-yard drive looked to have sewn it up but Wigmore was beaten twice more in a nightmare final ten minutes and Rothbury were left hanging on for the win.

Aydon Forest then came to Armstrong Park and took the points with a thrilling 5-4 win in a display of all-out attacking football from both teams. A Laidler free kick was headed in by Alan Arkle, Nick Gutherson scored with a fine shot, Laidler stuck away a penalty and Rex Ballantyne forced home in a goalmouth scramble that kept Rothbury in third place, two points behind Aydon and trailing leaders Highfields United by four points.

The club progressed in the Anderson Cup with a 3-0 victory at Belford and followed it up by thrashing Spittal Rovers 8-1 in the league. Gutherson netted a quick-fire hat-trick with Laidler (2), Bathgate (2) and Stewart the other scorers. However, the club's title hopes were blunted as Aydon Forest completed a double with a 3-1 win at Alnwick, the hard-working John Stewart netting a consolation in the dying minutes.

Rothbury romped into the final of the Sanderson Cup with a convincing 6-0 drubbing of Glanton. In the 43rd minute Laidler was brought down by Paxton and he dusted himself down to stick away the resultant penalty.

Five minutes after the interval Stewart's shot crashed back off the post and Gutherson followed up to put away the rebound. Another from Gutherson and a 25-yard Alan Arkle free-kick plus one from Ballantyne put Rothbury out of sight. Alan Arkle had the roof of the net bulging again from a Gutherson corner for the sixth.

Bogey-team Burnside came back from 2-0 down to leapfrog Rothbury in the table as they took the points with a 3-2 victory. Ballantyne had Burnside in all kinds of trouble in the opening twenty minutes and it came as no surprise when Gutherson headed in a corner to put Rothbury one up. Five minutes later Gutherson was held in the box and Laidler tucked away the penalty. Burnside hit back and in the 80th minute Jobson let fly with an unstoppable shot that whistled past Wigmore for the winner.

Rothbury then went behind to a shock goal at home to lowly Bamburgh, but went on to record a storming 9-2 win with Gutherson hitting FIVE, Stewart, Laidler, Straughan and the pick of the bunch - a 25-yard Ballantyne free kick - completing the hammering.

Rothbury had an off-day in the semi-final of the Anderson Cup but still went through in a 2-0 win over Spittal Rovers. Stewart headed in a Laidler cross just before the break but the Rothbury goal took a pounding after half time. The victory was sealed on the break as a long clearance by Mick Arkle found Ballantyne who in turn pushed through to Stewart who beat the already committed keeper to make it 2-0 in the dying minutes.

Spittal were a much easier proposition in the league the following week as Rothbury came away with a resounding 5-1 scoreline. Gutherson's double took him to an amazing 50 goals for the season with John Angus also scoring twice. Laidler hit the other.

Despite having Adam Robson sent off after just twenty minutes, ten-man Highfields kept their Championship hopes alive with a 3-1 over Rothbury. Gutherson scored again for the whites.

A 6-1 thrashing of Pilot followed and after the visitors turned up late they must have wished they hadn't bothered as Stewart netted the opener from close range in the opening minute. A Laidler header rebounded off the crossbar and Gutherson stooped to head in the second. Michael Arkle added the third and fourth before Ballantyne and Stewart both saw headers fly in during the last ten minutes to round off a great win.

A howling wind spoiled the game at North Sunderland as Rothbury were held to a 1-1 draw. From a long throw Bathgate back-headed across goal for Laidler to prod in from close range but a dubious penalty decision saw H. Day beat Wigmore to claim a point.

Glanton were again thrashed, this time by 8-1, as six goals in 25 minutes before half time shattered the visitors. Gutherson and Michael Arkle both scored doubles and Laidler, Alan Arkle, Stewart and Ballantyne all got in on the act.

The club hit eight again the following week as basement club Wark Castle were demolished 8-0, giving the Rothbury forwards plenty of shooting practice for their up-coming Cup finals. Gutherson, Stewart and Laidler all hit two each with Angus and Spiers hitting his first goal for the club the others.

Rothbury won the Sanderson Cup final at St. James's Park, Alnwick with a strong surge in the last 25 minutes as they twice fought back from behind to beat Highfields United 3-2. In the 25th minute United's Renton played in Athey who had a clear run on goal and beat Wigmore as he advanced to narrow the angle. Wigmore then pulled off a brilliant diving save from a Renton header to keep Rothbury in it and, urged on by a large noisy travelling support, Rothbury got on top after the break.

In a promising attack Gutherson was upended just outside the box. The free kick was pumped to the far post where Gutherson headed down and, to a tremendous roar, Straughan smashed the ball into the roof of the net for 1-1. Highfields hit back and when Ballantyne sent Johnson tumbling in the box, he got up and tucked away the penalty low in off the post.

Rothbury Captain Alan Arkle was replaced by John Angus in a dramatic move that paid off as Rothbury began to pile on the pressure. They were rewarded when Straughan fired in a powerful 25-yard drive to level once again. Rothbury's winner came as no surprise when Stewart headed a corner back across goal and Angus headed into the back of the net. Angus also rattled the crossbar in the dying moments as Rothbury deservedly took the silverware.

Belford were thrashed 7-1 on the final day of the league season with Gutherson, Laidler, Alan Arkle hitting one apiece and sub John Angus netting a hat-trick. Aydon Forest took the title.

Rothbury lost out in a tense, exciting Anderson Cup final to an extra time penalty as Highfields got revenge for their Sanderson heartache with a 4-3 win. Athey put United ahead following a goalmouth scramble and after Wigmore had pulled off a couple of tremendous saves Hall played in Renton who poked into the corner of the net to put them 2-0 up. This woke Rothbury up and a Bathgate long ball caught their defence square for Gutherson to fire in.

McClymont netted a low cross shot for 3-1 in the second half after Rothbury had a penalty appeal waved away when Laidler appeared to be held by Hall.

John Angus was again the Rothbury hero as he came off the bench to replace Ballantyne and he hadn't been on the field long when he was brought down in the box by Hossack. Laidler struck the penalty well but Turnbull flung himself across the goal to save magnificently. Rothbury's heads might have dropped but in the 75th minute in a determined effort Straughan was moved forward from centre half and he pulled one back. There were just seconds remaining when Straughan and Spiers combined with the latter drifting over a high, floating cross with Angus appearing through the crowd to jump and power in a header. He was still being congratulated by his ecstatic team-mates as the final whistle blew. Rothbury were on top for the opening 15 minutes of extra time but in the second period Michael Arkle brought down Johnson who again got up and slotted the penalty past Wigmore.

1973/74
Honours: Anderson Cup Winners

ROTHBURY BEGAN the season with a 3-0 win over North Sunderland but it took a late face-saver, Michael Arkle's shot being deflected past keeper Pile by a defender, to save a point at Longhorsley in a 1-1 draw the following week.

Newly-promoted Hedgeley were then on the receiving end of Rothbury's best football of the season and they were saved further misery as they game was restricted to just 70 minutes by bad light. Gutherson, Bathgate and Ballantyne gave Rothbury a 3-0 half time lead. Stewart added another before Gutherson grabbed two more to complete his hat-trick - one bizarrely as a defender hammered a clearance against him that ricocheted into the net in the 6-1 away win.

The next Saturday saw Rothbury 6-0 up and coasting at North Sunderland after 75 minutes, but the Fishermen hit back and almost gave the visitors a fright, reducing the arrears to 6-4. Gutherson hit another hat-trick, shooting in off the post, a chip and a drive, with Gray adding two more and A. Wood the other.

Rivals Aydon Forest left Armstrong Park with the two points after a 2-1 success, Straughan pulling one back with a 20-yard shot, before Highfields beat Rothbury 1-0 and the blip in form continued with a goal-less draw at Eyemouth.

After scoring just once in three games, Rothbury went crazy with a 10-1 trouncing of Hedgeley in the Anderson Cup first round. Gutherson hit an incredible FIVE, Gray three, Stewart and an own goal rounding it off.

A good 2-1 win followed at Billendean as Gray headed in a Stewart corner to level after Spittal had gone in front and Gutherson grabbed a late winner when he coolly rounded Chappell and shot into the net.

Highfields were then stunned at Armstrong Park as Rothbury won a top-of-the-table clash 8-3. Gray headed in Stewart's cross following a flowing four-man move but Athey scored from close range to level. Wigmore turned a Woolley corner into his own net but Gutherson blasted in an equaliser at the far post and Gray made it 3-2. Gutherson netted his second after the keeper had parried a Stewart shot before Stewart himself and Alan Arkle scored. Gutherson, who had an outstanding game, hit in a powerful volley for his hat-trick and added a fourth with a clever back-header as Rothbury opened up a five point lead at the top with the surprise win.

Gutherson hit another hat-trick at Amble Vikings in a 4-1 win that also saw John Stewart's 25-yard drive deflect in off a defender, but a point was dropped with a draw at mid-table Glanton before Rothbury maintained a two-point lead at the top of the table with an emphatic 6-1 win over Hedgeley at Armstrong Park. Hedgeley, members of the NNFL since 1923, were forced to resign from the League a fortnight later due to a player shortage. Bamburgh became the fourth team to resign from the troubled NNFL a week later. The club, formed in 1896, followed Warkworth and Embleton who had resigned from Division Two.

"We feel it is better to retire with a little bit of dignity than to go through the season being a laughing stock. It is not the fault of the players we have got or the League," said club secretary Eddie Horsfield after the side had crashed 12-1 against Lowick with just nine men - including a boy of 11 and another of 12. Hedgeley's resignation cost Rothbury four valuable points.

Bad weather left Rothbury inactive for a month and they were shocked at Armstrong Park on their return as Amble Vikings won 4-1. D. Gray scored the only goal. They got back on track with a 4-2 victory over Spittal with Gutherson, Laidler (pen), Ballantyne and Gray the scorers.

Rothbury went through in the Sanderson Cup with a 4-2 win over Aydon Forest in a game packed with goalmouth incident and controversy. Gutherson fired Rothbury in front in the 35th minute with a shot deflected in off a defender but Patterson shot home the leveller two minutes before the break.

Full-back Mick Wood hammered in a 25-yard shot for his first goal in almost three years to put Rothbury back in control but Smith fired home through a crowded goalmouth to make it 2-2. Ballantyne headed in from close range for 3-2 and Anderson added the fourth.

Rothbury also advanced in the Anderson Cup with winger Laidler hitting a 75th minute winner in a 1-0 success at Spittal.

The troubled League was concerned at the number of post-poned games and Secretary Barry Bilclough told the Gazette: "We are becoming increasingly concerned over the increasing number of postponements and are not satisfied with some of the reasons being given." Eyemouth went top of the league by two points but Rothbury had four games in hand and thrashed Longhorsley 9-2 with Gutherson hitting four, Laidler three and Ballantyne and Bathgate the others before slumping to a shock 3-1 defeat at second-bottom Belford. Gutherson had shot Roth-bury ahead after just three minutes.

Goalkeeper Wigmore was then injured during the game but played on in a 5-2 reverse at Burnside with Gray and Straughan the scorers.

More injury troubles were to follow as right back Malcolm Spiers was stretchered off with a broken leg 15 minutes from the end in a 6-0 win over Glanton. Gray and Stewart hit two apiece with a Laidler penalty and Gutherson the others before the game was abandoned as Spiers was rushed to Ashington General hos-pital.

Burnside were then dispatched 7-2 as Gutherson hit a hat-trick, Gray two, Ballantyne and a Laidler spot-kick keeping Rothbury in contention.

Having thrashed Glanton just a fortnight earlier, hopes were high for the Anderson Cup semi-final clash between the clubs but it took a last minute goal to win it at Wooler. A Laidler cross was headed in by Stewart with Rothbury on top but they struggled in the second half and a Paxton cross glanced off Henderson and rolled into the net for a fortunate Glanton equaliser. In the last minute Bathgate blocked a clearance and shoved through a good pass to Gray who beat Clark with a high shot and Rothbury breathed a heavy sigh of relief.

Rothbury rose to the occasion in the Anderson Cup final as they produced their best form to see off Amble Vikings 3-1 at St. James's Park, Alnwick and lift the silverware. Vikings were 1-0 up in 35 minutes as F. Young half hit a shot from 25 yards that deceived Wigmore and crept inside the post. But Rothbury dominated the second half and when a Gray shot was parried by W. Stewart, Gutherson pounced to level. In the 75th minute Anderson scored with a superb left foot shot through a crowded defence and into the corner of the net and in the final minute a defender handled under pressure from Gutherson and Laidler blasted in the penalty.

Vikings gained full revenge in the semi-final of the Sanderson Cup, though, and went through 5-3 after extra time. But it took an 89th minute equaliser kept them in it after Rothbury looked certain winners. Vikings went in front but Ballantyne restored parity before S. Wood banged in a volley to put Rothbury in charge. Vikings levelled with sixty seconds of normal time to play and added three more in extra time before Stewart pulled one back late on.

A three-nil defeat at Aydon Forest killed off Rothbury's Championship hopes and took the title to Alnwick. Although Ballantyne hit the bar late on, Rothbury were well beaten.

1974/75

Honours: Division One Champions, Sanderson Cup Winners, Anderson Cup Winners

MICHAEL ANDERSON and Nick Gutherson were to form the most formidable strike partnership in Northumberland as goal-crazy Rothbury romped to a superb Treble success, reached the quarter finals of the Northumberland FA Minor Cup and made an unsuccessful bid to move up the Football Pyramid into the Northern Alliance League after blowing the opposition apart.

Rothbury's opening league fixture of an amazing season was cancelled at Armstrong Park when the visitors, Percy Rovers, were unable to field a team. A number of the first team squad travelled instead to Milfield with the newly formed Reserve team in the Second Division of the NNFL and helped secure a 3-1 win in their first game. Anderson hit a hat-trick as the reserves battled to a hard fought win - and it wouldn't be his last as he stormed to become the League's Golden Boot with a simply sensational goal haul.

Rothbury went in front in the 20th minute when Wood sent Laidler clear down the left and his cross evaded the defence for Anderson to fire in from 12 yards. After soaking up some pressure from the Glendale side, Rex Ballantyne sent Anderson clear to smash in his second off the woodwork from 18 yards. Milfield pulled one back soon after but Anderson completed his treble with a long range shot that crashed down off the underside of the bar and in, the referee waving away the protests of the home team.

Anderson went nap when he starred for the first team in their opener the following week, crashing in five in a 7-1 demolition of Longhorsley at Armstrong Park. He put Rothbury in front in the 10th minute with a superb goal, Rex Ballantyne slipping him in to evade a tackle a crash a low 20-yard drive into the bottom corner of the net. Ballantyne added a second before the break and was unlucky to see an effort come back off the post just 30 seconds after the restart. Laidler crossed for Anderson to glance in a header for 3-0 minutes later and Mick Wood set him up for his hat-trick before Nick Gutherson created his fourth. Influential midfield playmaker Ballantyne combined with Laidler down the left to set up Anderson to make it 6-0. Long-horsley pulled one back late on, but centre half Stainbank sliced into his own goal to complete the rout.

It was a tougher proposition when Rothbury crossed the Border into Scotland for their next fixture against Eyemouth, but the long journey was worth it as their persistence was re-warded with the two points. Nick Gutherson had Eyemouth keeper Scott at full stretch to turn away a drive early on but a mistake by Straughan let in Aitchison to volley home the opener for the Scotsmen in the 12th minute.

At the other end Anderson was brought down in the box, but the referee ignored their appeals for a penalty and the red-hot hit-man fired just wide as Rothbury turned up the pressure.

Rothbury deservedly equalised on the hour when Gutherson challenged Scott for a high cross and when the keeper spilled the ball, Laidler was on hand to score from 10 yards.

They went in front when Alan Arkle's long ball found Laidler down the left wing and he crossed for Ballantyne to squeeze in a far post header from a narrow angle.

Rothbury sealed the win when Laidler picked up a clearance from Straughan in his own half and ran 50 yards before thump-ing the third past a helpless Scott.

The Coquetdale side kept up their unbeaten record and top spot in the table with a 3-2 win at title rivals Amble Vikings, where they turned in their best performance of the season so far. The game was switched to Alnmouth as a cricket match was taking place on Amble's ground. The game was played in blus-tery, windy conditions and was an incident-packed thriller.

Rothbury went in with a 1-0 lead at the interval when Laidler raced onto a through ball from Gutherson and picked his spot to slip the ball past keeper Stewart.

Rothbury doubled their advantage in the 50th minute. Anderson headed a Laidler cross goal wards and defender W. Stewart, under pressure from Gutherson, only succeeded in helping the ball into his own net.

But Amble hit back instantly, a mistake by Wigmore allowing them to score. Trustram then clipped the Rothbury bar with a chip before the Seasiders levelled with just 12 minutes to go. F. Young was brought down in the box and S. Young kept his cool to net from the penalty spot. Amble were now well on top but Rothbury broke and John Stewart hit the winner with 8 minutes left with a low cross shot from 15 yards.

Rothbury were given a surprise in the Second Round of the FA Amateur Cup at Armstrong Park when visitors Springhill went ahead in the third minute, a short goal kick mix-up between Wigmore and Henderson letting in Tait to walk the ball into the net. Rothbury were shaken and took some time to settle before they levelled when Gutherson knocked on to Laidler to fire in from 15 yards. Ballantyne then headed against the bar before they turned up the heat and added three more before half time. Springhill were on top for long spells in the second period and hit a second on the hour, but Rothbury advanced into the next round with the 4-2 win. Bedlington CW knocked Rothbury out of the competition 4-3 in the Third Round, but the result was no disgrace.

And Rothbury embarked on a tremendous run in the NFA Minor Cup, reaching the quarter finals of the competition for the first time.

After taking Nelson CW to a replay in the fourth round of the competition, Rothbury won 2-0 in a good game between two evenly matched teams. A Straughan penalty in the 80th minute put Rothbury in charge and Anderson pulled back from the bye-line for Rutherford to add the second eight minutes later and put Rothbury into the hat for the quarter finals, but the club crashed at West Allotment Celtic 4-0 to shatter their dreams of further glory.

Back in League action, Rothbury won their tenth successive game with a 13-0 annihilation of a young and inexperienced Embleton side at the coast. Hot-shot Anderson hit five and Nick Gutherson an amazing SEVEN in the goal blitz. Anderson opened the scoring after Gutherson flicked on an Alan Arkle free kick. Gutherson added the second soon after when he latched onto a Ballantyne pass to round the advancing keeper and roll the ball into the empty net. Gutherson pounced to net his second before Ballantyne headed in from a corner to make it 4-0 after 25 minutes.

Anderson headed in the fifth from a corner just before the break and he grabbed his hat-trick for number six from close range five minutes after the interval. Gutherson then pounced to net his hat-trick goal with a turn and shot from close range. Anderson was back on target with a left foot shot then Gutherson headed in number nine. He blasted in another three soon after, the pick of the bunch a fierce 15-yard volley from Arkle's downward header.

Ayton Ams. were also dished out an 8-1 drubbing at Armstrong Park before putting up a stern fight and only going down 2-1 at home the following week. They suffered a blow in the 75th minute with the score locked at 1-1 when midfielder Alan Morton was stretchered off with a broken leg after going for a fifty-fifty ball with Ballantyne. Rothbury went in front in the first half when Laidler crossed for Anderson to head in and Rothbury hit the bar as they looked to stretch their advantage. Ayton deservedly equalised in the 70th minute as Frater slipped the ball between a defender's legs and hit a powerful left foot drive bulging into the net. Morton's broken leg caused a 25 minute stoppage in play and with darkness creeping in at the restart, sub Straughan struck a late winner for Rothbury.

The Armstrong Park side then sent holders Amble Vikings crashing out of the Sanderson Cup with a comprehensive 4-2 away win. Anderson struck twice in the first half to put Rothbury in control, but Easton fired in a 25-yard free kick to pull one back in the 40th minute.

And Vikings levelled just two minutes after the restart as Easton's low centre beat everyone for Smith to side foot in first time past the stranded Wigmore. Rothbury got back on top and forced a succession of corners, making keeper Stewart produce some excellent saves. S. Wood smashed in a 25-yard drive to put them back in front and Ballantyne sealed the victory with a free kick from similar distance. However, Amble Vikings would go on to face West Allotment Celtic in the final of the Northumberland Amateur Cup at Portland Park, Ashington later in the season.

Eyemouth topped the NNFL First Division table at the end of January with 20 points and Spittal Rovers were in Second on the same total. Rothbury sat in third with 18 points but had 7 games in hand on Rovers and 6 on Eyemouth. And the leaders were left stunned when they were on the receiving end of a 9-0 thrashing at Armstrong Park with Anderson again the hat-trick hero. He put Rothbury in front before Phillip Bathgate almost added number two with a long range shot that crashed back off the bar.

In the 65th minute Anderson held off three challenges to make it 2-0 and Laidler hit the post before Henderson slid in for number three. Laidler crossed for Anderson to head in his treble and Straughan netted a penalty after Ballantyne had been brought down. As the visitors crumbled, Gutherson blasted in number six from 12 yards following a corner. Henderson added a second before an own goal and an Arkle drive rounded off the scoring as Rothbury sent out a message to the rest of the League.

North Sunderland were next to receive a 7-1 slaughter in their own backyard as Rothbury went rampant in the charge towards the League title. Gutherson and Anderson soon put Rothbury 2-0 up, but Giacopazzi in the Seahouses goal was in inspired form, making a string a fine saves. When he was beaten, North Sunderland twice cleared shots off the line. And in the 44th minute they broke up the park and Wright headed in a deep right wing cross at the far post.

In the second period Laidler was chopped down and got up himself to net the penalty before the prolific Anderson added another two to complete yet another hat-trick. Straughan added a second penalty and the hard working Henderson completed the massacre.

Rothbury went back to the top of the table when they sent RAF Boulmer crashing to earth with an 18-1 thumping at Armstrong Park the following week - the club's biggest win for many, many years and their best in the North Northumberland League.

Anderson plundered a hat-trick in the opening 15 minutes and Gutherson added another before Green pulled one back for Boulmer with a long range shot. But there was little respite for the airmen when an Arkle header and a Straughan penalty and close range effort made it 7-1 at the break. Anderson added FIVE more, Gutherson FOUR more and Henderson and Ballantyne got in on the act to complete the massacre.

Surprisingly, Rothbury required a last-minute own goal to see off the challenge of Belford Reserves at Armstrong Park a week later. Rothbury had a new goalkeeper, Allen, between the posts and they went in front when goal-machine Anderson headed in a Laidler cross. For all Rothbury's pressure they couldn't add to their tally and were stunned late on when Allen allowed a 30-yard free kick from full-back Gilchrist to slip through his hands and into the net.

With the clock ticking down and Rothbury increasingly desperate, a corner was swung in from the right sparking a scramble in the Belford box. Arkle kneed the ball goal wards, a defender cleared off the line but the ball struck another defender and rebounded high into the net.

On the same day across at Scots Gap, Northern Alliance neighbours Wallington made history with Mather netting in a 1-0 win over Morpeth Town to send the Greens into the semi-final of the Northern Alliance Challenge Cup for the first time.

Rothbury went into the Final of the Anderson Cup for the fourth season running with a 2-0 win over Eyemouth Utd over the border. But the margin of victory could have been much greater after a brilliant display. They hit the woodwork three times, had a goal given then disallowed and missed a penalty. Gutherson and Anderson both struck in the second half before Laidler's penalty was saved by Scott.

Bottom of the table Embleton gave Rothbury a scare at Armstrong Park when they went into an early lead and almost added a second. But Anderson hit another hat-trick and Gutherson, Stewart, Arkle and Ballantyne were all on target as Rothbury hit back to win 7-1.

The Championship bid showed no sign of let up as RAF Boulmer were thumped 9-2 in the return fixture. Anderson's sensational form in front of goal saw him notch another FOUR goals and Gutherson (2), Ballantyne, Laidler and Henderson added the others in another comprehensive victory over the struggling airmen. Malcolm Spiers made his first Rothbury appearance for a year in the game after coming back from a suffering a broken leg.

Eyemouth must have been sick of the sight of Rothbury and they went down 2-0 again in the Sanderson Cup semi-final with normally reliable keeper George Scott blundering to gift both goals. The match was played on a bitterly cold evening at Bamburgh and Eyemouth had the better of a tight first half, but

Rothbury came closest to breaking the deadlock when Anderson's overhead kick hit the bar and Henderson's follow-up was blocked on the line.

Rothbury again went close when Gutherson headed a corner on to Anderson, whose header looked to be over the line before Brown headed away. In the 75th minute Rothbury went in front when Straughan pumped a 55-yard free kick into the box that Scott misjudged and the ball sailed over his despairing out-stretched hands and into the net. Another free kick led to the second. Arkle flighted it in, and when Scott fumbled, Gutherson nipped in to score. Alnwick rivals Aydon Forest thumped Glanton 7-0 in the other semi-final as the defending Champions faced up against the Coquetdale men in both the Anderson and Sanderson Cup Finals - and they were hot on their heels in second place in the table, trailing by 5 points but with a game in hand.

An Anderson goal put Rothbury in front against Belford in a 4-0 away league win - but this time it was a Belford defender of the same surname who put through his own goal. Henderson hit the bar and went close with a drive from distance before he added number two. Gutherson struck twice late on to seal the comfortable win.

He struck another double in the Anderson Cup final as arch-rivals Aydon Forest were beaten 4-1 at St. James's Park, Alnwick. Forest had the better of the exchanges and could have been two up in the first twenty minutes; instead it was Rothbury who were two up at half time. Forest's Thompson shaved the wood-work with a thumping diving header and Bateman saw a shot scrambled off the line by keeper Allen. Davies then hit the underside of the Rothbury bar with a thumping 30-yard drive. Bathgate was making some positive forward runs and he spread play out to Anderson who crossed for Ballantyne to send a volley crashing into the net for a well-worked goal against the run of play. Just before half time Gutherson thundered home an Anderson pass to make it 2-0.

Early in the second half Rothbury failed to clear their lines from a throw in and Thompson netted from close in to pull it back to 2-1. Straughan then raced back to clear after Mick Wood's back pass went over keeper Allen's head. But Gutherson knocked the stuffing out of the Alnwick side with a third that had a bit of fortune about it. Laidler's shot looked covered by keeper Catlow but the ball took a wicked deflection off Gutherson and ran gently into the net at the other post. Soon after Anderson forced home the fourth following good work by strike partner Gutherson at the bye-line and the all-White shirted Rothbury had claimed their first silverware of the season, retaining the Anderson Cup.

Anderson was again on target with two more in a 3-1 win at Spittal to set up Rothbury for the First Division title.

The club made a bid to join the Northern Alliance League at this stage, and with Alston and Stockton resigning from the League, they were hopeful of the ambitious step up to join local derby rivals Wallington, Alnwick Town, Morpeth Town and Belford, who made the move two seasons previously. There was some doubt about Rothbury being able to continue using the Armstrong Park pitch, but it was suggested that with the Cragside estate in which it resides becoming a country park, its future was more assured. The Alliance at the time contained such teams as South Shields, Marine Park, Percy Main, Seaham, Workington Reserves from West Cumbria, Wallsend, Bede Colliery, Bedlington CW, Newcastle University, Throckley and Greenwell's, as well as the club's North Northumbrian rivals.

Rothbury dropped a point in a Wednesday night 2-2 draw at closest challengers Aydon Forest but secured their title credentials and displayed the necessity to test themselves at a higher level with 12-2 demolition of Glanton to put the club within two points of the silverware. Rothbury had played 20 games, winning 18, drawing 1 and losing 1 with 37 points while Aydon Forest had played one less, winning 15, drawing 2 and losing 2 with 32 points. Eyemouth had completed their fixtures and were in third with 28 points and Amateur Cup Finalists Amble Vikings were in fourth having played 19, won 13, lost 5 and drawn 1 with 27 points.

Glanton arrived at Armstrong Park with just eight players and had conceded five before a ninth man turned up. Rothbury were 8-1 up at half time with Anderson notching another hat-trick, Gutherson chalking up another 2, Arkle, Laidler and Ballantyne chipped in with one each. Gerald Paxton, who would later play for Rothbury, netted a penalty in reply for the beleaguered visitors. Common added another for Glanton in the second half but, after missing a number of chances, Arkle struck again before the lethal Anderson added another three to take his tally to SIX, taking his season's haul to well over 50 as the club raced to the title.

1975/76
Honours: Sanderson Cup Winners

ROTHBURY HAD reached the last eight of the Northumberland FA Minor Cup the previous season and kicked off the campaign with a 6-2 win over Milfield in the first round of the competition. With Henderson and Straughan playing for Alnwick Town, John Stewart at a wedding and Michael Anderson unfit, it was a weakened team that went twice behind before taking the tie.

The first league game was won convincingly, 5-1 at Lowick, before Wooler were seen off 6-0 at Armstrong Park with Gutherson hitting four and Stewart and Anderson the others.

A comfortable 3-0 win over Lowick followed in the NFA minor Cup second round with Anderson shooting the opener and almost immediately adding a second. Gutherson sewed it up with the third goal.

Rothbury then advanced in the Anderson Cup with a convincing 8-0 win at Broomhill. Ballantyne and Laidler both hit doubles with Anderson, S. Wood, Bathgate and Gutherson all adding to the tally.

It took a last minute leveller from Alan Arkle to save a point at home to old rivals Aydon Forest in the League, his lobbed free kick deceiving the keeper and slipping through his hands into the net. When the keeper had fumbled early on, Gutherson struck the opener, but Aydon hit back with two goals before Arkle's late point saver.

The club was always in control as they went into the last 16 of the NFA Minor Cup with a 5-2 success at North Tyne Champions Hexhamshire. Rothbury were easy winners with Gutherson striking a hat-trick and Anderson adding two more.

Rothbury followed this up with another 5-2 win at North Sunderland before crushing Belford 7-2 at Armstrong Park. Ballantyne, Anderson and Gutherson hit two-apiece with Stewart netting the other.

So it was a confident Rothbury that advanced into the quarter finals of the NFA Minor Cup as they beat Northern Alliance side Throckley Welfare 3-1 on merit.

Throckley took a quick lead but Rothbury equalised after forcing several corners as Gutherson let fly with a 20-yard shot that keeper Johnson couldn't keep out. Throckley attacked strongly in the second half but Alan Arkle and Ingham cleared the danger.

In the 75th minute Rothbury went in front when Ballantyne headed in from an acute angle after another corner had led to a goalmouth scramble.

Throckley threw everything into attack in an attempt to salvage the tie but they were hit with a sucker punch a minute from time as Anderson passed to the unmarked Laidler whose 20-yard shot beat Johnson low to his right. The victory was especially sweet for Rothbury as they had been refused admission to the Alliance at the beginning of the season.

Rothbury received a tough draw for the last eight however, pulling Northern Alliance League Stobswood out of the hat. Stobswood included Bains (former Newcastle United and South Shields), Glass (Ashington), Knox (West Brom trials and North Shields), Gibbard (Burnley junior) and keeper Ken Walton, formerly of Gateshead and South Shields in a vastly experienced squad.

The good league form continued with an 8-0 drubbing of Lowick. Gutherson, Anderson and Wood all struck twice and Laidler added another direct from a corner. He was unlucky to also see two free kicks crash back off the bar. Ballantyne added the other as it was all one-way traffic with Rothbury dominating.

They went one better with a 9-0 hammering at Broomhill the following week in what turned into virtually a practice match with Anderson grabbing a hat-trick, Gutherson (2), Alan Arkle, Laidler, Ingham and Bathgate taking the club into third spot behind Spittal Rovers and leaders Aydon Forest.

Rothbury then lost their first match for a year as they went out of the NFA Minor Cup in a 6-4 thriller at Stobswood. The home team built up a five goal lead before Rothbury began to play and they might have salvaged a replay but for some poor finishing.

Nichol blasted home from a half-cleared corner to put Stobswood 1-0 up and Sparrow netted from a centre for the second. Sparrow added his second before Mick Wood headed one off the line and John Stewart hit the post at the other end in a rare Rothbury attack just before the break.

Two cracking drives from Allison made it 5-0 to the favourites. Anderson pulled one back but Bains burst down the right and crossed for Sparrow to complete his hat-trick and make it 6-1.

In the last twenty minutes Stobswood ran out of steam and Anderson controlled a high pass and made it 6-2, then Gutherson netted for 6-3. Gutherson added another with a header to make Stobswood sweat and in a very exciting finish the home side were left hanging on. Alan Arkle was superb for Rothbury throughout.

In contrast, Rothbury then scraped through a drab Sanderson Cup tie at Eyemouth with a solitary goal the following week.

And the whites then slumped to their first League defeat in 14 months with a shock 3-2 loss to second-bottom Ayton Amateurs at a windswept Foulden. Nick Gutherson struck twice and Mick Wood was desperately unlucky when his shot struck the inside of the post, rolled along the line and bounced off the other post and into grateful Ayton keeper Henderby's arms.

A rousing 3-1 win at Wooler with both teams giving maximum effort got Rothbury back on track with Gutherson putting Stewart through and he outpaced the defence before coolly slotting past the advancing keeper for 1-0. Wooler levelled through Bissett but a Laidler free-kick put Rothbury ahead at the break. Stewart added the third before smashing a 30-yard shot against the post.

But Rothbury's title hopes were blown as they went down 3-2 at home to Eyemouth and slipped down to fourth in the table.

After a three-week lay off, Rothbury bounced back to beat Broomhill 6-1 with Gutherson netting a hat-trick. The ten-man visitors were no match for Rothbury, though it was not their best performance as they struggled to establish any rhythm. Ballantyne, Anderson and S. Wood completed the scoring.

The club fielded a new-look attack with Boardman coming in off the left and Laidler switching to the right and the new boy struck a goal in a 6-0 win over Ayton Amateurs in the Anderson Cup quarter final. Anderson and Gutherson helped themselves to two each and Laidler put away a penalty.

In the Anderson Cup semi-final Rothbury were the better team throughout and thoroughly deserved their 3-0 victory over Wooler. An early goal from Gutherson put them in charge and late strikes from Anderson and Laidler secured the win.

Another disappointing league result saw the side endure a frustrating goal-less draw at Belford with the wind spoiling the game. But in the Sanderson Cup, Rothbury advanced with a superb 3-1 win at rivals Aydon Forest. Anderson fired in a Laidler cross and then beat two men, rounded keeper Jamieson and shot into the empty net to put Rothbury 2-0 up half time. After Forest had pulled one back, Laidler crossed and Gibson put away a diving header to put Rothbury into the next round.

Rothbury then staged a thrilling fight back to salvage a draw in the NNFL at Eyemouth in a thrilling top-of-the-table clash. Rothbury were 2-0 down but Ballantyne's low cross was flicked into the net by Ingham to put them back in with a shout. When Ballantyne headed in the equaliser from a Laidler corner, it left the club requiring wins in their last four fixtures to retain the First Division title.

Their hopes were dashed in the next fixture as S. Wood was sent off and ten-man Rothbury crashed 2-0 at home to Spittal Rovers.

And a late penalty by Aydon Forest full-back Glass saw the Alnwick side lift the Anderson Cup at St. James's Park. When Ballantyne handled, Glass stepped up and drove the ball past Allan in the Rothbury goal to win it. Forest had outplayed Rothbury whose biggest danger had come from set pieces. But Rothbury went ahead against the run of play early in the second half when a Boardman cross was only partially cleared and Anderson followed up to make no mistake. Forest equalised in the 70th minute as Riddell powerfully rocketed in a near post header from a corner, and Glass finished the job.

Rothbury hit back from their Cup disappointment to thrash Ayton Amateurs 8-0 at Armstrong Park and they claimed the Sanderson Cup trophy with a 4-1 win over Spittal, but the match was marred when Rovers' Sandy Grieve broke his leg after 20 minutes with the score at 1-1.

Spittal captain Wallace put his side ahead from the penalty spot after Arkle was adjudged to have tripped Kelly but at the other end a Laidler centre deceived keeper Tait and dropped into the net behind him for 1-1. A 20-yard rocket shot from Gutherson put Rothbury ahead and further strikes from Boardman and Laidler clinched the Cup in a below-par performance.

1976/77

Honours: First Division Champions, Sanderson Cup Winners, Anderson Cup Winners.

THE CLUB got off to a storming start by winning their first six games on the trot, culminating with a 5-0 success at Wooler. The unstoppable Rothbury side saw Anderson beat keeper Guthrie with a low shot after chesting down a pass from Gutherson to make it 1-0. It took Rothbury some time to add a second, but when they did, Wooler's resistance crumbled. Gutherson netted a delicate lob for 2-0 and then added the third when he headed in the rebound when Guthrie parried out a Laidler shot. Arkle added a fourth before sub Phillip Bathgate completed the rout with a swerving 25-yard drive that deceived Guthrie.

Gutherson was back on the goal trail as he struck four to see of the challenge of second placed Lowick in a 6-3 away thriller. Gutherson put the Whites in front with an early header and struck again with a powerfully hit shot from Gray's right wing cross. He was denied a hat-trick when Robinson headed his shot off the line before Rothbury cruised into a 3-0 lead with a fine, flowing move. Ballantyne's pass found Laidler out wide and he crossed for Gray to sweep in.

It was looking easy for Rothbury at this stage but Lowick pulled one back when T. Crawford scored after good work by Robson and Hall. And Lowick struck again when M. Crawford hit the net. Gutherson completed his hat-trick with two further goals before Lowick reduced the deficit once again. But Wood and Gutherson netted further goals to underline the Coquetdale side's superiority.

Rothbury embarked on another fine run in the Northumberland FA Minor Cup and sent tough Ashington side Northern SC crashing out in extra time in a third round replay at Armstrong Park. Northern took the lead when Trewick raced through from the defence, played a short one-two on the edge of the Rothbury box, and cracked in a shot that Allen got his hands to but couldn't keep out. Blair then struck the post for the visitors with a snap shot.

Deep into the second half Boardman was brought on for Rex Ballantyne and his fresh legs soon earned Rothbury a leveller. The sub whipped in a cross for Gray to flash in a header that beat the keeper and goal-poacher Anderson made sure from close range.

Boardman was the Rothbury hero in extra time when he pounced to grab the winner after the Northern keeper parried a Laidler drive into his path.

But Rothbury's hopes further progression in the County's most prestigious lower league competition were dashed in the next round when Northumbria Police sent them crashing to their first defeat of the season, with speedy winger Russell tearing them apart in the final 20 minutes. Despite the 7-1 scoreline, Rothbury were far from outclassed. Rothbury were on top in the opening 20 minutes and went close when John Stewart and Anderson both shot inches wide. Midway through the half the Police went in front when Lambert headed in a left wing cross and just minutes later they added a second. Stewart headed narrowly over at the other end as a confident Rothbury hit back, but their possession broke down around the penalty area as the Police thin blue line held firm and their hopes were wrecked by Russell late on.

Neighbours Wallington fared better in the competition and the Greens went into the semi-finals with a 4-2 win over Newbiggin CW as Rothbury continued their top form in the league with a 4-1 win at Spittal Rovers in a game that was reduced to 35 minutes each way after some confusion over the changing rooms and the late arrival of some Rothbury players.

They were run close in a game at Milfield that saw Rothbury sweat in the closing stages after leading comfortably for 80 minutes. Gutherson headed them into an early lead and the advantage was doubled when Stewart drilled in following good work by Gutherson and Anderson. Rothbury were put under heavy pressure after Milfield scrambled a goal back ten minutes from time, but could have made the win more comfortable with a breakaway move that saw Anderson rattle the crossbar and Laidler fired the rebound wide with the goal at his mercy.

This was followed up with a confidence-boosting 3-0 win at Swarland, Gutherson steering in after Laidler's long-range drive was spilled and then Straughan's long ball put Anderson in the clear to chest down and shoot home low into the net. Anderson cut back from the bye-line for Gutherson to power in a header for the third. The team was missing the steadying influence of the classy Alan Arkle at the back, but Stewart performed well as an emergency full-back in his absence.

Rivals Aydon Forest had suffered some early set-backs when some of their young players were promoted to the club's senior team - Alnwick Town - but they sounded a warning to the rest of the league with a 6-1 drubbing of Milfield. Ian Tait, Clarke, Stewart Murray (2), Ray Murray and Henderson were on target for the Champions who had re-found their form and netted 33 with just one against in their last four fixtures.

But Rothbury weren't keen on letting them ruin their Centenary party and Swarland had keeper Munro to thank for keeper the score down to 5-0 in the return game at Armstrong Park. Ian Arkle made a very promising debut at full back and Philip Bathgate played at centre half with the influential Alan Arkle still out.

Gutherson struck with a well-placed shot in the 25th minute to make it 1-0. Ballantyne then added a second with a dipping shot from 25-yards that left Munro helpless after a five-man move. Gutherson had time and space to net again for 3-0. Anderson netted a penalty and then beat a couple of the defenders to cut in from the right and fire home the fifth.

Sanderson Cup holders Rothbury cruised into the semi-finals of the competition with an emphatic 4-0 win at Wooler. The home side managed just two shots on goal in the entire ninety minutes.

The lethal Gutherson-Anderson partnership was at it again for the first, Nick heading down for Mick to push the ball wide of keeper Boyd. Rothbury missed several chances before Anderson got on the score sheet again for the second. He completed his hat-trick by gliding in a Gutherson cross and he was rugby-tackled by Boyd for Laidler to step up and complete the scoring from the penalty spot.

The Anderson Cup was held on a League basis during this season and Rothbury were surprisingly held to a 1-1 draw by Milfield at Armstrong Park with a Laidler penalty miss with just five minutes remaining proving costly.

Rothbury missed a number of chances before taking a lucky lead when Anderson's cross hit defender Laylock's heel and span past keeper Chappell. But karma was restored when S.Wood's pass bounced off the referee and left Robertson clean through to slip the ball past Allen.

The marauding Anderson was brought down by Gargan in the 85th minute but Laidler was left with his head in his hands as he cracked the spot-kick wide.

Alan Arkle returned from his long layoff through injury as Rothbury got back on track in the Cup Group with a 3-0 win at North Sunderland. Gutherson's centre was only half cleared and Laidler volleyed in for the first, and Gray set up Stewart and Gutherson to seal it late on.

But the club went on a dip in form, losing an Anderson Cup group match 1-0 at Milfield and drawing in the league before going down to a shock 4-3 defeat at home to Spittal Rovers for the first of just two league defeats of the season - and all of a sudden they didn't look the Championship certainties that they had previously.

Rothbury went into a seemingly insurmountable 3-1 lead with Straughan (pen), Gutherson and Anderson stretching the net. Visiting striker Laverty levelled things with two fine headers and a gleeful Grecian hit the late winner when Allen dived to parry Campbell's shot into his path.

Rothbury scraped through into the Anderson Cup final with a 0-0 home draw with North Sunderland sufficient to see them through Group 2 which contained Lowick, Milfield, North Sunderland and Swarland. Seasiders Alnmouth topped Group 1 after Aydon Forest blew a 6-point lead at the top of the group also containing Spittal, Belford Res and Wooler.

Wallington were unlucky to go down 3-2 to Gosforth and Coxlodge during extra time in a replay in the semi-final of the Northumberland FA Minor Cup - but the Greens would go on to clinch the Northern Alliance title in a thrilling finish. They must have thought they'd blown it when they were beaten at home by Carlisle City in their final league game when a point would have secured them the silverware. City required just a point from their final game against Alnwick Town to snatch it from their grasp. Alnwick did their North Northumbrian neighbours a massive favour by beating the Cumbrians 2-0 at St. James's Park.

Rothbury were also left biting their fingernails as they were held to a 1-1 draw at home to title-challengers Lowick. The team did not play well again, but the point kept them four points clear at the top and virtually killed off Lowick's hopes. Both defences were on top in a tense game that saw Gutherson put Rothbury in front with a powerful shot that flew past Wigmore and crashed into the roof of the net. T. Crawford equalised with a header from a deep I. Johnstone free kick. Rothbury pressed hard for a winner but couldn't find their scoring touch that had served them so well throughout the season.

But Rothbury had something to cheer as they easily retained the Sanderson Cup with a comfortable 3-0 win over Swarland at St. James's Park, Alnwick. Gutherson sparked the celebrations by chasing a long ball and losing his marker to shot low past the advancing Munro. Alan Arkle cleared off the line at the other end before Anderson flicked a long clearance from Allen over his marker and raced on to shoot home. Stewart made it 3-0 before the break as Rothbury collected their first silverware of the season.

The club had a side playing in the Morpeth Sunday League and they were unlucky not to claim another trophy when they were beaten by Barrington Rangers in a Glaxo Cup Final replay after coming twice from behind at St. George' s Hospital in the first game to draw 2-2.

Rothbury recorded a 3-1 league win at North Sunderland on the Saturday, but the Monday night saw them soundly beaten 4-1 at fierce rivals and Champions Aydon Forest in the First Division as the chase heated up and left the Alnwick side trailing by just a point. Smith hit the first and had a shot handled on the line by Straughan for Glass to hit in the second from the penalty spot as Forest piled on the pressure. Gutherson gave Rothbury hope when he pulled one back but S. Murray hit a double to claim the points and leave Rothbury reeling on the ropes.

Lowick won 9-0 at home to Milfield to keep within two points of Rothbury, but they had played a game more and had just one fixture remaining - away to Aydon Forest.

Rothbury won the Anderson Cup with a 2-1 win over Alnmouth in the final and then completed a Centenary treble in style by sensationally crushing second-bottom Wooler 14-0 at Armstrong Park and following up with a 4-0 win over Swarland at home to regain the title. Aydon Forest thrashed Lowick 7-2 but slipped to a 4-3 reverse at home to fourth-placed Spittal on the final day. Rothbury had played 18 games, winning 14, drawing 2 and losing 2 to finish three points clear at the top. It was the second time in three seasons that the all-conquering Coquetdale men had raced to a clean sweep of the NNFL honours.

Rothbury Reserves finished second bottom in Division Two but ended the season in style with an 11-1 drubbing of mid-table Longhorsley.

LOCAL SOCCER TABLES

COQUETDALE LEAGUE
Division " A "

League table up to and including 10th April.

	P	W	L	D	F	A	Pt
Widdrington.	20	15	1	4	97	39	34
Longhirst ..	20	16	4	0	105	39	32
Choppington	19	15	3	1	86	31	31
Felton	21	13	6	2	80	42	28
Morpeth V.	21	9	9	3	56	62	21
Rothbury ..	19	8	9	2	55	59	18
Pegswood ..	19	8	9	2	56	64	18
Ellington ..	21	8	11	2	43	71	18
Linton	21	7	9	5	59	48	17
St. George's..	21	3	15	3	32	95	9
Wallington ..	20	2	14	4	24	69	8
Thropton ..	18	1	17	0	19	87	2

1954

1977/78
Honours: Subsidiary Cup Winners

ROTHBURY FINISHED the season with a trophy, two semi-final appearances and runners-up spot in their premier season in the Ashington & District Welfare League. Their dominance of the North Northumberland League, and with a number of clubs leaving the NNFL, meant that Rothbury were forced to test themselves against different opposition. The reserves, however, continued to play in the Second Division of the NNFL.

Rothbury were unlucky not to win their first game in the new league as they missed a late penalty and had a late 'goal' disallowed. The Rothbury team had a strange look with several new faces and Common was unlucky not to open his account when he hit the underside of the bar. Hosts Lynemouth had taken the lead but Common won the ball and slipped it through to Gray who sidestepped and challenge and fired into the net to make it all-square.

But Universal SC were hammered 4-2 at Armstrong Park the following week. Common had again hit the bar early on but opened the scoring when he dribbled past three men and smashed into the net. He then headed in a Laidler cross for his second. Anderson rounded the visiting keeper to roll in number three and new boy Common completed his hat-trick at the third attempt after his first shot was blocked by keeper Nicholson, his second came back off the post and he tucked away the rebound.

Whitehouse SC were unlucky not to take a point as Rothbury went away happy with the points from a 3-2 win. A Gray shot slipped through the keeper's hands for 1-0 and a Laidler penalty put Rothbury two-up. Whitehouse hit back to bring the game level but a Wood free-kick flew straight through the defensive wall to grab the points for the visitors.

A 6-1 demolition of Pegswood Welfare followed before Rothbury suffered their first defeat of the season, 4-3 at the Joiners Arms. Three players failed to appear and the club kicked off with only ten men. Common hit two goals. The club was unhappy that it was the third time certain un-named players had failed to show for away games.

Rothbury made several changes the following week and it paid off with a 6-2 win at Newbiggin CW reserves. A Wood free kick put Rothbury ahead but goals from Connell and Nicholson made it 2-1 to the Colliers. Anderson got on the end of a Laidler cross to make it 2-2 just before the break and seconds after half time Anderson struck again to put Rothbury in front. Common hit another hat-trick with a shot, a header and a cross-shot in off the post to complete the scoring.

In the first round of the NFA Minor Cup, Rothbury advanced after a hard-fought 4-2 win at home to Pegswood.

And the margin of victory should have been greater the following week as Rothbury needed a late winner to see off the poorest opposition they had faced, Alcan, 2-1. After a goal-less first half Common headed on a free kick that bounced off Trotter and went into his own goal. A short back pass from Stewart caught Allan out and Robinson nipped in to grab the equaliser. In the last five minutes Wood crossed and Anderson headed the winner past Taylor, much to Rothbury's relief as the win moved them to the top of the table.

But they were knocked off the top the following week after a 5-3 defeat at Area Workshops. They were 5-1 down at half time but improved after the break. And they suffered their first home defeat when Fell-Em-Doon recovered from going behind in Rothbury's first attack, Anderson turning in a long Laidler cross, to win 4-1.

Rothbury went out of the Minor Cup in the third round as a three -goal blitz in the last fifteen minutes by Dudley Welfare saw them crash out 5-2.

But they advanced to the second round of the Booth Cup with Phillip Bathgate heading the winner in a 3-2 victory over Whitehouse SC.

It took a winner in the dying seconds for Rothbury to grab the points at Constitutional SC. After missing a load of chances, Rothbury looked to have blown it when Constitutional grabbed a late equaliser. Laidler scored direct from a corner took put Rothbury in front but with the clock ticking down Greenacre levelled. In the dying seconds Malcolm Spiers sent sub Common clear to steer the ball wide of McCormack and steal the points.

Rothbury finally found their shooting boots the following week, thrashing North Seaton reserves 11-2 at Armstrong Park. Common hit SIX, Gray a hat-trick, Laidler scored from the penalty spot and John Stewart added the other. Rothbury substitute Gibson played for the visitors who were a man short – and, inevitably, scored for them.

A late goal from the visitors denied Rothbury victory as they were held 3-3 by Hirst Progressive but Rothbury were back in form for a 5-0 win over Whitehouse SC, who were totally outplayed with Alan Arkle in particular in superb form.

Stewart went clear and had time to pick his spot for the first. Arkle then headed in a Stewart cross for 2-0. A corner was helped on by Arkle and Gray applied the finish for the third. With Rex Ballantyne, who had been out injured all-season coming on for the final twenty minutes, Arkle crossed for Gray to head in the fourth. An Arkle header completed the scoring to round off a cracking personal performance.

Rothbury were back in the title race after a 3-2 win at the league leaders, Universal SC. But after a three-goal opening salvo, it was backs to the wall defending from Rothbury in the second half. A Paxton shot hit the post and the rebound was forced in by Laidler to put Rothbury in front. Gray headed through and Common picked his spot for the second. They were in dreamland two minutes later when Common beat a defender and pulled back for Gray to head in. Rothbury just weathered a second half storm to complete the double over Universal and keep up the pressure at the top.

Heavy snowfall wiped out the February fixtures and Rothbury went out of the Booth Cup when they returned to action, going down 1-0 to a goal mid-way through the second half for the Joiners Arms.

But in an absorbing tie in Rothbury's first appearance in the Aged Miners' Cup they staged a late rally for a thrilling 5-3 victory over Northern SC at Armstrong Park. Northern went one-up but Common dummied Atkins low cross for Anderson to thump high into the net for 1-1. Wood flighted a free kick over the wall for Common to run on and head past Henderson for 2-1. Two goals in two minutes from the visitors shook Rothbury but Bathgate headed in a free kick for 3-3. With the tension mounting Arkle powerfully headed in a Gray corner for 4-3 and Common got up to head in the fifth.

After the thrills of that fixture, it was a romp away to Newbiggin CW reserves in the quarter finals of the Subsidiary Cup, Common (3), Boardman (2), Gray, Anderson and Arkle scoring in an 8-1 massacre.

Poor Newbiggin were hit for eight for the second week running when they visited Armstrong Park in the League. Gutherson (2), Gray (2), Bathgate and another Common hat-trick saw off the visitors without reply.

But Rothbury's title hopes were dashed as after racing into a two goal lead at Hirst Progressive, the team collapsed. Anderson ran clear and shot in the opener with Common adding number two before Hirst hit back with six as Rothbury fell apart.

They cruised into the semi-final of the Alcan Cup with Common (2), Anderson (2), Atkin, Wood and a penalty from Rex Ballantyne seeing off Newbiggin CW reserves 7-2 this time.

Ballantyne was injured again in a tough 2-1 win at Central Club where Rothbury held out for the win.

Rothbury scored twice in extra time to go into the final of the Subsidiary Cup after beating Lynemouth 3-1. Lynemouth went in front in the 49th minute when K. Anderson scored. Philip Bathgate levelled from the penalty spot with just ten minutes to go, showing nerves of steel to shoot home. In extra time a Ballantyne corner whipped in the breeze causing panic in the Lynemouth defence and Hindhaugh sliced into his own goal. Anderson then latched onto a weak back pass and when his shot was blocked by the advancing keeper, Common joyfully followed up to hit in the rebound.

And two late goals, in the final ten minutes, from hit-man Common took Rothbury into the semi-final of the Aged Miners' Cup with a 2-1 win over Seaton Sluice.

Common hit another double, with Gray also scoring twice and young Kevin Proudlock the other in a 5-2 win at second-placed Pegswood that put Rothbury firmly in contention for the runners-up spot.

Rothbury squandered a number of chances and went out in the semi-final of the Alcan Cup, going down 3-2 at bogey-team Joiners Arms.

A 1-1 draw with the Joiners and a 4-3 win over the Central Club saw Rothbury complete their League programme and finish runners-up behind Universal SC.

In the Subsidiary Cup Final Alan Arkle kept Rothbury's hopes alive with a headed equaliser just 90 seconds from full time at the Hirst welfare pitch against Whitehouse. Whitehouse had struck the woodwork before Harmer gave them the lead when he finished off a good move. In the final minute Gray swung a free kick to the far post and Arkle powered in.

But Rothbury went out in the semi-final of the Aged Miners' Cup, going down 5-2 to Ashington reserves. A hat-trick by Tait and another by Storey put Ashington 4-0 up. Gutherson and Anderson struck to get it back to 4-2, but Johnson hit a fifth late on.

Rothbury won the Subsidiary Cup with a 2-1 win over Whitehouse SC in the replay. Anderson and Ballantyne scored to secure the trophy.

BROOMHILL.—A new football club has been opened here, and will play under the name of "The Coquetdale Rovers." W. Clancey is captain ; R. Wilkinson, vice-captain, J. Rutherford, secretary ; and J. Tait, treasurer.

1884

Robere et Sapientia

1978/79

ROTHBURY STRIKER Nick Gutherson was powerful in the air, had a great touch, control and vision, was quick and had a powerful shot with both feet - why he wasn't snapped up by a League club is a mystery. He started out banging in the goals at defunct neighbours Thropton at just 13 and hit around 1,000 in an amazing amateur career that spanned three decades.

Modest Nick told the Sunday Sun in 1989: "I haven't kept a record of the goals I have scored. I wish I had. I think I've managed between 15 and twenty this season. I don't think I've scored over 1,000 over the years, but I'm not far off."

He was on the goal trail again in 1978/79 with a hat-trick in the opening game of the campaign in a 4-1 win over Hirst Welfare at Armstrong Park.

Kevin Proudlock hit the opener from an acute angle before Gutherson netted with a header, a close range finish and a right foot shot in off the post.

He was suffering from the flu but played and flicked on a long kick from keeper Allan for Laidler to shoot into the net in a 5-2 home defeat at the hands of Hirst Progressive SC. Phillip Bathgate added the second with a header.

Keith Storey, Kevin Proudlock and Woodburn all returned to the Rothbury squad for the visit of Area Workshops. Straughan scored to put Rothbury in the lead but they were trailing 2-1 at half time. Laidler twice hit the bar and Straughan the post before Laidler levelled from a short Rex Ballantyne free kick. Proudlock crossed for Laidler to put away his second and supplied another delivery for Gutherson to head in and make it 4-2.

Rothbury travelled to Broomhill in the first round of the Northumberland FA Minor Cup and lady luck shone on the Co-quetdale side after a poor first half but a good second. Straughan, Laidler (penalty), a Lillico own goal and Nick Gutherson scoring to see Rothbury through 4-2.

Back in league action, a double from skipper Phillip Bathgate gave Rothbury a point their play hardly warranted. He smashed in a 25-yard volley and netted a header in a 3-3 draw at Whitehouse SC.

Rothbury were then forced to fight all the way for a win over Alcan after the Aluminium men had led 2-1 for most of the game. Cummings belted in the opener for the visitors but Gray netted from 8 yards to make it all square. Riddel put away a far post header to restore Alcan's lead but in the 70th minute Anderson headed in a Gutherson cross to level. Late in the game a Ballantyne cross was spilled by keeper Dixon and Anderson pounced on the blunder to head in the winner at the far post.

Rothbury's dreams of glory in the Minor Cup were shattered in the second round as five goals from Pegswood striker Rutter condemned them to a 6-2 home defeat in the competition.

And goals from Straughan (2) and Gutherson weren't enough away to Lynemouth in the League as Rothbury slumped to a 5-3 defeat.

A late Straughan goal then salvaged a point at Hirst Progressive with Rothbury going behind to a wind-assisted fluke. Bathgate levelled from the spot after Gray had been fouled but Sanderson crashed in to put Hirst 2-1 up before Straughan struck the late leveller.

The problems started piling up as two second half goals gave Universal SC a 2-0 win at Armstrong Park and a Bathgate penalty was Rothbury's only celebration in a 3-1 defeat at Fell-Em-Doon.

The reigning Champions and league leaders Universal were made to fight all the way after a Gray free kick had given Rothbury the lead in the return fixture, but Universal gradually got a grip on the game and condemned Rothbury to their third successive defeat with a 3-1 scoreline.

Ice and snow decimated the local fixtures lists and it was some weeks before Rothbury were back in action, turning in their best performance of the season after a long layoff to beat Alcan 3-0 on their own turf. Anderson had hit the bar before Laidler broke clear and slid the ball past the keeper with Straughan forcing in from close range. Graham lobbed his own goalkeeper for a spectacular own goal in the 30th minute and five minutes after the break Anderson left his markers trailing in his wake and beat Dixon with a low shot.

Spot-kick king Philip Bathgate put a penalty in off the post and Anderson set up Laidler for a tap in as Rothbury drew 2-2 at Hirst Central and then picked up 2 valuable points with a 3-2 win at the Constitutional club.

The return fixture was unfit to play at Armstrong Park for the horrendous snow - in March - so the game was switched to Lynemouth with Anderson striking a leveller in a 1-1 draw.

Subsidiary Cup holders Rothbury went out in the first round of the competition to a narrow 2-1 defeat at North Seaton Welfare, Phillip Bathgate scoring the only goal from the penalty spot.

After the snow had played havoc with the Rothbury fixtures, they finished a comfortable mid-table fifth in their second season in the Ashington & District Welfare League - but they finished the season without any silverware for the first time in eight years.

1979/80

THE SMACK of studs as players knock the mud from their boots, before feeling the new cold concrete floor of Armstrong Park's dressing rooms through their socks as they throw their shirts, damp and brown with dirt, into the kitbag in the middle of the floor. Tearing off tape and un-rolling ankle bandages; jeans and jackets hanging from the pegs and rolled up on the wooden benches, with jokes and laughter ringing around, the smell of sweat and Deep Heat in the air. The banter of a winning dressing room, swearing and mickey-taking. A club official calling for someone to come and help take down the nets.

Two more teams left the North Northumberland League - Shilbottle Colliery Welfare and HMP Acklington tending their resignations - as the league was reduced to just 14 teams, its lowest number for years.

Rothbury continued in the Ashington & District Welfare League, but the jokes were thin on the ground in the dressing rooms as the club got off to a bad start with a 3-2 defeat at newly-promoted Northern SC.

Rothbury had enough chances to claim a draw and went in front when Gutherson rounded keeper Scott and rolled into the net. Young debutant Eddie Sutton had a few chances and set up strike-partner Gutherson to make it 2-2, but Rothbury went down.

And they threw away a 4-1 lead to get beaten 5-4 at home to Universal SC the following week. Gutherson struck twice and Chisholm added another. Gutherson hit the bar before he completed his hat-trick with a 20-yard shot after the break.

Some respite came in the form of a 2-1 win at NNFL side Craster in the first round of the NFA Minor Cup, but Rothbury made hard work of the victory. They suffered a set-back in the 15th minute when Rex Ballantyne limped off to be replaced by Bill Snowdon and Craster went in front when Burrows headed in from a corner. Chisholm's shot rattled the bar but the bounce fell kindly for Gray to make it 1-1 and Gray forced in a second to win it in less than convincing fashion.

The club then drew 2-2 at Area Workshops, coming from 2-0 down to snatch the point. Bathgate tucked away a penalty for the first and Paxton crossed for Gutherson to net the equaliser.

And another draw was earned at Newbiggin CW, despite Rothbury leading 3-1 late in the second half, they were pleased to take a point as they were left hanging on by a late fight back. Gutherson cut in from the left and shot in from a narrow angle to make it all square after the Colliers had gone in front and Gray turned in a low cross to put Rothbury ahead. Gutherson headed in Gray's accurate cross for the third but Newbiggin hit back strongly and Rothbury were relieved to get away with the 3-3 scoreline.

Rothbury hit five at home to Progressive the following week - but it still wasn't enough as they conceded seven. Gray, Gutherson, Gibbon (own goal), Chisholm and Bathgate were on target in the amazing game.

And a controversial refereeing decision cost Rothbury their place in the third round of the Northumberland FA Minor Cup. With Rothbury leading New Delaval Star 3-2 with a couple of minutes to go at Armstrong Park, Clark's blatant handball was ignored by the referee and he ran on to force the ball over the line after it had come back off the post. Brannigan had fired the opener past Neville Laidler to put Delaval in front in a fast paced game but Gutherson calmly rounded the keeper to make it 1-1. Laidler parried a free-kick and the quick-thinking Brannigan pounced to put Delaval back in charge. Gutherson headed in a Malcolm Spiers cross to level and completed his hat-trick with a sensational goal to give Rothbury the lead for the first time in the game. He chased and harried four defenders before turning and firing an unstoppable 25-yard drive into the roof of the net.

Rothbury were hard done by as they went out 5-0 in the re-play.

They gained their first win 2-1 at Whitehouse SC, but had played better and lost during the campaign. Rothbury were quick off the mark as Ballantyne side-footed in after the keeper had blocked Chisholm's shot and Graham hit a dipping 20-yard drive into the net for the winner.

A second victory followed, 4-3 at Newbiggin CW in the Booth Cup, and the Joiners Arms were beaten 3-2 at Armstrong Park as the good run continued.

Two Rothbury players and a number of supporters failed to turn up after a wrong match cancellation blunder on the team sheet, and Gutherson equalised with a well-placed shot after Rothbury fell behind. The Joiners went 2-1 up with a deflected shot after the break but Gutherson struck again when he thundered in a low right foot shot low inside the near post for a fine solo effort. Graham blasted in the winner.

Rothbury then came back twice from behind to draw 2-2 with a young Nelson CW side with plenty of chances created. Stewart prodded in the first leveller and Common, on as a sub, pounced to equalise the second time.

Rothbury travelled to bottom of the table Fell-Em-Doon and came away happy with a 4-0 victory. Bathgate was again spot on with a penalty before Gutherson made it two with a low shot. Gutherson ran through and drew the keeper before firing past him for 3-0 and completed yet another hat-trick when he pounced after the keeper had fumbled a Proudlock cross.

Rothbury gave their supporters some anxious moments with a second half fade out as they progressed in the Booth Cup with a 3-1 win at Lynemouth.

Gutherson made it 1-0 with a left foot shot then played in Stewart to slide the ball under the keeper for 2-0. When Gutherson scored the third from a Gray free kick Rothbury were cruising but after a second half stutter they held out under heavy pressure.

Penalty-King Bathgate again scored from the spot in a 3-1 defeat at Hirst Universal before frost and snow knocked out Northumberland's sporting fixtures in February.

When Rothbury returned to action they went into the Booth Cup semi-final with a 3-2 home win over Second Division club Wallsend Rising Sun.

A superb Gutherson header put Rothbury in front but they were under pressure for much of the rest of the first half. Just a minute after the break an Owen volley made it 1-1 before Common put Rothbury back in front following good work by Ballantyne and Chisholm. Bell's shot skidded through Rothbury keeper Dodds' legs for 2-2 but Gutherson sent a flying header crashing into the roof of the net from a Proudlock corner to put Rothbury into the last four.

Northern SC were beaten 3-1 at Armstrong Park and back in the North Northumberland League, Rothbury reserves knocked favourites Spittal reserves out of the Robson Cup with a 2-1 win to go into the final of the competition with a Nicholson header and a C. Gray volley from a Don Jeans cross putting them in the final. They also beat Alnmouth 1-0 to go into the Runciman Cup final.

Goals from Ballantyne and Proudlock were not enough as Rothbury crashed out of the Booth Cup semi-final 4-2 at the hands of Shankhouse. And the reserves went down 2-1 to Craster in the Robson Cup final.

Rothbury doomed Whitehouse SC to relegation on the final day of the season with goals from Chisholm and Gutherson enough to win a scrappy game and secure Rothbury a top-half of mid-table finish.

forwards.

NEWCASTLE B v. ROTHBURY (ASSOCIATION.)—Played at Rothbury on Saturday, and after a fast and exciting game resulted in a victory for the visitors by three goals to one. Arkle, W. Peters, and Brumwell played well for Newcastle; while Benson, Davy, and J. Worsnop rendered good service for Rothbury. Teams :—Newcastle : Goal, Horsley ; backs, A. Peters and T. Arkle ; half-backs, T. Smith, T. Squire, and W. Peters ; forwards. Simpson, J. A. Peters, Brumwell, Balfour, and Weddell. Rothbury : goal, Mitcheson ; backs, A. Benson and W. Davy ; half-backs, J. Mackay, J. Clarke, and J. W. Firth ; forwards, J. Worsnop, Hogarth, F. Worsnop, Green and Foggin.

1884

1980/81

ROTHBURY BROUGHT in a number of new faces with John Kidd, Keith Storey, Gordon Mackenzie, Gerald Paxton and keeper Stephen Bolton joining the team but they suffered a dismal opener in the Ashington and District League First Division as Stobswood scored three times in the last 15 minutes of the first half to take control at Armstrong Park. John Kidd gave them a glimmer of hope but Stobswood struck twice more to take it 5-1.

Rothbury then thrashed Northern SC by a huge ELEVEN-NIL away with Gutherson hitting four, Laidler three, Gordon Mackenzie and Proudlock one apiece with two own goals rounding off a superb turnaround.

But Rothbury could have no complaints as they went down 2-0 at Newbiggin CW the following week as it was the 75th minute before Newbiggin keeper Barron was forced into any serious action. They were then outclassed in a 10-3 demolition at Progressive with Bathgate, Gutherson and a Jobson own-goal the only highlights.

Rothbury rang the changes following that heavy defeat with four players dropped to the reserves and two more to the subs bench as they drew 2-2 with Area Workshops. Gordon Mackenzie was pushed and when Bathgate hit the resultant penalty the keeper parried it out and although Bathgate miss-hit the rebound, it went in for 1-0 in the 15th minute. Lewis beat the Rothbury offside trap to restore parity. The young Eddie Sutton and Kevin Proudlock came off the bench and Sutton received a pass and shrugged off a couple of challenges before the ball ran clear but his determined harassment of the Workshops centre-half forced him to turn the ball into his own net to put Rothbury back in front.

Paxton was robbed by Lewis who crashed a shot past Bolton to level and leave Rothbury third from bottom.

Rothbury went into the second round of the NFA Minor Cup with a 3-1 win over Central Club. A Sutton cross was deflected into his own net by a defender and as Rothbury continued to dominate, a Proudlock shot skidded against the post and was cleared. Disaster struck when Roxby let fly from 25-yards to beat Bolton, but when a Bathgate free kick was headed on by Gutherson, Sutton pounced to score.

Sutton added his second from a Gutherson centre to put Rothbury into the next round.

The steadily-improving Rothbury then came away from Universal with a point after a 3-3 draw. Bob Pile started the game in goal for Universal and kept the score down to 1-0 with Fenwick netting. When Pile was eventually replaced he went up top and almost immediately equalised. A Bathgate penalty made it 2-1 to Rothbury but Universal hit two more and Ballantyne rounded the keeper to hit the equaliser with just ten minutes to go.

Rothbury made several changes after conceding another ten in their next fixture and were then outdone by former players Malcolm Straughan and Michael Anderson who tore them apart in a 6-1 defeat at the Joiners Arms.

Gordon Mackenzie scored but Rothbury crashed out of the NFA Minor Cup second round 3-1 at Hirst Progressive.

The club was relegation-haunted at Christmas and wasn't helped when Bathgate and Fenwick had a wasted journey to Ashington for a game played at Armstrong Park as Rothbury went down 6-1 to Progressive. Gutherson scored the only goal.

They won their first game since mid-October with a 5-4 success at North Seaton. Gutherson, Proudlock, Ballantyne and Bathgate scored before Storey rose to head in the winner from a free kick.

But any hopes of a revival in fortunes were shattered as Rothbury crashed out of the Booth Cup 5-1 at home to Newbiggin CW with Neville Laidler playing in goals. Gutherson hit the only goal again in the final ten minutes.

Stephen Bolton was recalled to the number one spot and long-time club servant Bill Snowdon and Tom Dixon came in in the heart of defence as Rothbury showed more effort and commitment but still went down 7-3 at home to Pegswood.

Rothbury were having team difficulties and could only field ten men as they sank to bottom of the table with Nelson leap-frogging them in a 4-2 defeat.

They were relegated with a 4-1 defeat at Stobswood with the side again only starting with ten men as two players turned up late thinking it was a 3.00pm kick-off. By the time they arrived Stobswood had scored twice and missed a load of chances to increase their haul.

In the first round of the Aged Miners' Cup Gutherson headed in a Sutton cross and Proudlock fired home but Gosforth St. Nicholas hit NINE to send the club crashing out.

Few gave relegated Rothbury any chance in the John Murphy Cup semi-final against Progressive, but they battled away for the 90 minutes and Gutherson headed in low from a John Kidd cross but Rothbury were beaten 2-1 in a season they just couldn't wait to end.

GRAND FOOTBALL MATCH.

Northumberland & Durham Football Association
Challenge Cup Competition.
RANGERS (Holders) *V.* ALNWICK.

THE above MATCH will be played on SATUR-
DAY Jan. 20, 1883, in the FOOTBALL
FIELD, HOWLING LANE.
Kick off at 2·15.
Admission—Threepence.   Ladies Free.
Spectators are requested to keep clear of the
touch-line.   R. C. STEPHENSON, Hon.-Sec.
Fenkle Street.

1981/82

ROTHBURY HAD several new faces in the team they made a satisfactory start to life in the Second Division of the Ashington and District League with a 4-3 win at fellow-relegated North Seaton. New striker Ivan Dodds hit two with Gordon Mackenzie and John Sampson netting the others. Stuart Mackenzie played his first full game on the right wing for the reserves in the Second Division of the NNFL and showed a lot of promise in a 1-1 draw with Belford reserves.

Rothbury then went down 4-3 at home to Bedlington side Percy Arms in a good end-to-end game with a fast pace throughout. Kevin Proudlock hit two and Gordon Mackenzie the other but injury-plagued Rothbury saw Storey, Bathgate and Gutherson all limp off.

Ivan Dodds was again on target with Gordon Mackenzie also netting in a 3-2 defeat at the Sun Inn in an uninspiring performance with only Ballantyne in midfield and Kidd at the back playing to anything like their true potential.

Rothbury got back on track with a 5-1 derby win over Whittle Colliery at Armstrong Park. Sampson fired Rothbury in front then Ballantyne was unlucky to see his shot crash back off the crossbar. Dodds added number two and Durham the third just before the break. Durham also crashed in the fourth after Ballantyne cleverly ran over the ball allowing him to get the shot away. Proudlock's swerving, dipping shot flew past keeper Latto for 5-1.

Ballantyne was out injured for the visit to Whitehouse but Gutherson returned from injury and shot high into the net from 20 yards. Unfortunately, he limped off injured shortly after and Rothbury went down 4-1.

Constitutional Club the thrashed Rothbury 6-3 with the defence often under pressure and keeper Neville Laidler overworked. Sutton shrugged off Down's challenge and placed the ball wide of Freeman for the first. Gutherson pounced after a defender lost control for the second and Shotton netted the third.

Rothbury then took a point in a twelve goal thriller at Hirst Central. The whites were 2-0 down but then took a commanding 5-2 lead with goals from Dodds (4) and Robert Laidler. A Proudlock penalty made it 6-4 but Hirst hit back to level the game at 6-6.

Rothbury keeper Neville Laidler was then carried off injured in the next game as Rothbury went out of the NFA Minor Cup 4-3 at Lowick. Substitute Goodfellow took over between the sticks and a Gutherson downward header from a Mackenzie cross put Rothbury in front. Sutton hit the bar before Proudlock shot low through the keeper's legs for 2-2. Gutherson rammed in the third after the Lowick defence failed to clear, but it wasn't enough and Rothbury crashed out.

League leaders Northern SC then suffered a shock as Rothbury came away with the points from a fantastic 5-4 win that they thoroughly deserved. Keith Appleby replaced the injured Neville Laidler as goalkeeper and Rothbury were 3-1 up at half time with goals from Dodds and a Gutherson volley and side foot past the keeper. Dodds fired in his second from 12 yards and completed his hat-trick when he ran through to beat the keeper.

Rothbury's improved form continued with Storey working hard in midfield and Appleby superb in goal, but they went out of the Booth Cup 2-1 at home to Newbiggin CW, Gutherson converting a Dodds cross for the only goal.

Appleby was again on top form, making some good saves as Rothbury found the right formula at last and disposed of North Seaton 4-1 at Armstrong Park.

It was goal-less at half time but Gutherson crashed past Barron from six yards for the first and turned in the second from close range. Five minutes later Ballantyne set up Dodds who beat two men in the box and pulled back for Gordon Mackenzie to side foot in via the post. North Seaton pulled one back but Proudlock drilled in from 18-yards in the last minute to cap off a fine team performance.

Ballantyne, Storey and Proudlock then bossed the midfield in a 5-2 win over Whitehouse before Rothbury slipped up again and went down 5-2 at Sun Inn.

Rothbury then threw a point away in a 5-5 derby thriller at Whittle Colliery. Ballantyne, Mackenzie, Proudlock (pen), Laidler and Gutherson all scored.

Two welcome points were deservedly picked up in a 2-0 win at Percy Arms with goals coming from Ballantyne, who curled a free kick in off the post, and Gutherson, who followed up to score after Ballantyne had set up Mackenzie whose shot was blocked. Rex Ballantyne gave Rothbury that bit extra with John Kidd being the pick of the team in a game where the referee had called both teams into the centre circle before kick-off and warned them about using foul and abusive language - the FA having asked match officials to clamp down on it.

There was no official referee at Rothbury's next fixture, the Rothbury sub having to take the whistle after he failed to show up, and they produced their best performance all season with a 3-2 win and the double over leaders Northern SC. A Wareham own goal and a Proudlock penalty after Mackenzie had been fouled saw the game locked at 2-2, but in the final minute Ballantyne's clever lob beat Lowter at the near post and Sutton followed up to make sure.

The improving Rothbury then coasted to an easy 6-1 CISWO Cup win over Fell Em Doon with Ballantyne at the centre of most of Rothbury's attacks and Sutton and Gutherson combining well up front.

But in a lacklustre display against old NNFL rivals Aydon Forest the match never rose to any heights and ended in a 1-1 stalemate. Gordon Mackenzie appeared to be tripped in the box but with Rothbury appealing for a penalty the ref waved play on and an unlucky defender turned the ball past his own goalkeeper for 1-0. Davies pushed the equaliser past Appleby after the Rothbury defence hesitated.

The clubs faced each other again the following week in the CISWO Cup quarter final. In a better game, Aydon bossed the first half but the teams went in goalless at the break. A Saunders penalty put Forest in front but Rothbury levelled when Proudlock also put away a penalty, sending the keeper the wrong way from the spot to force a replay.

Back in the league, Rothbury were outplayed by Bomarsund for 65 minutes and 1-0 down, but Gutherson fired into the roof of the net following a corner and they won it when sub Stuart Mackenzie crossed and Proudlock headed firmly past Doughty.

Bomarsund turned the tables the following week with a 2-1 reverse and Rothbury went out of the CISWO Cup with a 6-4 defeat at Aydon Forest in the replay.

Rothbury made up for the disappointment by advancing into the semi-final of the Alcan Cup with a 2-1 success at Fell Em Doon. Rothbury missed a number of chances and had Keith Appleby to thank for a fine save in the last five minutes to secure the win. Rothbury played some good football with Gutherson heading in the opener from close range. Later, Ballantyne played a first time ball inside the full-back and Sutton didn't break stride as his shot flew low into the net for what proved to be the winner.

Top scorer Gutherson was out injured for the fixture at home to Constitutional Club and proved a big miss as Rothbury were twice behind but hit a last-minute equaliser to grab a point. Sutton raced on to flick past the keeper for the first and, with the seconds ticking away, Proudlock's low shot flew across the face of goal and crashed in off the post.

Rothbury then slipped to successive defeats, 3-1 at home to Aydon Forest with the visitors in complete control and 4-2 away to Fell-Em-Doon where Rothbury created and missed a number of chances which proved their downfall.

Boss Thompson Rutherford couldn't believe it as Rothbury were beaten 2-1 by Percy Arms in the Alcan Cup semi-final - but hit the woodwork on four occasions and had a late goal disallowed. In an incident-packed match Gutherson made it 1-1 before the Percy keeper was carried off with cracked ribs after colliding with Sutton. Ballantyne had the ball in the net late on but another player was in an offside position and following a scramble in the Percy six-yard box several Rothbury players appealed that the ball had crossed the line before it was hacked clear.

Fell-Em-Doon turned up half an hour late and were thumped 5-1 at Armstrong Park as Rothbury strolled through the game and the impressive Eddie Sutton hit a hat-trick with Nick Gutherson netting the other two.

In the final league game of the season, second-placed Central Club took the points with a 6-2 drubbing at Armstrong Park. Chick Chisholm and John Kidd scored.

Rothbury crashed out of the Northumberland Aged Miners Cup 1-4 at home to NEI Parsons from Wallsend. Parsons went in front but Gordon Mackenzie levelled before the break. Parsons went back in front in the 70th minute and the final scoreline flattered them a bit.

FOOTBALL. FOOTBALL.

MORPETH HARRIERS V. WEST END,

In Grange House Field, Morpeth,

On July 10th, (Miners' Pic-Nic).

Admission 3d.

.1886

1982/83

ROTHBURY HAD played several friendlies, practice matches and held training sessions throughout the summer so it was with a sense of disappointment that they went down 2-1 at home to North Seaton on the opening day of the season in the Ashington & District Welfare League. They let themselves down badly in a game they didn't deserve to lose, having the better possession and with keeper Wigmore having little to do, the only Rothbury goal was scored by the previous season's top gun, Nick Gutherson.

Central Club were unable to field a team against Rothbury in the next fixture and the Ashington side signalled their intention to withdraw from the League.

Rothbury then crashed to their second defeat, 3-1 at Bomarsund, with Chisholm heading in a Sutton cross in a much-improved performance.

But the poor run continued as Rothbury crashed out of the Booth Cup 4-0 at Sun Inn. The club battled to their first point in a 2-2 derby draw at Shilbottle. In an exciting game on a windswept pitch Rothbury had most of the play and went ahead through Sutton in the 25th minute. Albert Straughan equalised ten minutes later, but Rothbury rained in shots from every angle and couldn't believe it when they couldn't find the net. Eventually, Sutton left the home defence in his wake and slotted past Sample to put Rothbury back in front. Les Cairns rifled the leveller into the roof of the net from 6 yards late on.

With Ballantyne suspended, Rothbury found themselves 2-0 down at half time at Fell-Em-Doon. But Gutherson led a second half fight back, heading in a Laidler cross for 1-2 and Sutton hit a superb equaliser, having a clear run on goal and gliding a shot over stranded keeper Wanless' head as he advanced.

In the NFA Minor Cup Rothbury were 1-0 up for a long time against visitors New York, but went out 2-1 as the visitor's fitness levels told at the end. A Sutton long range drive deflected and looped over keeper Gillespie's head to give the Coquetdale men a fortuitous lead that they couldn't hang onto.

The first win came with a 5-3 success at Whittle Colliery before Rothbury were thumped 6-3 at home to Fell Em Doon, with visiting striker Watt scoring four, hitting the bar and being brought down for a penalty, leaving the club sitting ninth in a twelve team Division.

Bomarsund took the points at Armstrong Park with a 4-1 success before Rothbury got their first home success of the season with a 4-1 win over Kings Arms.

Proudlock hit two, Gutherson one and Kings Arms defender Thorburn scored a comical own-goal from 30-yards with Kidd, keeper Appleby and Paxton performing well.

Rothbury then struggled to field a team, taking just the bare 11 to Percy Arms, and were soundly beaten 7-2 with Gutherson and Sutton scoring for Rothbury and Sanderson, Haggerty, Reay, Fennell (2) and Reid (2) on target for Percy Arms.

North Seaton beat struggling Rothbury 5-0 and Aydon Forest won 4-1 after Gutherson had left their defence stranded to race through and beat the keeper to put Rothbury one up.

Rothbury breathed a huge sigh of relief as they broke their losing sequence and dominated the first half in a 2-0 win over Constitutional Club at Armstrong Park. When Ballantyne was tripped, Proudlock sent keeper Ducat the wrong way from the spot to give Rothbury a deserved lead. In the second period Constitutional were on top but Rothbury weathered the storm and when Sutton crossed deep, Gutherson headed back across goal and Proudlock nipped in to beat Ducat again. Tom Dixon, Ballantyne and Mick Arkle were the star performers.

Rothbury were then unlucky not to claim a point off Aydon Forest, going down to a last minute goal in a 3-2 defeat. Forest sub Belisle won it when he hit a shot in off the foot of the post.

Gutherson and man of the match Ballantyne scored for Rothbury.

In the CISWO Cup Rothbury won 1-0 at Shilbottle with Arkle
and Ballantyne controlling the match and a Proudlock snapshot
high into the roof of the net winning it.

Rothbury should then have won comfortably at the Kings
Arms but saw a last minute equaliser deny them in a 3-3 draw.
Rothbury went in front in the 8th minute when the keeper could
only fingertip a Storey header into the roof of the net. Rothbury
were 2-1 down at the break but were in complete control in the
second period with Arkle hitting the bar and Gutherson heading
just wide before Arkle headed in a Storey cross for 2-2. Gutherson then sent Sutton clear to round the keeper and put
Rothbury in the driving seat. Douglas headed low into the Rothbury net with time quickly running out.

The official referee failed to show up at Armstrong Park as
Rothbury drew 2-2 with Whitehouse SC in game that threatened
to deteriorate into a bad-tempered affair. Rothbury were 2-0
down but Arkle drove in to pull one back. A Storey hip-high
cross was spilled by keeper Cunningham and Gutherson pushed
into the empty net for 2-2. Arkle almost won it late on, but his
header came back off the bar.

Rothbury nosedived out of the CISWO Cup 4-0 at Fell Em
Doon and despite enjoying much of the play, they gifted the
home team a couple of goals.

They were then left to reflect on a succession of missed
chances as Whittle Colliery took the points with a 1-0 win. The
skilful Graeme Foggon was drafted in for his debut from the reserves, but was taken off injured leaving Rothbury having to
play the final 30 minutes with only ten men.

Rothbury were dumped out of the Alcan Cup 1-0 at home to
rivals Aydon Forest. Appleby, Sutton, Kidd and Dixon all played
well but a Brian Thompson goal won it for the Alnwick side.

And with Rothbury frustrated by the non-appearance of the match official again, Shilbottle manager Peter Egdell took the whistle for a 5-1 home defeat in the final game of the season. Gutherson found the bottom corner from a Proudlock corner for the Rothbury goal as a disappointing season ended on a low note.

1983/84

THE SECOND Division of the North Northumberland League was scrapped during the summer of 1983 with 17 teams forming the only Division. It was Rothbury Reserves, bolstered by several first team players, who drew 3-3 with newly-formed Seahouses on the opening day of the season. Rothbury were 3-1 down to the youngsters from the coast but salvaged a point with two goals in the final ten minutes. The club then withdrew from the Ashington & District Welfare League with Rothbury moving back into the NNFL lock, stock and barrel with the Reserves being disbanded. But the team then went down 5-2 at another new club, Felton, with Gordon Mackenzie netting the first and when Gordon Turnbull pumped a free kick into the Felton area, keeper Sample missed it allowing Nick Gutherson to run in the second.

Gutherson hit two more with an own goal and a first for the club from skilful midfielder Graham Foggon earning the points in a 4-3 success over Wooler before Rothbury secured a tremendous 3-0 win over Percy Rovers. Gordon Mackenzie scored the first following good work by Kevin Coe and added a second when he raced clear to place his shot wide of the keeper. Rothbury added the third in the second half.

But after a couple of impressive performances, Rothbury then fell to a 2-0 home defeat at the hands of lowly Craster, with Stuart Mackenzie hitting the bar with their best chance. In another blow, the clubs new goal nets had been stolen before the fixture and old ones had to be repaired and hung out for the game.

The new-look Rothbury proved a handful for young Berwick side Springhill but could only come away with a point in a hard-earned 1-1 draw then Bamburgh where thrashed 5-1 at Armstrong Park in a game totally dominated by the Coquetdale side.

Tom Dixon side footed in the first after a Kevin Proudlock penalty had been parried out by the visitor's keeper. Gordon Mackenzie added the second and then saw a shot smack off the bar before Gutherson intercepted a back pass to roll in the third. Stuart Mackenzie made it four and Proudlock got it right from the penalty spot the second time, netting the final goal.

Rothbury were unlucky to crash out of the NFA Minor Cup in the first round after outplaying Springhill for practically the entire game at Armstrong Park. On-form Gordon Mackenzie hit two more and Proudlock finished an impressive Rothbury move for another in the 85th minute, but Springhill got the crucial goals to send Rothbury tumbling out at the first hurdle 4-3.

Keith Storey was the man of the match in the heart of the Rothbury defence in an entertaining 0-0 draw with Felton but Rothbury also went out of the Sanderson Cup 3-1 at Wooler. Kevin Coe looped in a shot from Gutherson's low centre but Wooler resisted a second half onslaught to progress.

But Rothbury did go into the second round of the Anderson Cup with a 3-1 success at Longhorsley. Stuart Mackenzie hit the post in an early raid then Dixon gave Rothbury the lead. Coe beat two men and centred for Gordon Mackenzie to smash in the second via the underside of the bar. The new Longhorsley team pulled one back but Proudlock finished them off.

A 1-0 defeat at Belford reserves saw Rothbury 8th in the table with 15 points, Highfields United sitting on top with 25 after 13 games.

Nick Gutherson was on target as Rothbury were beaten 3-1 at Spittal - who had four players under 16 in their line-up.

But Bamburgh were then smashed 11-1 in front of the Castle as Rothbury finally found top form. Tough-tackling Gordon Mackenzie kept up his brilliant form by hitting FIVE, Proudlock hit a hat-trick, including two penalties, and Coe, Storey and Foggon completed the rout.

Rothbury's erratic form continued as they were beaten 4-1 at home by North Sunderland in the Anderson Cup with the visitor's nippy frontmen too much for the defence. Gordon Mackenzie scored from a Coe cross.

Rothbury then hit five in the first half in a comfortable 7-1 win at Wooler. Gutherson and Stuart Mackenzie both hit hat-tricks with Proudlock netting the other with a stunning 35-yard drive.

A fortunate deflection saw Longhorsley take the points in a 2-1 defeat, but Rothbury were back on the goal trail the following week as Shilbottle were trounced 8-2. Proudlock hit three and an own goal, Sutton, Coe, Stuart Mackenzie and Gutherson completed the scoring. Rothbury did their goal difference a power of good, taking the goals scored in their last six games to a stunning THIRTY-EIGHT with a 10-3 romp at Seahouses as they totally overwhelmed a young team. Proudlock struck two more, Sutton added one and made two more with Storey, Kidd, Dixon and Gordon Mackenzie rounding off the annihilation.

Six more were added in the Bilclough Cup with a success at Shilbottle - but the home side managed four themselves in an open, attacking game. In the first minute Sutton drove in a fierce 30-yard drive off the post and Keith Appleby blasted in the second. Sutton rose to head in number three and Gutherson also used his head for the fourth. An own goal and a strike from Proudlock saw Rothbury through into the next round.

Graham Foggon put in a good display and scored twice in a 4-3 win at Craster. Gutherson slid in the opener from 10 yards then Foggon drove in his first after Gutherson and Sutton combined to create the chance. Sutton cracked against the post and Gutherson tapped in the rebound then Foggon hit the winner with a 20-yard shot.

Glanton were then beaten 3-0 on their own turf and after Stuart Mackenzie shot the first past Dodds, Rothbury never looked back. Proudlock netted a penalty and Coe forced in the third from an acute angle.

But Rothbury then turned in a depressing performance, their worst of the season, as they went down 2-1 at Longhorsley, a Gordon Mackenzie penalty raising the only cheers.

In a hard game at home to Alnmouth, Rothbury went down to their second straight defeat with a 4-2 reverse. Dixon went up to challenge the keeper and the ball fell free for Gordon Mackenzie to ram in from close range and Proudlock placed in a penalty after Sutton had been brought down.

The rot was stopped with a 1-1 draw at home to Spittal but Rothbury were short of four regulars and their fine performance deserved more. Eddie Sutton had a great game throughout and when a Foggon drive hit the bar he was unlucky to see his follow up header also rattle the woodwork. Sutton then forced the keeper into a fine diving save as Rothbury kept up the pressure. Rothbury went behind against the run of play but from a Keith Appleby corner, Sutton span and fired in the equaliser. Neville Laidler made a couple of good saves at the other end.

Rothbury were left shocked as they went out of the Bilclough Cup in the semi-final with a 2-1 defeat at the hands of Percy Rovers. Rothbury went two behind and after Gordon Mackenzie had pulled one back they just couldn't score again and Rovers had to hang on for the win.

In the final league game Rothbury were given a lesson in taking chances as they went down 4-2 at North Sunderland.

ROTHBURY v. TYNE A TEAM (A.)—The return match between these clubs was played at Rothbury on Saturday. The wind spoiled combined play, though several played well individually. F. E. Messent for the Tyne was best, but was invariably tackled before getting dangerous. On the same side Burnett (captain), McNabb, Morrison, and Charlton did well; while Manners of Morpeth Harriers worked hard. F. Worsnop, on the Rothbury side, was in best form, and J. Hutchinson tackled well and made some huge kicks. The half backs did better against the wind than with it, and saved well on many occasions. A very even game ended in a draw, no goals being scored. Teams :—Rothbury : C. Mitcheson, goal ; J. Hutchinson and J. Mackay, backs ; J. Elliott, J. Cowley, and J. Armstrong, half backs ; A. Benson, E. Hogarth, F. Worsnop (captain), C. Hogarth, and G. Burn, forwards. Umpire, Rev. B. Smith. Tyne : W. Shaw, goal ; C. H. Parker and T. Smailes (Morpeth Harriers), backs ; Manners (Morpeth Harrier) and L. McNabb, half backs ; F. E. Messent, Leathart, Morrison, Charlton, M. Burnett (captain), and L. Shann, forwards. Umpire : Bowman.

1885

1984/85

Honours: Division One Champions, Anderson Cup Winners.

ROTHBURY HAD a number of skilful young players such as Mark Bruce, whose ball-skills, close control and talent almost earned him a place in League football as he had trials for Darlington Football Club; Graham Foggon, Keith Storey, Kevin Proudlock and the Mackenzie brothers, Stuart and Gordon in the team at the time. The veteran Rex Ballantyne added experience and Nick Gutherson and combative big centre forward Eddie Sutton led the line with a solid defensive partnership of John Kidd and Paul Appleby at the back. The balance and creativity in the squad ensured that Rothbury would prove a stern test for rivals Highfields United for the title.

The team made a solid start to the season and by January were sitting second in the table. A 4-2 defeat of Glanton at Armstrong Park ensured that they kept up the pressure on the leaders. Rothbury went in front when Foggon headed on for Bruce to net from close range but lowly Glanton levelled with a fine Chick Chisholm effort. The visitors took a shock lead when Arkle fired a low shot into the bottom corner from the left edge of the area.

Foggon restored parity after the break and Gutherson got on the score sheet with a low shot that squeezed under diving keeper Dodds and rolled over the line. The win was secured when a Dixon free kick was headed back across goal by Gutherson for Proudlock to nod in.

They were at home again the following week and dished out an 11-1 drubbing to Wooler - the club's biggest win for a number of years. Gutherson turned in a low cross for the opener and Gordon Mackenzie rounded Clarke a couple of minutes later to make it two. Proudlock and Foggon then linked up for the latter to leave the keeper helpless with a bending shot. Wooler pulled one back through Clark. Kidd then scored a cracker, running sixty yards and beating four men before firing home as he cut in from the left to make it 4-1. Gordon Mackenzie robbed a defender to notch his second for number five and Gutherson made it six after the break with a tap-in. Proudlock netted the from the penalty spot for the first of a hat-trick before Foggon scored the eighth. Proudlock added 9 and 10 to complete the treble and Bruce volleyed in the eleventh to complete the rout.

Rothbury had won 8, drawn 2 and lost just one of their opening 11 fixtures to tally up 18 points. Highfields were on top of the table with a point more, having won 9, drawn one and lost one.

Rothbury kept up their fine form to advance into the semi-finals of the Sanderson Cup with a resounding 5-2 victory over North Sunderland at Armstrong Park. Storey set up Gutherson to net the first and Proudlock added a second after a move involving Gordon Mackenzie and Gutherson. Stuart MacKenzie made it 3-0 with a low left foot drive from 18 yards. North Sunderland's Laidler beat Rothbury keeper Neville Laidler with a deflection that the scrambling Kidd couldn't prevent from crossing the line to pull one back. Rothbury added two further goals before North Sunderland hit a late consolation.

Wooler made an amazing turnaround as they bounced back from their 11-1 drubbing at Armstrong Park to thrash Seahouses 10-2 away in the League on the same day for their first win of the season.

And Rothbury were hit by a bombshell as they were held to a surprise 1-1 draw by the Glendale side four games later as they dropped a vital point on Highfields United. Rothbury had hammered Felton the week before, but lost their way when Punton lobbed the advancing Neville Laidler to give Wooler a shock lead. Rothbury hit back immediately as Proudlock beat a defender to the ball and drilled past the helpless Clark.

The stutter continued as Rothbury dropped further points at home to Alnmouth and then lowly Hipsburn the following week with a goal-less draw, Eddie Sutton coming closest to breaking the deadlock with a chip that the visitor's keeper got a fingertip on to touch onto the crossbar. Highfields ran riot with a 7-2 hammering away to Glanton, and Rothbury must have thought they'd blown it.

The North Northumberland League was in somewhat of a crisis at the time, with a huge fixture backlog forcing the league two months behind schedule.

"We have lost 50 fixtures, or eight weeks football. And we have two months to catch up," said League secretary Norman Laidler.

"This is the worst it has ever been. Teams will have to fit the fixtures in at night, and most will be playing on a Friday or Monday as well as a Saturday."

Rothbury rediscovered their scoring touch when the Mac-kenzie brothers shared the goals between themselves in a 5-1 win over Belford Reserves at Armstrong Park to get back on track. Gordon hit a first-half hat-trick and Stuart added two more after the break.

But the slump continued and a mid-week defeat at Al-nmouth saw the club slip into fourth place behind Highfields, Lowick and Percy Rovers, but with two games in hand. Rothbury had scored 66 goals and conceded 30 with top club United scoring 86 and conceding 31 - and looking odds on to take the title.

Rothbury bounced back with a 4-2 win against Springhill at home. They went behind when Robson's in swinging corner kick was deflected past Laidler by a defender for an own goal. But Rothbury didn't hit the panic button and equalised after a long spell of pressure when Stuart Mackenzie lifted the ball over the defence for Sutton to run on and power in a header. Rothbury made it 2-1 when Ballantyne swung over a corner for Storey to head in. And it was 3-1 before the interval when Sutton released Gutherson down the left and he crossed for Proudlock to roll into the net.

Rothbury had a man sent off before Ballantyne set up Stuart Mackenzie to add the fourth. Springhill scored again late on but the points were in the bag.

A brilliant Paul Appleby goal won the Anderson Cup for Rothbury as they beat Belford reserves 1-0 in the final at Berwick Ranger's Shielfield Park. The final generated a tremendous atmosphere with the travelling Rothbury fans keeping up a constant crescendo of noise and it was fitting that Appleby should be the hero as he played tremendously throughout the ninety minutes.

Rothbury had the better of the first half and went close through Gutherson and Proudlock before Belford keeper Chappell made a fine diving save to keep out a long range Appleby drive. Belford came out after the break and increased the pressure but found Appleby in inspired form, shackling the threat of danger man Peter Turnbull and encouraging his hard pressed team-mates. Belford missed a glorious chance when the ball fell

Peter Rutherford unmarked six yards out but he hammered wide.

Rothbury began to get back into the game and when Proudlock was fouled down the left, he picked himself up and floated in the free kick for centre back Appleby to rise and power a magnificent header past the helpless keeper. Rothbury went on to control the game and had two shots cleared off the line by Belford stalwart Bissett in a fast flowing final. And the first silverware of the season was raised to great cheers ringing around the stand.

The league was boiling down to an exciting climax with any one of three clubs in with a chance of winning it. Highfields United were firm favourites, but had slipped into second spot behind Percy Rovers, who could seal the title with a win at Armstrong Park to third place Rothbury. All three clubs could finish on 39 points with two games to go.

Eddie Sutton was the star as he smashed in a four blitz to shatter Percy Rovers' hopes in a thrilling 6-1 demolition of their rivals. In a tremendous display by the powerfully-built brickie, the Alnwick team was simply blown apart. Highfields hammered Glanton 6-2 on the same day, leaving Rothbury requiring to beat basement club Seahouses by seven clear goals on the Tuesday night to take the title on goal difference from United.

It seemed a mammoth task, but the players responded tremendously to the noise created by a large coach load of travelling fans and hammered in TWELVE without reply. Veteran hit-man Nick Gutherson was the star of the show as he helped himself to SEVEN goals. Rothbury were five-nil up at the break to the despair of the watching Highfields United manager who literally had to look on from the sidelines as the trophy slipped from his grasp to be adorned with the Red and White ribbons of Rothbury in one of the most exciting finishes the North Northumberland League had ever seen.

1985/86

Honours: Sanderson Cup Winners, Bilclough Cup Winners.

AFTER THE double success the previous season, Rothbury promised to deliver again. They fell just short of an amazing treble as they were beaten on the final day of the season, when a point would have secured the McEwan's NNFL title.

The club continued the season were they had left off, romping to five wins and two draws from their opening fixtures and when they were beaten 2-1 at Armstrong Park by Percy Rovers in the New Year, it was their first home defeat, excluding County Cup ties, for some time.

Rovers went ahead in the 55th minute when Bobby Pile broke clear and took the ball around the advancing Neville Laidler to slide in. The deadly Pile went around Laidler again 10 minutes later to add the second. With ten minutes to go Gutherson controlled a perfect cross from Graham and belted the ball past Murray but Rothbury couldn't score again. The club were top of the table as the League returned to the two Division format with nine teams in the First and eight in the Second.

Rothbury went through in the Anderson Cup with a 3-1 success over fancied Alnmouth with the midfield trio of Stuart Mackenzie, Kevin Proudlock and Rex Ballantyne setting up the win. A Foggon free kick put Rothbury in front before Proudlock hit a superb second, receiving the ball on the half way line and evading three tackles then crashing the ball into the net from 18 yards. Proudlock played in Sutton to make it 3-0.

With the Anderson Cup being played in Group stages again, Highfields looked certain to advance to the semi-finals with a 4-3 win over Rothbury.

But in the League the following week, Rothbury retained their grip at the top of the table with a 2-0 win at Highfields.

Lowick were then seen off 2-0 at Armstrong Park in an easy win that should have seen Rothbury hit more. Sutton created the opening for the first with centre-half Kidd cracking it in off the underside of the bar. Proudlock went down the left and his low cross-shot flew in to double the advantage.

Rothbury then condemned Alnmouth to their first League defeat with a 3-1 success at Armstrong Park. But they had to do it the hard way after the tough Eddie Sutton was sent-off after 30 minutes for punching Hutchinson. Proudlock flicked in the first and Gutherson added the second before Sutton was given his marching orders. Hindhaugh blasted one back but Gutherson rolled the ball wide of Catlow for the third in a great victory.

Rothbury's slim chances of making the Anderson Cup semis disappeared with a 2-2 draw with Highfields and in the Sanderson Cup semi-final the game was spoiled by a strong wind that blew straight down the pitch throughout in a 0-0 draw with Alnmouth that required a replay.

Gutherson was on target at Shielfield Rangers in the second round of the Bilclough Cup but, with both teams having chances to win it, the game was drawn 1-1 and another replay was required.

The Champions kept up their challenge for retaining the title with a good 3-1 win against Acklington Res. at the prison. Nick Gutherson scored two and Proudlock the other in what was shaping up to be another very tight title race.

Rothbury went into the final of the Sanderson Cup with a 4-1 win over Alnmouth at Wooler in the replay and they took just five minutes to break the deadlock with a stunning, well-worked goal. Ballantyne played it wide to Gordon Mackenzie whose first time cross into the box was headed down by Gutherson for Proudlock to volley into the net. Keith Storey was carried off injured and with Rothbury unsettled, Alnmouth began to get on top and Hindhaugh slammed in the equaliser.

Early in the second half Gordon Mackenzie crossed and the unmarked Gutherson headed in off the post to put Rothbury back in charge. Mark Bruce then won a race against the Alnmouth keeper and slipped it past him for 3-1. In the 85th minute a Sutton centre was turned into the net by a defender for the fourth.

It took a disputed winner just two minutes from time to see Rothbury progress into the Bilclough Cup semi-final. The replay at home to Shielfield Rangers looked to be heading for extra time when Gutherson hit a disputed winner, controlling a corner at the near post and ramming into the roof of the net with Shielfield claiming handball.

Rothbury were held in a midweek draw against Shilbottle that put pressure on themselves before Lowick were trounced 7-0 with Gutherson hitting three and Sutton, Bruce, Kidd and Foggon the others to keep up the heat at the top of the table.

Rothbury and Alnmouth drew once again after extra time in an exciting and controversial Bilclough Cup semi-final at Wooler. Alnmouth went ahead and it was against the run of play when Rothbury equalised in the 29th minute with a well-taken effort in off the post. Hutchinson put Alnmouth back in front ten minutes later. Rothbury grabbed a controversial equaliser in the 70th minute when referee Brian Boyd whistled for offside against Rothbury, but as Alnmouth prepared to take the free kick, linesman Neil Simpson flagged for the ref's attention and, after a lengthy discussion, a penalty was awarded for shirt pulling. An incensed Alnmouth took a couple of minutes to calm down before Proudlock netted the spot-kick. Two minutes into extra time Taylor drove in for 3-2 to Alnmouth but Rothbury came back again to force the replay.

The Sanderson Cup Final was Rothbury's fifth match in eight days but they ran out deserved 3-1 winners over Percy Rovers to take the trophy.

Gutherson's inch-perfect pass put in Proudlock round the back of the defence and he blasted past Murray on the volley to put Rothbury in front in the 31st minute. On the hour, Rovers equalised. Kidd was beaten by a bad bounce that left Bobby Pile clear on goal. Laidler blocked his initial shot but Pile followed up to score.

Bruce put Rothbury back in front when Proudlock's header put him through and he placed his shot past Murray from 12 yards. Bruce struck again shortly after when he headed in a Gutherson cross for the third and killer goal.

Rothbury then dumped Alnmouth out of a Cup semi-final replay again with a 2-1 win in the Bilclough. Alnmouth were 1-0 up at half time but after the break Gutherson headed in a Bruce cross at the far post. And a fine individual goal from Eddie Sutton took Rothbury into the final. He received the ball on the edge of the area and beat two men before firing low past Catlow from 15 yards to break the Seasiders hearts.

The Green and Whites had to win an all-important winner-takes-all final game of the season while Rothbury needed only a point from the game to claim a back-to-back Championship. The first half was very scrappy with so much at stake but the game improved after the interval.

Benny Dodds hit his first goal for Alnmouth to give them the lead in the 66th minute, shrugging off a challenge and slipping the ball low past Laidler.

Rothbury poured forward in search of a leveller and left gaps at the back which were exploited by Alnmouth with just ten minutes to go. Richard Jobling attempted an ambitious overhead kick that deceived Laidler, squirmed through his grasp and into agonisingly dropped into the net at the near post, leaving the keeper blowing out his cheeks in disbelief.

John Common side-stepped two defenders to grab a goal back in the last minute, but Rothbury crashed to only their second defeat of the season and Alnmouth took the title by a measly two points. Having won eleven and drawn three, it was hard to take.

But smiles were back on Rothbury's faces as they took the Bilclough Cup with a 2-1 win over Percy Rovers. Nick Gutherson rounded off a fine 23-year football career by scoring the winning goal in a hard-fought final. But while Gutherson looked to retirement with cheers ringing in his ears, the unlucky Rex Ballantyne, who had also announced his intention to retire after the game, ended in agony as he suffered a recurrence of an old injury and had to limp off. Midfield maestro Ballantyne had also been a tremendous key player for sixteen years

Rothbury were in front in the tenth minute, Sutton finishing off a good move with a low shot into the corner of the net. They suffered a blow when Ballantyne was forced out to be replaced by Graeme Foggon and Rovers equalised on the stroke of half time. Gordon Mackenzie's throw-in back to Laidler was robbed by a forward and knocked across the face of goal to Pile who tapped in.

In the 80th minute Gutherson was the hero when a perfect pass by Foggon put him through and he rounded the keeper and slotted the ball into the net for a fairy tale finish.

Probables—Goal, R. A. Oldham, West End; backs, J. Taylor, West End, J. Ferguson, Tyne; half-backs, M. Manners, Morpeth, A. H. White (captain) and W. Blackett, East End; right wing, T. K. Dobson, North-Eastern, and W. Thompson, Shankhouse; left wing, R. Aitkin, West End, and W. Muir, East End; G. Matthews, Shankhouse, centre. Possibles—Goal, J. Wood, Shankhouse; backs, Rev. F. E. Ainger (captain), Rothbury, and A. Perkins, Elswick Leather Works; half-backs, C. Ritson, Shankhouse, J. Beattie, Elswick Rangers, and J. Atkinson, Barrington; W. H. Ainger, Rothbury, and A. Beattie, Elswick Rangers, right wing; S. Wood, Boundary, and Young, Bedlington, left wing; Stewart, Elswick Rovers, centre.

The Aingers star in a Northumberland County trial match in 1886.

1986/87

ROTHBURY'S IRON GRIP on the NNFL was beginning to falter. Percy Rovers took sweet revenge for their two Cup final defeats at the hands of Rothbury the previous season as they romped home 5-1 at Armstrong Park in the first game of the campaign.

Rothbury then played some good attacking football but defensive blunders cost them dearly in a 4-2 defeat at Shielfield Rangers. Paul Appleby raced through from centre-back to score and Rothbury added a second after a defensive mix-up, but it was too little, too late.

A player shortage forced retired Nick Gutherson back into action and he opened the scoring as Rothbury raced into a 2-0 lead in 15 minutes, but was later forced to leave the field with a leg injury with a much-changed Rothbury falling apart under pressure and crashing 4-2 to Highfields United.

The first point of the season was gained with a 3-3 draw at Lowick. Bruce made it 1-0 in the fourth minute, rounding Guthrie and slamming in low and hard from an acute angle. A looping header made it 1-1 and Hogg struck to put Lowick 2-1 up. Stuart Mackenzie opened the defence for Proudlock to level and a Bruce cross was headed in by John Common to put Rothbury back in front in the 77th minute. With the clock ticking down, a 25-yard drive flew in to make it all-square.

And with Eyemouth making their first visit to Armstrong Park in over ten years, a hard struggle led to another point with a 1-1 draw. The tremendously skilful Bruce caused Eyemouth problems and Rothbury equalised in the 82nd minute when Kidd stretched to prod over the line.

Bruce was in top form and was fouled repeatedly as Belford had no answer to him in a 4-1 Sanderson Cup first round win. Stuart Mackenzie hit two with Kidd and Sutton the others.

Champions Alnmouth and Rothbury both looked to be struggling in a 2-2 draw at the coast in the next fixture. Keith Appleby smashed in a 30-yard drive and Chisholm fired home from 15-yards from a Sutton pull-back.

Rothbury went out of the NFA Minor Cup in the first round with a 5-3 home defeat in a hard-fought tie at home to Byker SHFC. Strikes from Bruce and Chisholm gave Rothbury an early lead but Bruce's second was just a consolation.

And despite goal-tormentor Bobby Pile playing in nets for Percy Rovers, Rothbury went down 4-2 at Armstrong Park in an Anderson Cup Group stage game. Coe and Proudlock scored and Paul Appleby and Kidd played well in the heart of the defence despite leaking goals.

Wooler were beaten away 3-1 in another Anderson Cup group game before Rothbury found themselves 3-0 down at half time at top-of-the-table Highfields United. Rothbury dominated the second half with the wind at their backs and after a Sutton first time drive flew in off the post and Bruce added a second with a low shot, they were unlucky not to salvage a point.

Rothbury coasted into the next round of the Sanderson Cup with a crushing 6-0 win over Alnmouth. Skipper Proudlock put away a penalty and added the second with an unstoppable high shot into the roof of the net from a Sutton pull-back. From a Coe free-kick Proudlock rose to head in for his hat-trick. Sutton blasted in from 20-yards then Proudlock struck again from the penalty spot for his fourth. Left-back Neil Corbett sent Bruce clear and with just the keeper to beat he placed in a low shot for number six.

But the form deserted Rothbury in the League as Alnmouth took the points at Armstrong Park the following week with a 2-1 win, missed chances costing Rothbury dearly with Chisholm crashing in from 18-yards for the only goal.

Rothbury's chances of progression in the Anderson Cup were dashed as a controversial goal two minutes from time condemned them to a 3-2 defeat at Shielfield Rangers.

Rothbury were sixth in the table of ten teams with 9 points, Highfields United clear at the top with 21.

In the Anderson Cup Rothbury then thrashed Shielfield Rangers 6-2 and could have had six more with an emphatic display that saw Bruce hit four and Proudlock and Mick Arkle the others.

But chance after chance was again wasted in the League with a 4-4 draw at home to Belford Reserves - and it took a last minute equaliser to salvage a point. Paul Appleby put past his goalkeeper brother Keith to put Belford one up but Common levelled after Bruce and Sutton had missed good chances. Bruce jinked down the right and pulled back for Coe to flash in a low drive for 2-1 but a surprise 25-yard drive from Miller restored parity. A brave Bruce diving header made it 3-2 but Belford scored two more before a desperate last-gasp clearance bounced off Sutton and rebounded into the net.

Rothbury fielded a weakened team and went out of the Anderson Cup with a 4-1 loss at Percy Rovers. A Proudlock penalty provided a late consolation.

And in a disappointing display at home to Lowick where it took 25 minutes for either team to manage a shot on goal, Rothbury again went down 3-1. Ballantyne briefly returned to action and his low cross caused problems with Chisholm firing first-time into the corner of the net.

With Rothbury already out of the Group stage of the Anderson Cup, a 3-3 draw with Wooler in the competition was pointless and exasperated when influential defender John Kidd was carried off.

Rothbury were on top for an hour but were robbed of a seemingly easy win as Wooler fought back in the last 25 minutes. Bruce and Coe combined to set up Chisholm and his low shot went into the corner to put Rothbury in front. Bruce was then fouled as he went around the goalkeeper and took the penalty himself to make it 2-0. Vince Bissett stooped to head in a Court cross for 2-1 but Rothbury were back in control when a Foggon cross was half cleared and Coe volleyed in from 15 yards. After Kidd had gone off, Strangeways headed in a corner from 2 yards and with 90 seconds to go Laidler blocked two close-range shots and Strangeways tucked away the third.

Rothbury finished mid-table with Sutton and Chisholm on target in a 2-2 draw with Alnmouth, an Appleby own goal and Phelan scoring for the Seasiders.

League Secretary Norman Laidler said that in 36 years in football he couldn't remember a worse fixture backlog in April so the Robson and Anderson Cup Group Leagues were to be scrapped for a home and away basis the following season.

In the Sanderson Cup semi-final, Rothbury came from behind to beat Shilbottle 3-1. Richard Robson volleyed home a right wing cross to put the Colliers 1-0 up in the fifth minute. But Rothbury held out and equalised in the 50th minute when Kevin Proudlock netted a diving header. Sutton added a second ten minutes later, and with Rothbury on top, Proudlock added his second in the dying moments to give Rothbury a deserved victory.

One of the largest crowds ever to watch a NNFL match turned out to see Percy Rovers and Rothbury in the Sanderson Cup Final at St. James's Park, Alnwick.

Rovers took their first trophy of the season with a 3-0 win as they looked to take the treble. A Michael Rogerson penalty opened the scoring but Rovers didn't add a second until the 75th minute. Bob Pile crossed to the back post and Ray Smith knocked it in. Three minutes from time Rovers were celebrating again as Rogerson turned a Smith pass past Appleby.

1987/88
Honours: Sanderson Cup Winners.

MARK BRUCE shot wide from a good position and Proudlock blazed a penalty over the bar as it just wasn't Rothbury's day on the season's opener as they went down 5-1 at home to Alnmouth. An Eddie Sutton shot was pushed onto the bar by the visiting keeper and Stuart Mackenzie tapped in the rebound for the goal.

In the Bilclough Cup preliminary round Springhill had keeper Neil Easton to thank for keeping them in it with a last minute penalty save from Proudlock - but Rothbury advanced into the first round with a 2-1 win in the replay.

Lowick maintained their unbeaten start to the season with a 4-1 win over the Armstrong Park side that then crashed 3-5 at home to Percy Rovers. The visitors deadly trio of Ray Smith, Michael Rogerson and Bob Pile all struck to put Rovers three up after just ten minutes, but Rothbury's battling performance made them labour for the win.

Rothbury advanced in the Sanderson Cup with a 7-3 mauling of Eyemouth Ams - but went out of the NFA Minor Cup 5-4 to Steamboat.

A 3-3 draw at second-bottom Belford did little for either club with Rothbury stuck in ninth spot, four from the bottom and the magic seemed to have gone.

A double sending-off didn't help matters in a heated game against Felton at Armstrong Park with Rothbury going ahead but being pegged back by two second half goals. And the struggle was really on after a 1-1 draw with basement-club Wooler.

Bruce gave Rothbury hope of a revival with a dazzling display, teasing the Shielfield Rangers defence all afternoon and rounded it off with a brilliant solo effort fitting reward for a player whose skills had tormented the Berwick side in a 6-2 win.

And after a long lay-off due to bad weather, Rothbury were back with a 6-0 thumping of North Sunderland.

Rothbury's form continued with a battling 4-3 Anderson Cup win over Felton, and a point was picked up at Felton's ground in the League a week later - a Michael Lillico own goal making it 1-1 but Rothbury had picked up just 10 points from 14 games and remained in trouble hovering just above the relegation zone. Back to back wins against Eyemouth (3-1) and a Sanderson Cup victory against Lowick (4-2) returned some confidence.

And when the club travelled to top-of-the-table Percy Rovers, instead of looking like a team that had won every fixture, Rovers looked more like a team facing relegation as they struggled to beat Rothbury 1-0 with an appalling display.

A Peter Saunders shot deflected off a Rothbury defender and looped in for a fluke own goal to take the points for the Alnwick side.

In the Sanderson Cup Shielfield Rangers had four men away on duty with the East of Scotland side and they never troubled an in-form Rothbury outfit. Gutherson opened the scoring in a 5-1 win and the impressive Bruce added the second. Gutherson headed in at the far post for another. Rothbury punished a defensive error soon after before Gutherson snapped up a chance for his hat-trick.

Alnmouth beat Rothbury 3-0 in the NNFL but the result was overshadowed by a horrific injury to Alnmouth's Bob Wilson who broke his leg in two places in an innocuous-looking challenge on John Kidd.

A 2-2 draw with Lowick earned another point and Rothbury eased comfortably away from the relegation pack with a 2-0 win over Shielfield Rangers at Old Shielfield.

If the league performance had been disappointing, an eighth placed finish Rothbury's worst since re-joining the NNFL, the club destroyed Alnmouth with a classic display of counter-attacking football to the lift the Sanderson Cup - and then they had to hand it straight back.

A dreadful administrative mix-up led to the victorious 4-0 winning Rothbury team being presented with the Runciman Cup!

Bruce embarked on the first of many dazzling runs and crosses that was only partially cleared and Rothbury took the lead. Alnmouth dominated the rest of the half with only some good goalkeeping from Keith Appleby and bad-luck denying them a leveller. The Seasiders' Hutchinson hit the post with a rasping shot but Rothbury soaked up the pressure and struck a second on the break in the 65th minute. The brilliant Bruce latched onto a pass and slipped the ball home for number three. Sub Andrew Crewther intercepted a weak back pass to add the fourth in the 85th minute and send Rothbury's travelling support into raptures.

With League safety assured, a depleted and youthful Rothbury side was beaten 6-1 at home by Shilbottle on the final day of the season.

1988/89

ROTHBURY WERE a team in transition in season 1988/89. While some experienced players remained the backbone of the team, a number of youngsters were breaking into the squad. Seventeen-year-old attacking left back Neil Corbett and midfield battler Andrew Stewart were established players with sixteen year-old forward Lee Coppock and left winger Michael Hutchison, and fifteen year old utility player Jon Tait taking their place alongside players such as the veteran former Wallington star Mick Arkle, keeper Terry Foreman, John Kidd and skipper Kevin Proudlock.

Though only in their twenties, Gordon MacKenzie, Kevin Coe, Gordon 'Shack' Hardy and Keith Appleby, along with strikers Roy Hamilton and Chris Oliver, were the mainstays of the side.

Jon Tait was still two months short of his 16th birthday when he netted on his McEwan's North Northumberland League debut, following up to fire a parried shot home from close range in a 3-1 defeat at Glanton & Hedgeley on the opening day of the season.

Worse was to follow as Rothbury crashed to a 3-0 home defeat against Longhoughton at Armstrong Park the following week, a 15-yard shot from Lawrence Gaines and a Russell Turnbull penalty putting the visitors in control before the break. Rothbury played some neat football as they hit back strongly and won themselves a penalty, which was missed, before they were killed off when Gareth Williams shot home from six yards to wrap up the points.

The side gained their first point of the season in an amazing game at Felton where they found themselves 4-1 down at the break and then 5-1 down just after the re-start. But Rothbury showed great spirit to fight back and complete a 'great escape' netting 4 times, including two in the last five minutes, to draw 5-5.

They then crashed to a 4-2 home defeat to a strong High-fields United Reserves at Armstrong Park but the young side was praised in reports that claimed they 'had some talented ball players and could develop into a useful side in a year or two's time.'

This was reinforced in a trip to unbeaten League leaders Lowick who were given a mighty fright. Lowick's Geoff Hulley and Alan Fairbairn hit the woodwork before bottom-of-the-table Rothbury hit back with some flowing football had two shots cleared off the line as their 'very promising young players' were again praised in the press. Fairbairn crashed in a half- volley in the 67th minute to claim the points, but Rothbury were begin-ning to grow in confidence and they claimed their first win of the season up in Berwick.

Highfields were left stunned as the went down 4-3 after tak-ing the lead with the shrewd mix of youth and experience in the red and white' s side playing the offside trap to perfection to frustrate the home team.

More teenagers joined the team, with prolific schoolboy goal scorer Paul Arkle and brave goalkeeper David Richardson signing up. Talented defender Alistair Kidd played only a hand-ful of games before breaking his leg and tragically never kicking a ball again.

Rothbury were drawn at home to Gosforth KOSA in the Northumberland FA Minor Cup and crashed out of the competi-tion at the first hurdle. A defensive slip-up just as Rothbury were getting on top cost them dearly. Gosforth went in front on the half hour when keeper Terry Foreman got his hands to a powerful shot but could only push it onto the underside of the bar and it dropped just over the line. Rothbury hit back five minutes later when Andrew Stewart crossed for Kevin Coe to flash in a header that the keeper parried out and Michael

Hutchison was on hand to lash the rebound right-footed into the roof of the net.

The defensive blunder came five minutes after the break to gift Gosforth the lead and they sealed the win with five minutes to go after Rothbury had dominated and looked the better side.

Rothbury had dragged themselves up to a respectable mid-table position after 18 games, winning seven, drawing two and losing nine of their games with Lowick, Percy Rovers and Scottish side Eyemouth LR dominating the top of the League.

But the early promise displayed in the young team began to peter out as some of the lads drifted back to watching Newcastle United on a Saturday and the club had to recall some veteran players. Evergreen striker Nick Gutherson was forced back out of retirement three years after he thought he had hung up his boots due to a player shortage - and he smashed in SIX in a 13-0 annihilation of basement club North Sunderland. Then 39, Nick bemoaned the fact that the young lads in the village had stopped playing on a Saturday in favour of playing in the successful Rothbury Reserves team that was a force to be reckoned with in the Third Division of the Morpeth Sunday League.

Nick told the Sunday Sun: "It saddens me when I see talented, skilful youngsters in Rothbury who are not interested in playing football regularly. I have had 26 years of pleasure playing football. They don't know what they are missing."

"I would love to be able to stop playing. I retired three years ago, but when Rothbury found themselves short of players they asked me to make a comeback. I am by no means the oldest player in the league. A bloke called Johnny Duncan at Belford still plays, and he's 10 years older than me. I think it's a shame us old stagers have to play. If we didn't club's would fold. There are teams who turn out with just nine men. I am not fit and shouldn't really be playing." Duncan would amazingly go on playing for Belford well into his fifties.

"The youngsters in the village are not interested. They would rather go to Newcastle to watch a match, or go to the pub to play pool."

NNFL Secretary and Northumberland FA official Norman Laidler agreed with Nick and said: "People like Nick Gutherson and Johnny Duncan, who is in his 35th year playing football, have a decent lifestyle. I think living in the country helps. I am still refereeing and I'm nearly 60. I referee games where the grandchildren of blokes I have refereed are playing. There are 400 players and officials turning out in the NNFL every Saturday afternoon. It is surely better to kick hell out of a football than to cause trouble. It is a shame Rothbury are having trouble finding younger players. I think one of the reasons is that they have a Sunday team. Some of the young lads prefer to watch Newcastle United on Saturday and play on Sunday."

Shilbottle were beaten 2-1 at Armstrong Park and had winger Nigel Sample sent off in a tough encounter. Rothbury's Keith Appleby and new-signing Morris Adamson had both hit the woodwork before the Colliers went one-nil up before the break when Robson played a neat one-two and went around keeper Foreman to score. But Gutherson sent over two inch-perfect crosses in the second period from which Keith Appleby and Kevin Coe rose to head home.

But up at Wooler, the home side stretched their unbeaten run to nine games as Rothbury went down 6-0. Les Porteous shot home from six yards to put Wooler in front after just three minutes and Barry Guthrie headed in a David Henderson corner to make it two on the half hour. Another Henderson corner saw Vince Bissett claim the third. Young keeper David Richardson made a good save to keep out a Barry Forrest shot but Brian Martin nipped in to net the rebound and Richardson again dived to make a great save from Martin, but Guthrie snapped up the loose ball to make it five. He was denied his hat-trick ten minutes from time when left-back Jon Tait made a last-ditch sliding tackle as he bore down on goal, but the ball span past the advancing Richardson in crept inside the post for number six.

Despite the disappointing showing in the League, Rothbury battled their way through to the Anderson Cup final where they went down 2-1 to Percy Rovers at St. James's Park, Alnwick in a disappointing game watched by a large crowd.

Bobby Pile was tripped in the box and Ian Rogerson slotted home the resultant penalty to put Rovers 1-0 up in the 70th minute and Pile himself added the second with ten minutes to go when he was sent clean through and coolly slipped a shot under the advancing keeper. Rothbury pulled one back three minutes later from a corner, but couldn't force the issue and went home empty handed.

As the season limped to a close some of the youngsters were back knocking pool balls around the green baize - but with some reward. Darren Arkle would go on to be one of the best players in the county and had trials to play for the England national pool team in 2005.

1989/90

T HE BBC Road to Wembley cameras were at Alnwick Town to capture the FA Cup fever in the town as a large crowd turned out to watch the preliminary qualifying round of the greatest Cup competition in the World, with the St. James's Park side drawing 1-1 with Peterlee.

Rothbury also drew, 3-3 at home to Hedgeley on the opening day of the season, but then had a long four-week lay-off due to postponements as the campaign got off to a sluggish start.

Highfields United were beaten 4-3 at home before Shilbottle's promising start to the season continued with a hard-earned 1-0 win at Armstrong Park. Coe, Kidd, Foggon and Gutherson were best for Rothbury and they had a shot cleared off the line. Alan Straker's goal won it for the Colliers.

Amble Town went top of the table with their fifth straight win as they thumped Rothbury 5-1 at the coast then Rothbury earned a point with a 3-3 draw at Alnmouth. Rothbury played some very attractive football and Gordon Mackenzie calmly lobbed in the opener. Eddie Sutton rounded a hesitant keeper and fired in the second. Nick Gutherson beat the offside trap for the third in the 85th minute of a very sporting and entertaining match.

Local rivals Hedgeley went into second place with a 3-2 win over Rothbury before Wooler romped away with the two points with an easy 5-1 win at Armstrong Park. Ex-Rothbury keeper Keith Appleby made a superb penalty save from Proudlock before Barry Forrest destroyed the Coquetdale side. Gordon Mackenzie was on target again and Rothbury's misery was completed when Gordon 'Shack' Hardy was rushed to hospital with a suspected broken leg.

Rothbury went into the second round of the NFA Minor Cup with a four-goal spell 15 minutes either side of the interval sending Hexham & District League leaders Corbridge United crashing out 4-1. Stuart Mackenzie headed on a Gutherson cross and Sutton controlled and tucked away. A Sutton flick-on sent Gutherson clear for the second and a superb bending Mick Arkle free-kick that crashed into the top corner from 20-yards to make it 3-0. Mick Scales' through ball put Gutherson clear for the fourth. With a comfortable lead, Rothbury allowed the visitor's back into it and after Stephen Bolton had made a couple of good saves, Corbridge pulled one back.

In the First Round first leg of the Anderson Cup Rothbury were crushed 5-1 at home by Amble Town, but a 1-0 victory over Springhill in the League rocketed the club up the table from third bottom to seventh place.

Hexham then beat Rothbury 3-2 in the NFA Minor Cup and with Rothbury trailing heavily, the second leg of the Anderson Cup first round was always going to be a struggle and they went down 4-1 at Amble to crash out 9-2 on aggregate.

Second Division North Sunderland were on the receiving end in the Sanderson Cup as Rothbury thumped them 7-1. Longhoughton were beaten 3-1 in the league but a goal from Alnmouth sub Billy Douglas fifteen minutes from time saw Rothbury beaten 3-2 after leading for a long stage of the game.

Rothbury then became only the second club to take a point from dominant Amble Town with a 2-2 draw - and it was a relieved Town who came away with the draw after fighting back from 2-0 down. Rothbury were hovering just above the relegation zone but showed they were anything but a bad team as they nearly shocked the league leaders. In the 16th minute a back header from Derek Hope fell short of the keeper and Eddie Sutton nipped in to score. Sutton then hit the woodwork as Rothbury dominated. In the second half Rothbury had three shots cleared off the line before they stunned Amble with a second well-taken goal from 8 yards. Bobby Pile bundled one in in the 75th minute and Peter Embleton spared Amble's blushes in the 80th minute with a sweetly-struck shot from 18 yards.

Rothbury had a chance to win it in the dying seconds but Shanks pulled off a great save to deny them a richly deserved victory against the best club in the NNFL.

A good 5-2 win at Lowick followed but Wooler then beat Rothbury 3-1 with Kevin Proudlock spraying the ball around well in midfield and Stuart Mackenzie a handful up front. Mackenzie hit a consolation that his hard work deserved in the 85th minute.

Rothbury went out of the Sanderson Cup 2-1 at Longhoughton before a superb solo show from Nigel Sample saw Shilbottle beat Rothbury 3-1. Rothbury were missing key players Coe, Mackenzie and Arkle, but had good performers in keeper Bolton, Kidd and Proudlock.

Further defeats followed at Eyemouth (5-1) and Longhoughton (5-3) that saw Rothbury go three-nil up in 15 minutes - and blow it. John Common, Eddie Sutton and Nick Gutherson scored.

Rothbury drew 0-0 at Springhill and basement club and relegation favourites Highfields United fielded three or four experienced players who made a difference as they held Rothbury 2-2 in an entertaining match with a lot of good football. But if Rothbury were to compete with the likes of Amble Town, changes would have to be made. Town won the Sanderson Cup with a 3-0 win over Wooler, the Anderson Cup with a 4-1 win over Wooler and took the league for a superb treble by six points from Alnmouth, amassing 34 with Rothbury finishing sixth on 17.

1990/91

MARK BRUCE struck twice, once from the penalty spot, but Rothbury were beaten 5-2 at home by Shilbottle on the opening day of a disappointing season in 1990/91. The club bounced back from this set back and trounced Lowick 6-1 away. Lowick went in front through Craig Dixon but after Nick Gutherson had seen a header hit the bar, it was all Rothbury. Eddie Sutton ghosted through the defence to make it 1-1 and Gutherson headed in to put Rothbury in front. Kevin Proudlock volleyed in the third and a Bruce cross-shot flew in for number four. A late Mick Scales double rounded off a fine performance.

And local rivals Wallington were then seen off 3-1 at Armstrong Park. Kevin Coe and Kevin Proudlock both scored before John Smith brought down Sutton in the box and Bruce tucked away the penalty.

Rothbury then crashed to a 3-1 defeat at Hedgeley but Springhill were beaten 3-1 at Armstrong Park, before Rothbury slumped to an embarrassing 7-1 reverse at Armstrong Park at the hands of Wooler, with Barry Forrest their main tormentor. Longhoughton then beat Rothbury 2-0.

The red and whites tightened up and stopped the rot by beating Percy Rovers reserves 3-1 with a Sutton drive opening the scoring. Sutton then beat a defender and his cross-shot gave Balmbra no chance for the second. Stuart MacKenzie came on as a substitute and almost immediately added the third. Fletcher pulled one back for Rovers with 20 minutes to go.

Longhoughton completed a double with a 4-3 win at Armstrong Park that left the club perilously close to the relegation zone, but Rothbury got some Christmas cheer with a 2-1 win at Belford in an uninspired game with the minimum of goalmouth action.

Belford then took a point from Armstrong Park in the return fixture before Rothbury's season hit a new low with a horror show at Shilbottle. Rothbury were 2-0 down at half time but fell apart and collapsed like a pack of cards in the final twenty minutes as they were annihilated 11-0, completely over-run by the Colliers who went back to the top of the table.

Amble Town reserves visited Armstrong Park in the first round of the Bilclough Cup and went away victorious after a 4-2 win.

But Rothbury made it into the semi-final of the Anderson Cup with a Stuart MacKenzie hat-trick enough to see off a late fight back from Lowick as Rothbury took the tie 3-2.

Wooler then rocked Rothbury 2-0 and Lowick took the points at Armstrong Park with a solitary goal enough to drop Rothbury to third bottom in Division One.

Rothbury dug in for a vital 4-3 win at basement club Springhill and drew 2-2 at home to Alnmouth for another important point. Nick Gutherson headed in a far post cross and a Kevin Coe pin-point header capping a fine solo performance.

Rothbury totally outplayed Wooler in the Anderson Cup semi-final and were desperately unlucky to go out 1-0 to a Barry Forrest goal in the 75th minute. Rothbury dominated the game and missed a number of chances.

And in the Sanderson Cup quarter final, Rothbury also went out, beaten 3-0 by Alnmouth. A 1-0 win over Hedgeley saw the club finish in eighth spot in the league, above Wallington, Longhoughton, Percy Rovers reserves and Springhill.

1991/92

Honours: Sanderson Cup Winners, Bilclough Cup Winners.

ROTHBURY GOT OFF to a flyer with a 3-1 victory at Wooler and then thumped Percy Rovers reserves 3-0 at Armstrong Park as the red and whites enjoyed a successful season. Against Rovers Stuart MacKenzie shot through a crowded area and latched onto a poor back pass to round the keeper and add his second. Eddie Sutton added the third in the 80th minute.

But Rothbury went out of the Anderson Cup in the first round, going down 2-0 at home to North Sunderland. Their league form also suffered with a 1-1 draw away at Longhoughton and a 6-2 drubbing at home to Braeside.

Sanderson Cup holders Reston Rovers received the backlash as they were sent tumbling out of the competition 3-1 at home to the Coquetdale men. Eddie Sutton put Rothbury 1-0 up at the break and Stuart MacKenzie added two more. John Kidd sliced into his own goal to give Rovers a consolation.

And the club advanced in the Northumberland FA Minor Cup with a 5-2 win at home to Newcastle Bakers Oven.

Back in League action, Rothbury went up to neighbours Hedgeley and came away smiling after a 4-1 win. They were 3-0 up at half time through Andrew Stewart, Bruce and Stuart MacKenzie. Sutton added a fourth after a goalmouth scramble. Hedgeley full-back Williams pulled one back with a long-range shot that beat keeper Ian Fenwick.

And Rothbury moved up to seventh in the table with a 6-1 drubbing of Amble Town reserves at Armstrong Park. Stuart MacKenzie hit two, as did Bruce, with Ian Armstrong and Andrew Stewart also on the score sheet.

In the second round of the NFA Cup rampant Rothbury travelled to Tyneside and disposed of Walker Stack Fosse 5-2 for their fifth successive victory. Stuart MacKenzie opened from a pinpoint Proudlock cross and Armstrong rammed in the second. Bruce made it 3-0 before he missed a chance to seal it from the penalty spot. Walker pulled two back before a speculative Stuart MacKenzie lob flew in and he blasted in a Bruce cross for his hat-trick.

Two successive 1-0 defeats, away at Lowick and at home to Shilbottle at a very foggy Armstrong Park were a setback, but the club advanced into round four of the Minor Cup with a shock 4-1 win over Newcastle DHSS, one of the competition's fancied sides, at Armstrong Park. The social had no answer to the commitment and enthusiasm of Rothbury who went 1-0 up in the 15th minute when Scales slid in Bruce whose shot was saved and Stuart MacKenzie followed up to stretch the netting.

Andrew Stewart struck twice in five minutes to put Rothbury 3-0 to the good. Donnelly pulled one back but McKenzie sealed the impressive victory with his second of the game.

In the quarter final of the Sanderson Cup, an Ian Fenwick goal after 60 minutes, sweeping a shot past Keith Appleby, saw Rothbury win 1-0 at local rivals Wallington.

Rothbury then put a dent in North Sunderland's title aspirations as the Seasiders had to battle from behind to salvage a point at Armstrong Park. Rothbury were in excellent form and the brilliant Kevin Coe fired in an absolute screamer from 25-yards. Five minutes later, in a goalmouth scramble, former Berwick Rangers ace Stuart Romaines rifled into the roof of his own net. But North Sunderland hit back with two late goals to rescue a point.

Rothbury went out of the NFA Minor Cup fourth round to a sickening goal in the last minute of extra time at home to Tyne & Wear Fire Brigade. Rothbury were reduced to ten men after just 30 minutes in the best Cup tie seen at the ground in years. Stuart MacKenzie hit the post with a long range shot before Ian Fenwick volleyed Rothbury in front. Ian Armstrong then punched a shot off the line and was dismissed, but Simpson put the penalty wide for the firemen. They drew level in the 60th minute when Bolton could only parry a Taleman shot into the net. And five minutes later Felvus' speculative shot flew in to make it 1-2. With just nine minutes of normal time to go, left back Neil Corbett embarked on a surging run and was upended in the box, with Bruce coolly sending the keeper the wrong way from the spot. The firemen also had a man sent off in extra time but clinched the tie in the dying seconds when Connelly broke Rothbury's hearts by squeezing in a low shot.

Rothbury just held on for a point in a 3-3 draw at home to Wallington the following week. Fenwick fired in a long throw from Coe to put Rothbury ahead but Sammy Lough levelled. A Bruce penalty hit the post after he had been brought down by Appleby but a Proudlock pass put in Stuart MacKenzie to hammer Rothbury back in front. With Wallington being run ragged, MacKenzie volleyed in his second from 15 yards to make it 3-1. Lough struck again in the second period to reduce the deficit and John Kidd sliced into his own goal for the equaliser. Rothbury were now defending desperately and the Greens were unlucky not to win it when Moffat hit the bar and John Smith fired wide from a good position.

Bruce hit a hat-trick in a 3-3 draw at Alnmouth that kept Rothbury in mid-table, seventh in the Division.

And Bruce hit two more in a 2-2 draw at North Sunderland in the Bilclough Cup with keeper Stephen Bolton the hero, saving an amazing FOUR penalties in the shoot-out as Rothbury took it 2-0.

A 5-1 win at Belford followed then Rothbury beat struggling Percy Rovers reserves 3-2 at Armstrong Park. Bruce bent a free kick over the wall and into the top corner before adding a second from the penalty spot. Mick Scales volleyed in the winner from a Bruce cross.

Lowick travelled down to Coquetdale and went away with the points from a 3-2 win before Rothbury dispatched Belford 4-1.

Runaway League leaders Shilbottle were sent out of the Bilclough Cup in the quarter final with Kevin Proudlock drilling in the only goal after 15 minutes. The visitor's hit-man Bobby Pile was injured and limped off with no substitute available and a Colliers full-back walked off the pitch in a fit of bad temper to leave them with just nine men at the final whistle.

Rothbury were leading 1-0 deep into extra time in the semi-final of the Sanderson Cup through a Bruce goal when a thunderous Ken Lyle drive flew into the top corner from fully 35 yards to earn the Seasider's a replay. But Rothbury came back from behind to take it 3-1 and march into the final. Jackie Allan put Alnmouth in front but Gordon Turnbull stabbed in the equaliser from goalmouth scramble following a corner. Mick Scales was brought down and Bruce sent the keeper the wrong way from the spot to make it 2-1 and Bruce later converted a Stuart MacKenzie cross to ensure the win.

Rothbury took the Sanderson Cup silverware in the first ever floodlit final at St. James Park, Alnwick with a 2-1 win over Braeside. Mark Bruce put the Coquet men ahead in the 10th minute with an exceptional goal, even by his high standards. He cut inside two defenders and crashed his shot into the top corner for a sensational strike. Soon after it was 2-0 when Braeside failed to deal with a corner and Stuart MacKenzie scrambled home. Braeside pulled one back five minutes before the interval, but for all their heavy pressure after the break, Rothbury held out to claim the trophy.

Rothbury were given a fright by Division One strugglers Percy Rovers reserves in the Bilclough Cup semi-final at Hedgeley, though, fighting all the way for a 2-1 win. Leading scorer Bruce put Rothbury ahead but Peter Saunders volleyed the leveller. Rovers keeper Nesbitt fumbled a shot and the outstanding Kevin Coe was on hand to stab in the winner.

Rothbury moved up to third in the League with a string of three wins, 3-1 at home to North Sunderland, 2-0 at home to Hedgeley and 1-0 away to Wallington.

Braeside were again the victims of a 2-1 win as Rothbury claimed their second trophy of the season in the Bilclough Cup final, with the red and white's defence gaining the edge. Bruce made it 1-0 ten minutes into the second half but Colin Smith rammed in the equaliser just sixty seconds later. Four minutes later Kevin Coe won it when a high ball was lofted into the box and he rose to powerfully head past the stranded keeper. Braeside were reduced to ten men for swearing at the referee as their frustrations got the better of them.

The Berwick side did gain some revenge in the final League game of the season with a 5-0 win - but with keeper Stephen Bolton unavailable, top marksman Mark Bruce had to play in nets for 45 minutes after stand-in Ian Fenwick was injured.

1992/93

WALLINGTON'S Martin Roberts and Graeme Foggon were added to boss Nick Gutherson's team and Rothbury displayed their title aspirations with a good 4-3 away win at Lowick on the first day of the season. In the 9th minute Mick Scales drilled in a low shot to put Rothbury ahead and Mark Bruce side-footed in a Neil Corbett cross just after the break for the second. Stephen Bolton struggled to deal with a heavy back pass and Murray forced the ball over the line to put Lowick back in the game. Hogg drove in a 20-yard free-kick to equalise. Goals from Stuart MacKenzie and Bruce put Rothbury 4-2 up and Rothbury held out after Dave Miller made it 3-4 late in the game.

But Rothbury were over-run in the last 30 minutes at home to Braeside as they were soundly beaten 4-1 after Ian Armstrong had shot the Coquetdale side in front.

A John Bain hat-trick was the major factor in a 5-2 home defeat at the hands of Springhill, with Kevin Proudlock and Stuart MacKenzie on target for the red and whites.

Rothbury's good away form continued however, with a solid 3-0 win at local rivals Hedgeley Rovers. The unmarked Bruce slipped the ball past keeper Mason to open and Stuart McKenzie blasted in a fierce volley to double the advantage. Hard-working midfielder Martin Roberts drilled in the third in the 78th minute.

North Sunderland outplayed Rothbury at Armstrong Park but had to settle for a point in a 1-1 draw. Bruce got to the bye-line and crossed for Stuart MacKenzie rifle home but Robert Locke beat keeper Stephen Bolton from a cross to make it all-square in the 75th minute.

Rothbury claimed their first home win beating Percy Rovers 3-2, bouncing back from 2-0 down to see a Stuart MacKenzie double and a solitary Bruce strike claim three good points and move Rothbury into second in the table.

But Percy turned the tables the following week, claiming only their second win with an Ian Rogerson goal all that could separate the teams. In the Bilclough Cup, Second Division Craster Rovers were kippered 4-1 at the coast and an above average crowd turned out and were treated to a great Rothbury display in the first round of the Northumberland FA Minor Cup as North Shields Nautilus were disposed 3-1 after extra time. Kevin Proudlock rattled the bar, a John Kidd header was hacked off the line and Nautilus keeper Brannigan made some brilliant saves as Rothbury dominated the goal-less ninety minutes. Five minutes into extra time a 30-yard drive flew past Bolton and crashed into the Rothbury net to give the visitor's a surprise lead. But Kevin Coe, one of Rothbury's most consistent performers over the years, showed his great class on the ball and his low shot crept inside the post with just 10 minutes to go. Stuart MacKenzie bundled in a Bruce cross to put Rothbury ahead and Bruce's skill and ball control created himself a yard of space to hit the third.

Rothbury and Amble Vikings both seemed to be suffering Minor Cup hangovers as they laboured to a 2-2 draw at Armstrong Park the following week. Graham Foggon and Mark Bruce scored for Rothbury with Martin Douglas and Keith Morley on target for Vikings.

With Shilbottle's pitch unplayable, a league fixture was switched to Armstrong Park and the points shared in a 1-1 draw that left Rothbury fifth in a table topped by Braeside. The Shilbottle keeper had an inspired game but was beaten by a close range Adamson shot for 1-0. With snow billowing down out of the slate grey skies, Bobby Pile hit the leveller.

Rothbury made a disastrous start at home to Northumberland CC in the Minor Cup when they found themselves two down after only twelve minutes at Armstrong Park. Foggon then hit the woodwork twice before a three-goal blast in five minutes saw Rothbury in front. Foggon, a speculative Roberts effort and Adamson forcing in to put Rothbury in the driving seat. Adamson went through and slipped past the advancing keeper to make it 4-2 but Northumberland CC from the Newcastle District Welfare League pulled one back after a defensive mix-up.

In the Bilclough Cup, Rothbury went through 4-2 on penalties after a 2-2 draw at home to Longhoughton. Adamson drove in the first and when Roberts was fouled, Bruce added a second from the spot. Stephen Bolton saved Longhoughton's third penalty and the fourth was blazed over the bar as Rothbury progressed.

In the New Year Rothbury made it into the last eight in the Minor Cup for the first time in many years with a hard-fought 3-2 win over Kenton at a mud-bound Armstrong Park. Bruce brought down a perfectly-flighted long ball from Kevin Coe to shoot Rothbury ahead in the 20th minute and Stuart MacKenzie was unlucky not to add another as his shot was hacked off the line. Foggon then chipped inches over and Morris Adamson hit the post as Rothbury were on top. But they were stunned on the hour when Fennelly blasted a loose ball past Bolton. Stuart MacKenzie crossed for Bruce to head Rothbury back in front but Kenton's big number nine Scott levelled when his cross-shot dipped over the back peddling Bolton and dropped in at the last moment. With just ten minutes to go Adamson brought a ball under control and coolly placed the winner past keeper McDermott.

Sanderson Cup holders Rothbury squeezed into the next round with a narrow 2-1 win over Shilbottle, Bruce and Stuart MacKenzie cancelling out a Bobby Pile strike to keep the 'Cup Kings' on the glory trail.

Rothbury beat Wooler 2-0 before disposing of Alnwick Town reserves 2-1. Mark Bruce put Rothbury in front and solid centre half John Kidd hit his first of the season with a volley to win it on the hour.

But the red and whites went out of the Minor Cup in the quarter finals after a 2-0 defeat at Northern Alliance Division Two leaders Gosforth Bohemians. Rothbury made the worst possible start and were two down inside six minutes. It could have been worse as a third was disallowed for offside just moments later. But Rothbury weren't disgraced and created some decent chances as they got more into the game.

The title ambitions remained intact, however, with a 2-1 win at North Sunderland. Mick Robson put the home side in front but Martin Roberts and Stuart MacKenzie hit back.

In a dour derby Rothbury claimed three more points with a 2-1 home win over Wallington - but after dominating for long spells it took a Mark Bruce goal just four minutes from time to seal it.

Rothbury were frustrated by Wallington's tight defence but went ahead when Kevin Proudlock deceived keeper Keith Appleby with a lofted drive that ended up in the back of the net. Jimmy Moffat levelled in the 65th minute but, with the clock ticking down, leading scorer Bruce latched onto a weak clearance and side footed past Appleby's despairing dive.

Rothbury crashed out of the Sanderson Cup in the quarter final with a 3-1 defeat at Alnwick Town reserves and further disappointment followed with a 3-1 loss at Shilbottle.

The title hopes took a set back with a 2-2 home draw against Hedgeley. Kevin Coe grabbed a double, powerfully heading in a Foggon corner for a great goal and applying a faint touch to divert in a Roberts free-kick minutes later.

A 2-0 win over Wooler and a good 3-2 victory away to Braeside kept Rothbury in with a shout, lying in fourth place in the table trailing leaders Alnmouth by nine points.

A 4-2 defeat away to Amble Vikings, with Stuart McKenzie and Bruce on target, was a set-back but John Kidd drove home the loose ball from a corner and Kevin Proudlock tucked away a penalty in a 2-0 win over Lowick. The title hopes were dashed, though, by a 5-2 defeat at Shilbottle.

In their penultimate game Rothbury went up to Springhill and came away with the three points after a 4-1 success over the Bilclough Cup winners. Proudlock's low drive in the 50th minute put Rothbury in front but Johnny Bain levelled. Stuart MacKenzie hit two and Bruce rounded off the scoring.

Alnmouth clinched the North Northumberland League title on the last day of the season with a 4-2 win at Armstrong Park. The visitors outplayed Rothbury, who hit two consolation goals in the last minute, Foggon crossing for Stuart MacKenzie to head in and Bruce, who had been strangely quiet throughout, being tripped and converting the resultant penalty with the last kick of the game.

Unveiling a memorial seat for former goalkeeper Neville Laidler in 2009.

1993/94

THE CLUB was in a strong enough position to enter a reserve team in the Second Division of the NNL along with League newcomers Chevington and Stobhill Rangers but had lost central defender John Kidd and influential midfielder Kevin Proudlock to retirement whilst Mark Bruce had taken his skills to Wallington. But the club had signed prolific goal scorer Bobby Pile from Shilbottle, and Nick Gay and Barry Forrest from Hedgeley.

Gay opened the scoring after just ten minutes in an opening day 3-0 win over North Sunderland. Gay was again on target after the break and Ian Armstrong headed in a rebound for the third. But Rothbury were then subjected to a 2-1 defeat at home to Springhill. Rothbury went behind but Gay crossed for Pile to head in the leveller. Former Berwick Rangers legend Eric Tait fired in a blistering free kick that had Stephen Bolton diving full stretch to save, but in the 55th minute Millar's opportunist strike won it.

Rothbury beat Spittal Rovers A 2-1 at Berwick before beating Ashington Town 5-2 at home. The newly-promoted Ashington side had been the Northern League club's reserve side but had broken away from the Portland Park set-up for financial reasons in a change sanctioned by the League.

Kevin Proudlock volleyed Rothbury ahead and Kevin Coe was unlucky to hit the bar during the onslaught. Nick Gay put Barry Forrest clear to make it 2-0. But Ashington weathered the storm and Kevin Stocks squeezed in a shot for 2-1. A Gay header increased Rothbury's lead before Gary Caldow pulled one back from the penalty spot. Gay then headed in a Forrest cross for his hat-trick and Gordon MacKenzie rifled in the fifth in the 88th minute.

Rothbury went through to the second round of the Bilclough Cup with a 1-0 win at North Sunderland that saw Gordon Mackenzie's speculative 25-yard shot crash in to win it for the Red and Whites.

Amble Vikings then visited Armstrong Park and went away with the points in a 5-1 massacre - this just a week after they had drawn 2-2 with Rothbury Reserves in the Bilclough Cup, before going on to win 6-2 after extra time in what they admitted had been their toughest game of the season. Barry Forrest scored.

Rothbury sent Alliance Division Two side Wallsend Rising Sun crashing out of the Northumberland FA Minor Cup 3-1 in a first round tie at Armstrong Park. Rothbury went behind on the half hour to a bizarre goal as Johnstone's 30 yard shot beat Bolton and trickled into the net. After a comedy of errors a Wallsend defender sliced into his own goal to level things up and in the 70th minute Gay blasted Rothbury in front. Pacey reserve striker Martyn Smith added a third five minutes later.

League leaders Berwick Harrow beat Rothbury 1-0 before the Coquetdale side cruised into the third round of the NFA Minor Cup with a 4-0 victory at Hexhamshire.

Gay made it 1-0 and a Gordon MacKenzie penalty two. Steven Brewis stabbed after a mistake and Stephen Virtue set up Gay to knock in his second and the team's fourth.

A good crowd turned out to see Rothbury draw 3-3 in the derby clash with Wallington at Armstrong Park. Gay shot Rothbury into the lead after Appleby had parried his initial shot but a mistake by Gordon Turnbull let in Eadington to equalise. Stocks made it 2-1 to the visitors but Peter MacDougal hit back with his first goal for the club. Andrew Stewart then headed Rothbury in front after Appleby had palmed a cross onto the crossbar. Jimmy Moffat levelled after a Mick Scales shot came back off the post. A 2-2 draw up at Lowick saw the club sitting third bottom in the table with a disappointing eight points from seven games.

North Sunderland secured their fifth win on the bounce when they beat an unlucky Rothbury 5-2 on a windswept pitch.

Mark Romaines powerful shot from the edge of the box flew in to make it 1-0 but after a sustained period of Rothbury pressure, Marflitt headed a Foggon cross into his own net. Stuart MacKenzie volleyed in at the back post from a corner to put Rothbury in front. Thomson rifled in the leveller after several goal-line clearances and Dave Stanton turned his marker and curled into the top corner to put North Sunderland 3-2 up in the 75th minute. Rothbury thought they'd equalised five minutes later when left-back Jon Tait fired a half-cleared corner into the net from 25 yards, but they were denied by a controversial linesman's flag. The decision unsettled Rothbury and Stanton and Robson added two more for North Sunderland in the final five minutes.

A Kevin Henderson-inspired Amble Town sent Rothbury crashing out of the NFA Minor Cup in the third round with Henderson twice smashing against the bar before Rothbury took a surprise lead. Henderson levelled after the break and added a quick-fire 11 minute hat-trick as the hosts and Cup favourites ran out 6-1 winners.

Then having done the spadework with a 4-1 win at Berwick, Rothbury produced a workmanlike performance to see of the challenge of a lively Spittal outfit 5-3, taking the Anderson Cup first round tie 9-4 on aggregate.

Disaster struck for the visitors after only eight minutes when Andrew Stewart's left wing cross was sliced into the net by a defender. Worse followed three minutes later when Kevin Coe challenged the visiting keeper for a cross, leaving Stuart Mackenzie a simple two-yard tap in.

Spittal settled and pulled one back through the League's top scorer Darren Amory. But within five minutes Rothbury had restored their two-goal advantage, Bolton's long kick falling to MacKenzie to chip in his second. Just before half time Bolton fumbled a low drive and Hossack was on hand to notch the visitors second. The second half was scrappy, but in the 65th minute the Spittal keeper flapped at a cross which fell to Chris Gray on the edge of the box and he volleyed into the top corner. Ten minutes later Gordon MacKenzie crossed to the far post where Nick Gay stooped to head in the fifth. Amory scored the visitor's third with a couple of minutes remaining after Rothbury failed to clear a corner.

Rothbury's first game of the New Year ended in defeat in a tough match that was liberally laced with petty shenanigans as Berwick Harrow won 2-1 at Armstrong Park.

Rothbury were punished for some slack finishing on the half hour when a ball over the top of their back four let in speedy Harrow forward Jamie Stewart, and he neatly lobbed Bolton to break the deadlock. Just before the break Rothbury debutant Simon Wilson cut in from the right and his low driven cross flashed across the face of goal, evading everyone. Michael Strangeways made it 2-0 in the 66th minute when he put the ball smartly past the advancing Bolton.

Rothbury were rewarded for their efforts in the 80th minute as a long clearance by Kevin Coe was chased by Stuart MacKenzie and, after colliding with the visiting keeper and a defender, he span around to tap into the empty net. Rothbury almost stole a last-gasp equaliser in the final minute, but the ball was twice scrambled off the line.

Basement club Belford were thrashed 5-1 at Armstrong but gloss was taken off as the visitors Thompson was taken from the field in an ambulance after suffering a bad ankle injury.

Rothbury were 3-0 up at the break with an Andrew Stewart cross hitting the bar and ricocheting in off the back of an unlucky defender, Gay netting and Graham Foggon cracking in a superb 18-yard strike. Foggon added the fourth before former Hedgeley hit-man Wilson plundered his first Rothbury goal for number five.

An injury-time winner from Peter Embleton took Alnwick Town reserves back to the top of the table as Rothbury were unlucky to go down 3-2. Rothbury led until the 80th minute when Ray Smith levelled before Embleton's last-gasp sickener. Martin Roberts sent Foggon away down the right and his low cross was turned in at the near post by Stuart MacKenzie to give Rothbury the lead. Rueben Stuart headed in an equaliser after the break but MacKenzie fired in his second low from the edge of the box to give Rothbury the advantage.

And Rothbury were then put on the back foot in the quarter finals of the Bilclough Cup when two Gary Irving penalties gave North Sunderland the edge with a 3-2 win in the first leg. North Sunderland went in front in the 20th minute when an in-swinging corner struck Nick Gay on the hand and Irving stepped up to thunder in the spot-kick giving Bolton no chance.

Rothbury levelled five minutes before half time when they were awarded a free kick 25-yards out. Graham Foggon squared it to Kevin Coe and his dipping shot beat the Seahouses keeper.

Rothbury went in front shortly after the break when Stuart MacKenzie was brought down in the box and brother Gordon rifled in from the penalty spot. North Sunderland were awarded a dubious second penalty with 20 minutes to go as Bolton slid out and appeared to make a brave save at an in-rushing striker's feet. But, to the Rothbury player's disbelief, the referee pointed to the spot and Irving slammed home the equaliser. Five minutes from time Mick Robson clipped the winner over Bolton.

A 2-1 defeat at Berwick Harrow followed before Rothbury sent Spittal A out of the Bilclough Cup quarter-finals with a 2-0 win.

Amble Vikings were thrashed 5-1 at Armstrong Park as Stuart MacKenzie and Peter MacDougal both had shots cleared off the line with the red and whites dominating. A spectacular Gordon MacKenzie headed own goal gave the visitors the lead but Rothbury hit back in determined fashion with three goals in the first six minutes of the second half, Wilson, Coe and Stuart Mac-

Kenzie netting. MacKenzie added a second and Peter MacDougal grabbed the other.

The club went out of the Anderson Cup quarter finals 6-3 on aggregate as a Stuart MacKenzie lob was the only bright spot in a 3-1 defeat at North Sunderland.

But Rothbury beat injury-hit Alnmouth 2-1 to advance into the Bilclough Cup final. The semi-final tie was hastily re-arranged to Embleton after the Shilbottle pitch was declared unfit and Stuart MacKenzie lashed a Coe free-kick into the net to give Rothbury the lead. Raynor broke through the Rothbury defence and followed up as his initial shot was parried by Steven Bolton to net the equaliser. On the hour Stuart MacKenzie and Nick Gay combined, with Gay drilling in the winner from 10 yards.

Back in league action Rothbury bounced back from a shock 2-0 defeat at basement club Belford to thump Spittal Rovers A 4-2 at Armstrong Park. But they found themselves a goal down after just 30 seconds in the sleety conditions when Hossack screwed the opener past Stephen Bolton.

Rothbury equalised in the seventh minute when Spittal failed to clear Kevin Coe's in-swinging free kick and Simon Wilson drove the loose ball back across goal for Peter MacDougall to apply the decisive touch. Stuart MacKenzie put Rothbury in front in the 22nd minute when he chased Graeme Foggon's through ball to slide it past the advancing keeper and Nick Gay crashed in a third just before half time to put Rothbury in a commanding position. Spittal pulled one back when prolific scorer Darren Amory scrambled one over the line before the Red and Whites sealed it late on, Chris Gray hammering a shot against the bar and sub Michael Hutchison reacting quickest and firing in the rebound.

Both sets of players stood around the centre circle with bowed heads as a minute's silence was held before kick-off for respected Rothbury FC President Jack Tait who had passed away aged 96 before the club went down to a 2-1 home defeat to Alnmouth. Jack had been a familiar sight to Rothbury players and fans, arriving across the dips in the fields behind the far goal at Armstrong Park from his Cragside home in a jacket and flat cap for every home fixture before taking up his usual spot near the half-way line. Tommy Taylor gave the visitor's the lead in the 35th minute when he broke clear from Kevin Coe and smacked in a low shot from eight yards. But Rothbury equalised in first half stoppage time, Graham Foggon's chip splitting the defence for Stuart MacKenzie to smash in a left foot volley.

The winning goal came on the hour. Alnmouth were awarded a penalty for holding in the box; Bolton flung himself to the right to parry the spot-kick, dived to push out the rebound and blocked a third effort with his body, but Straughan followed up to shoot through the packed six yard box and into the corner of the net. The Bilclough Cup final was drawn 2-2 with Springhill and had to go to a replay.

Nick Gay struck four times as Rothbury completed their league programme with a 6-3 win over Lowick. Stuart MacKenzie and Simon Wilson added the others to see the club finishing comfortably in mid-table in 8th spot with 20 points. The reserves finished tenth in the Second Division, two off the bottom, with 16 points.

And Rothbury were left deflated in the Bilclough Cup Final replay when a John Hall goal in the dying seconds took the trophy to Springhill for the second time in three seasons.

The game looked to be heading for extra time when former Berwick Rangers star Charlie Elvin sent McGonigal clear with a perfectly weighted ball through the mud. He raced on and squared it to Hall who gratefully side-footed home from six yards.

The winner followed a frantic final ten minutes where Graham Foggon, Simon Wilson and Kevin Coe all went close to winning it for Rothbury.

There was a doubt as to whether the game would go ahead as a thunder and lightning storm brewed ominously over Alnwick's St. James's Park before kick-off. The game started under the floodlights half an hour late and with the pitch saturated and muddy following the downpour.

Elvin went close for Springhill with a drive just the wrong side of the upright and a delicate lob which fell on the roof of the net before Rothbury were forced to re-organise in the 25th minute. Centre-backs Chris Gray and Gordon Turnbull both went for a high ball and suffered a clash of heads, splitting both brows. Turnbull was replaced by Darren Arkle while Gray was off the pitch for 15 minutes receiving treatment before coming back on heavily bandaged. Springhill failed to capitalise on their temporary advantage, though they did force keeper Stephen Bolton to make a number of saves as they forced numerous corners. At the other end, midfield battler Peter MacDougall cracked an effort just over from the edge of the box. And Rothbury almost went in front in the opening seconds of the second half when Foggon bent in a free-kick from near the corner flag that keeper Manual mishandled and Bell hacked off the line.

Springhill broke the deadlock in the 68th minute when Innes Gray arrived at the edge of the box and struck a low shot through the crowded area and into the corner of the net. But Rothbury hit back immediately, Gordon MacKenzie lofting a free-kick into the box for his brother Stuart to charge in and head powerfully past Manual.

For all Rothbury's late pressure, Hall finished the last minute breakaway move to win it for Springhill 2-1.

1994/95

ROTHBURY WERE 2-0 down at home to Spittal on the opening day of the new Halifax Property Services NNFL season but started the fight back when Stuart Mackenzie cracked in an 18-yard drive just before half time. Strike-partner Stephen Virtue fired in the equaliser after good work by Micky Hutchison down the left in the 75th minute and Virtue was just off target to win it with a delicate lob that beat the keeper all-ends-up but fell just past the post. Hutchison, Virtue and Chris Bews were superb for Rothbury and they were well supported by midfielders Coe and Mackenzie.

An under-strength Rothbury side then brought about their own downfall by gifting visitors Alnmouth three goals in a 4-1 home defeat. Debut keeper Malcolm Wilkinson got his hands to a Johnny Davis penalty but the power took it over the line and a Gordon Mackenzie penalty was the consolation.

Stobhill Rangers then won 4-3 at Armstrong Park before Rothbury travelled to Tyneside for a NFA Minor Cup first round tie and came away with a 5-3 win from Wallsend Lindisfarne. Steven Ballantyne came in at centre half for his first team debut and Kevin Coe was switched to midfield. Hutchison confidently fired in a penalty and Coe headed in from a corner. Virtue added the third with a well-struck volley and then headed in an Armstrong flick for the fourth. In-form Virtue grabbed his hat-trick when he smashed in the fifth from six yards in a much-improved team performance.

A 3-0 defeat at Craster's Windmill Park put Rothbury out of the Sanderson Cup but Rothbury grabbed a good 4-2 win at Alnmouth in the Anderson Cup first round, first leg. Stephen Virtue took advantage of hesitancy in the home defence to bundle in the opener after just sixty seconds. Gordon Turnbull and Ballantyne were winning the aerial battle at the back but Alnmouth struck twice. Stuart Mackenzie equalised and a Hutchison cross was fired in at the near post by Kevin Coe to put Rothbury back in charge. Hutchison took the ball through the middle, coolly rounded the keeper and fired into the net for 4-2.

In Division Two, hugely-promising 16-year-old Stuart Foreman hit a hat-trick in his first season of NNFL football in a 5-0 win for the reserves over Hedgeley Rovers. Fellow 16-year-old strikers Kim Fenwick and Michael Gutherson were also on target in the rout.

Rothbury crashed 7-1 at Acklington Prison and were stunned to go down 3-0 at home to Alnmouth in the second leg of the Anderson Cup to slump out 5-4 on aggregate. A Stuart Mackenzie header was cleared off the line with ten minutes to go.

Rothbury met Shilbottle CW at Armstrong Park for the first time since the Colliers had been promoted to the Northern Alliance in the second round of the NFA Minor Cup and were unlucky to go down 4-2 after their best performance of the season. With a bit of luck they could have pulled off a shock result. After Shilbottle took the lead Stuart Mackenzie intercepted a back pass to make it 1-1. A Dodds penalty put Shilbottle back in front but Virtue crashed in the equaliser from a good Hutchison run and cross. After the break a stretching Ballantyne fouled Dodds and he got up to put away his second spot-kick. A Forrest header made it 4-2. Craster also put Rothbury out of the Bilclough Cup with a 1-0 win at Windmill Park.

Rothbury's hearts were then broken by an injury-time winner from Wallington's Jimmy Moffat in a passionate derby in front of a large crowd that saw five players booked and two sent off. Ian Armstrong drilled in low in the 13th minute but Wallington's attractive play was rewarded in the 60th minute when former star Mark Bruce's cross was turned into the net by the unlucky Gordon Turnbull for an equaliser. Rothbury were shattered when Moffat lashed in a low shot with just seconds to go for Wallington' s first win over Rothbury since they re-joined the NNFL.

Berwick Harrow then hit four without reply at Armstrong Park that left the club languishing at the bottom of the table with just two points from nine games.

But Rothbury showed little sign of a festive hangover in the New Year as fellow-strugglers Springhill were hit for six without reply at Armstrong Park. In the tenth minute Virtue turned a defender on the edge of the box and crossed for Stuart Mackenzie to score with a thumping header. Mackenzie added his second with a low drive then Virtue slipped in the third after half an hour. Andrew Stewart's perfect chip made it four and Chris Bews raced clear and slotted under the despairing keeper for the fifth. Kevin Coe headed a Gordon Mackenzie free kick into the roof of the net to round off the scoring in the final minute.

The improved form continued with a 1-0 home win over Amble Vikings that moved the club up the table two places, but

Rothbury suffered a blow as they lost striker Stephen Virtue in only the third minute with a broken ankle that put him out of the game for six months. A good ball from Stewart was fired home by the hard working Stuart Mackenzie for the winner in the 18th minute. Stewart was also hurt in a clash that left his head requiring stitches.

Ian Armstrong scored but Rothbury went down 5-1 at second-top Berwick Harrow before drawing 3-3 at Wallington on a wet pitch in a derby thriller. Mick Leyburn scored his first goal for the club with a curling left-foot strike from 20-yards and young striker Michael Gutherson lobbed in the second on his debut. Centre-back Paul Appleby went half the length of the pitch and fired past ex-Rothbury keeper Bolton to put Rothbury 3-2 up, but Moffat struck late on again to salvage a point for the Greens.

Rothbury were hit by injuries and suspensions and took youngster Stuart Foreman from the reserves for a promising debut as Rothbury completed a fine double with a 2-1 win at Amble Vikings. Mick Leyburn put Rothbury in front in the 30th minute when he rolled a defender and floated a shot over the keeper and into the net. Amble levelled but two minutes into injury time Steven Brewis drove over a low cross and Michael Gutherson was the hero as he powered in a near post diving header.

The good form continued with a 5-1 home victory over Lowick that saw Paul Appleby open with a 20-yard shot. Further goals from Leyburn, Coe and Armstrong put Rothbury out of reach. Leyburn added his second when Straughan put him clear and Keith Appleby saved a penalty as Rothbury pulled clear of the relegation danger zone.

Rothbury then pulled off a shock at runaway league leaders HMP Acklington with a surprise 1-0 win. With the prison defence appealing in vain for offside, Stuart Mackenzie raced clear and fired the only goal. Rothbury's excellent form had earned 16 points from seven games since the New Year - but the prisoners remained 15 points clear at the top of the table.

A Mick Rogerson double for Craster brought the run to an end as Rothbury went down 2-0 at home to Craster but three points were picked up in a 2-1 success at North Sunderland.

Craster beat Rothbury 3-1 in the return fixture and Lowick romped to a 4-0 victory over the Coquetdale side. With several players injured or unavailable, Stuart Foreman and Jon Tait returned to the team, with Paul Ebdon going on the bench, for a 4-1 win over North Sunderland on the final day of the season. Ian Armstrong hit two and Gordon Turnbull another before a fine, flowing move sent Foreman away down the right and he kept his cool and waited for the advancing keeper to commit himself before slotting home. The win moved Rothbury up to seventh in the table.

Football Fixtures.

ALNWICK ASSOCIATION FOOTBALL CLUB FIXTURES
FOR THE SEASON 1884-5.—FIRST TEAM.

Oct. 25, 1884.	Rangers	at	Alnwick.
Nov. 1	Jesmond	at	Jesmond.
22	Newcastle	at	Newcastle.
Dec. 6	North Eastern	at	Newcastle.
13	Rothbury	at	Alnwick.
20	Heaton	at	Alnwick.
25	Berwick	at	Berwick.
Jan. 3, 1885.	North Eastern	at	Alnwick.
17	Rothbury	at	Rothbury.
24	First Round of Senior Cup Competition.		
Feb. 7	Second Round of Senior Cup Competition.		
14	Newcastle	at	Alnwick.
21	Third Round of Senior Cup Competition.		
Mar. 7	Rangers	at	Newcastle.
	Fourth Round of Senior Cup Competition.		
14	Jesmond	at	Alnwick.
21	Final Round of Senior Cup Competition.		
28	Heaton	at	Heaton.
Easter Monday	Berwick	at	Alnwick.

1995/96

A NEW SPONSOR meant a new name and Rothbury got off to a flyer in the Beattie NNFL with a 4-3 home win over Stobhill Rangers. Rothbury included new signings Stuart Conway and Mark Evans and had youngsters Michael Gutherson and Stuart Foreman up front. With keeper Keith Appleby unavailable, Lee Straughan played in goals. Stobhill took the lead but Gutherson fired in a free-kick to equalise. Two deflected goals put Stobhill 3-1 up before Paul Arkle bent a free-kick around the wall to pull one back. Midfielder Arkle hit a second to level after a goalkeeping error. Foreman was unlucky as he rattled the bar but won it when he squeezed in from an acute angle with just three minutes left.

Paul Arkle's good form continued as he shot Rothbury ahead at home to Amble Vikings, but Rothbury missed a number of chances and were punished as Amble hit back with three.

Keith Hughes then hit a late winner as Red Row beat Rothbury 2-1, with Gordon Mackenzie netting from the penalty spot after Hutchison had been fouled.

Centre-back Paul Appleby returned from injury for the NFA Minor Cup first round at home to Lemington Rangers and Gutherson grabbed an extra-time winner as Rothbury went through 3-2. Lemington were awarded a penalty in the 20th minute after a Gordon Turnbull foul, but they missed a glorious chance to take the lead with a poor spot-kick. They did go in front, however, ten minutes later. Phillip Arkle and Evans combined to set up Paul Arkle to shoot home for 1-1. Gutherson fired home from a Foreman pull back to put Rothbury in front but with ten minutes to go a header crept in through a crowd of players to take the tie into extra time. Foreman cleverly beat two men near the corner flag and hung over a pin-point cross that Gutherson powered in with his head.

Sammy Lough was on target twice for Rothbury in a 2-1 win at HMP Acklington. He netted his first with a twenty-yard free kick and fired in the winner from close range after his first effort was blocked in Rothbury's best performance of the season so far. But Rothbury went out of the Sanderson Cup in the first round with a 2-0 defeat at Alnmouth and two points were dropped at home to Red Row as Scott Fulton equalised with the last kick of the game in a 2-2 draw. Evans had put Rothbury in front in the fifth minute but a poor second half showing cost them.

Rothbury advanced in the County Minor Cup with a 2-0 success at Embleton then a second half goal burst rocked Lowick away in the league. Stuart Mackenzie and Lough put Rothbury two up then Paul Appleby's 60-yard punt up field bounced high over the advancing keeper for the third. Gutherson tucked away an Armstrong cross for 4-0 and when a Stuart Mackenzie shot was spilled Gutherson followed up for the fifth. Lowick struck twice in the last ten minutes.

Rothbury went out of the Bilclough Cup at holders Craster, but it was a close call in a 4-3 reverse. Stuart Mackenzie, Gutherson and Andrew Stewart scored.

Three goals in three second half minutes sank Ashington White House in the NFA Minor Cup. Paul Arkle's terrific strike flew in off the post, Foreman's tricky footwork created himself an opening and when the keeper parried his shot Lough crashed in the rebound and Foreman received the ball just inside the Ashington half and dribbled all the way into the box, rounded the keeper and netted a superb goal for a quick-fire 3-0 lead. Whitehouse hit back with two headed goals but Rothbury went into the fourth round.

The club was presented with new strips by the Rothbury Home Bakery before a 3-0 win at home to Spittal Rovers. A brilliant Paul Arkle free-kick put Rothbury one up in the eighth minute and Foreman beat two men and drilled the second low into the net. A Mark Bruce chip completed the scoring and moved an impressively strong Rothbury squad into fifth place in the table, five points behind leaders Amble Vikings.

Rothbury were unlucky to go out of the NFA Minor Cup in the fourth round at home to the league leaders after extra time to a hotly-disputed winner. A Tindale half-volley from the edge of the box put Vikings in front and it was against the run of play when Shanks fired in the second from six yards. Stewart fired in a cross at the far post to get Rothbury back in it and minutes later a Gordon Mackenzie corner squirmed through keeper Mark Robson's hands and into the net for the equaliser.

In extra time Shanks was flagged offside following a shot but the referee waved play on, Rothbury failed to clear properly and Shanks, who had been offside in the build-up, shot home from a cross to Rothbury's anger.

Michael Gutherson struck in a 1-0 Anderson Cup victory at home to Spittal A before Rothbury went down 6-4 to Stobhill Rangers in a cracker at Morpeth.

Rothbury were down the Wansbeck again the following week and had Gordon Mackenzie and Bruce on target in a 2-2 draw with Morpeth Town reserves at Craik Park.

Rothbury then dominated but had to come from behind to beat struggling Craster 3-1 at Armstrong Park. A Bruce free-kick was fired home at the far post by Stewart for the equaliser and Lough and Evans were opening up the Craster defence with probing passes. With time running out, and urged on by skipper Gordon Mackenzie, a Stewart shot finally put Rothbury in front and Gutherson gave Rothbury a sigh of relief with the third.

Stuart Mackenzie hit a hat-trick and Bruce scored twice with Evans, Foreman and Gutherson also scoring in an 8-2 win at HMP Acklington to move Rothbury into second in the table.

Hard-working midfield battler Andrew Stewart scored twice more with Gutherson adding another with a 3-0 win over Springhill keeping Rothbury in contention. But a 3-0 defeat at

Amble Vikings moved the coastal club seven points clear of the Coquetdale men.

The Vikings then sent Rothbury crashing out of the Anderson Cup with a 4-0 reverse and a 3-1 home defeat at the hands of Lowick saw Rothbury slip into fourth place.

Rothbury were missing Paul and Phillip Arkle, Steven Brewis and Bruce and called up Morris Adamson and Jon Tait for a very tight, hard-fought battling 2-1 win over Morpeth Town reserves at Armstrong Park that took Rothbury back into second spot. Morpeth took the lead but Foreman was causing them all sorts of problems and he fired a superb shot over the keepers head to level. In the final minute, Stuart Mackenzie cut inside and fired the winner into the roof of the net.

Evans scored twice and Stewart added the other in a 3-1 win over Alnmouth and Craster looked doomed to relegation as they fought hard for First Division survival but went down 2-1 to Rothbury at Windmill Park. Craster keeper Duncan Glen was in inspired form, denying and frustrating the visitors on a number of occasions with some brilliant spectacular saves. Rothbury went in front in the 35th minute when Bruce was tripped in the box and Gordon Mackenzie rifled in the penalty. Glen got his hands to the ball, but couldn't stop it crashing into the roof of the net. Mackenzie also curled a 20-yard effort against the bar following a good four-man move. Craster equalised in the 50th minute when the unmarked veteran Dougie Hogg thumped in a header from six yards. A Mark Bruce diving header won it for Rothbury in the 70th minute of a game that saw seven bookings.

Rothbury finished in third place, level on 35 points with Morpeth Town reserves, Amble Vikings taking the Championship with 54 points.

1996/97

AN UNFORTUNATE own goal from big centre half Gordon Turnbull saw Rothbury lose 1-0 at Stobhill Rangers on the opening day of the new season but a point was picked up with a 1-1 draw at North Sunderland, Paul Appleby scoring from a corner and Tony Gilholm earning the Seahouses men parity.

Michael Gutherson and Micky Hutchison hit the net in a 2-2 draw at home to Lowick the following week as Rothbury got off to a slow start.

But hopes were raised when title favourites Amble Vikings were trounced 3-1 at Armstrong Park. Ian Armstrong capitalised on a mistake between the keeper and a defender to make it 1-0 and eight minutes later Stuart Foreman doubled the lead. Bobby Pile pulled one back after the interval but Foreman added his second to secure a tremendous victory.

The club went out of the Northumberland FA Minor Cup in the first round after a disastrous trip to Haltwhistle Red Star that saw the Rothbury team coach break down on its way to the fixture. A Michael Gutherson header from a Foreman cross provided the goal but it wasn't enough in a 2-1 defeat and the club went down 2-0 at home to Red Row Welfare seven days later.

Rothbury then went out of the Bilclough Cup with a 3-2 home defeat at the hands of Wooler. Andrew Stewart powered in a header off the underside of the bar and Stuart MacKenzie fired in a second late on. He was also unlucky not to level when his shot struck the inside of the post and bounced out.

In a very physical game at Alnmouth another point was earned with midfielder Andrew Stewart again on target for the opener with Tommy Taylor grabbing an injury-time leveller to leave Rothbury third bottom above Lowick and basement boys Springhill.

Stuart Foreman crashed in the goal of the game with an unstoppable 30-yard drive but Amble Vikings had already hit six to gain revenge for their earlier League defeat as Rothbury remained in trouble.

Breathing space was secured as bottom club Springhill were hit for six themselves at Armstrong Park. The visitors were destroyed by flying wingers Micky Hutchison and Stuart Foreman. Andrew Stewart had celebrated becoming a father in the early hours of the morning and his fine form on the pitch continued when he curled a free kick into the corner of the net from 25 yards. Springhill equalised almost immediately but Michael Gutherson strongly held off a challenge and smashed into the net to put Rothbury back in front. A Straughan volley and a Stuart MacKenzie lob put Rothbury well in control before Straughan added his second from a Hutchison corner. Goalkeeper Keith Appleby came up the park and blasted in a late penalty for number six.

Goals from Micky Hutchison, Lee Straughan and Michael Gutherson then saw Rothbury rocket up the table with a 3-2 win over Red Row. But the optimism was dashed as young strugglers Springhill gained revenge for their previous 6-1 mauling with a shock 4-2 win over the red and whites. Darren Dillon, Charlie Mace, Les Turnbull and an Atkinson penalty put the basement boys in control before Jon Tait curled a left wing corner directly into the net in the 80th minute and Andrew Stewart added a second and some respectability to the scoreline two minutes from time.

In the Anderson Cup first round first leg Rothbury drew 2-2 at Belford with Gutherson and a 20-yard cracker from Foreman keeping them in with a shout. And Rothbury found themselves sixth in the League table after a good 3-2 away win at Shilbottle which left them trailing runaway leaders Stobhill Rangers by 11 points. That lead was extended to 14 a week later as the Morpeth side took the points with a hard-fought 4-3 win at Armstrong Park. Foreman gave Rothbury the lead but a Ross Dillon shot and a Paul Appleby own goal saw Rangers go in front. Peter Farrier extended their lead before Appleby atoned for his error and pulled one back to make it 2-3. Simon Wray added number four for the visitors before Michael Gutherson added the third.

The season was kept alive with a 3-1 win over Belford (5-3 agg) in the quarter final of the Anderson Cup with Straughan scoring twice. He shot home from a Gutherson flick on for the first and latched onto Appleby's long clearance to bang in his second. Gordon MacKenzie added a third from the penalty spot.

Michael Gutherson scored in a 1-2 home reverse to North Sunderland with a bizarre 35-yard Stuart Romaines shot flying over Appleby's head to win it for the Fishermen.

But an improved performance saw Alnmouth crash 3-1 at Armstrong Park with Ian Armstrong slamming in a superb 30-yarder to cancel out Alnmouth's opener and Gutherson stabbing in to put Rothbury in front. Foreman added the third when he went clear and fired into the roof of the net.

Bobby Pile hit a hat-trick as Amble Vikings thrashed Rothbury 5-1 in the Anderson Cup semi-final.

Lowick beat Rothbury 3-0 but a 3-2 win at home to Belford eased the club up and secured a mid-table finish. Rothbury twice came from behind with a Gordon MacKenzie penalty, a hooked shot from Stuart Foreman restoring parity and Stuart MacKenzie grabbing the winner to complete a disappointing season on a high.

1997/98

THE OPENING fixtures of the North Northumberland League programme were wiped out by the funeral of Princess Diana. Diana had been killed in a car crash in Paris and more than a million people lined the streets of London to pay their respects at her funeral. A further 2.5 billion people worldwide watched the funeral on television.

Princess Diana's coffin was draped with the Royal Standard and covered with white lillies and a floral arrangement. The streets of Rothbury were strangely quiet as people stayed in to watch the sad occasion.

The George, Alnwick inflicted a 4-1 defeat on Rothbury as the season got underway and worse was to follow as Rothbury were sent crashing out of the Bilclough Cup in the First Round by their own reserve team in a penalty shoot-out thriller at Armstrong Park. With reserve team keeper Malcolm Wilkinson called up into the first team for the tie, midfielder Jon Tait was forced to don the gloves and became the hero for the underdogs with a string of stunning saves. Striker Lee Straughan broke the deadlock just after the hour for the first team when he coolly side footed past the outstretched leg of the advancing Tait and into the bottom corner for the opener, but the reserves hit back and in the final minute as Paul Arkle drifted a deep free kick into the box and nippy hit-man Michael Tall arrived at the back post to nod in the leveller from close range.

Tait pulled off a number of diving saves in extra time and Stuart Foreman was unlucky when he rattled the underside of the bar but the tie went to penalties. Reserve striker Kim Fenwick blazed the first spot-kick over but Tait got his fingers to skipper Gordon MacKenzie's to tip it onto the post and out. Michael Tall rammed his effort into the roof of the net but Keith Appleby levelled when Tait got his hands to the penalty but the power took it into the net. Tim Winston then gave Wilkinson no chance before Andrew Stewart fired down the middle and Tait saved with an outstretched leg. Phil Winston put the reserves 3-1 ahead with a confident strike and with the pressure on Paul Appleby, who had to score to keep the first team in it, he could only cringe as Tait flung himself full stretch to save his powerful effort and book the reserves a Second Round meeting with Shilbottle.

The Second Division reserves went ahead against the high-flying Colliers at Armstrong Park to the delight of manager Don Jeans when Peter Higgins' shot from a corner came back off the bar and skipper Jon Tait, in a more familiar midfield role, stabbed the rebound into the net. But a stunned Shilbottle levelled 10 minutes later through Mark Dodds and Richie Robson struck to put them ahead. Rothbury reserves equalised in the 35th minute when a mazy Jon Tait dribble was brought to an abrupt halt in the box and Phil Winston crashed in from the penalty spot. Dodds grabbed the winner just 15 minutes from time when he created space for himself and unleashed a low left foot shot. The Colliers admitted afterwards it had been one of their toughest games of the season.

A number of the Rothbury reserves side that pulled off a surprise Bilclough Cup win over the first team in 1997/98.

Red Row beat Rothbury 2-1 and Champions and League leaders Amble Vikings extended their unbeaten run to five games with a 4-2 win at Armstrong Park. Bobby Pile opened for Amble when he turned twisted in the box before hammering into the net. Gordon MacKenzie equalised from the penalty spot but a Sutton own goal under pressure from Stu Marshall, a Micky Lowes 30-yarder and a second from Pile left Rothbury in tatters, though they did grab a late consolation.

Rothbury picked up their first points of the season with a 3-1 win at Spittal Rovers A, Straughan, Stuart Conway and a Gordon MacKenzie penalty bringing sighs of relief.

But Rothbury were left with a mountain to climb in the Anderson Cup after going down in the first round first leg to a 4-0 defeat at home to the Vikings.

And they were dumped out of the NFA Minor Cup at the first hurdle 3-2 at home to Heddon, despite playing their best football of the season with Kevin Coe dominant in midfield. A Michael Gutherson cross was powerfully headed past his own goalkeeper by Graham right on the stroke of half time but Heddon drew level when Walton headed in a far post cross. Hogarth fired in from 15 yards to put the visitors in front on the hour, with Coar stabbing in a free kick at the near post for 1-3. Stuart Conway and Michael Hutchison came on for Rothbury and they pulled one back in the dying minutes when Gordon Turnbull's shot was handled on the line and Ian Fenwick smashed the resultant spot-kick into the roof of the net.

North Sunderland then beat Rothbury 2-0 as the pressure mounted. A point was picked up with a 3-3 draw at home to Spittal Rovers A that saw midfielder Andrew Stewart carried off the field and raced to hospital with a bad injury that marred the game. Mark Caine put Spittal in front but Stewart levelled before getting hurt in a tackle. A Turnbull own goal made it 1-2 but Foreman and Conway netted to put Rothbury in front. Dave Buglass hit a deserved equaliser for Rovers.

Just a week after Shilbottle had sent the reserves out of the Bilclough Cup, Rothbury won their first home game of the season with a 3-2 victory over the Colliers. A spectacular 40-yard Kevin Coe chip gave Rothbury the lead and with the pace of Michael Hutchison and Stuart Foreman causing problems down the wings, a poor clearance let in Michael Gutherson to volley in the second. Gutherson stabbed home a Foreman cross to make it 3-0 but a Robson penalty unsettled Rothbury and they had to endure a nervous finish after George Brown hit a second from six yards.

If the win had given the club some confidence, it was shattered with a 9-2 demolition at Amble Vikings in the second leg of the Anderson Cup, seeing Rothbury crash out 13-2 on aggregate. Bobby Pile hit a treble, as did Stu Marshall with Simon Common (2) and Martin Lazonby completing the damage.

Basement club Belford moved off the bottom of the table with a 3-0 win over Rothbury that left the club with only Red Row below them. Stuart Foreman struck twice and Phillip Arkle added another in a 3-3 draw with The George, Alnwick at Armstrong Park but the pressure was eased with a 6-4 win at home over struggling Red Row Welfare.

Foreman took advantage of a mix-up in the defence to go around the keeper and roll the ball into the empty net before the visitor's Rob Wilcox broke his leg immediately after the restart and was taken to hospital in an ambulance. Gav Keen equalised from 20 yards but Ian Armstrong blasted Rothbury back in front with a shot too hot for the keeper to handle. Mark Bruce made it 3-1 after the break, coming on for Hutchison, and Paul Appleby netted from close range to stretch the advantage. McInally made it 4-2 but Bruce added a fifth. Rothbury were wobbling after a Craig Smith double took it back to 5-4 but Stuart Conway shot home from a rebound to make it six.

Rothbury were then in front twice in a scrappy draw with Alnmouth, Foreman shooting home from 10 yards and a deflected Paul Arkle shot earning a valuable point.

Boss Nick Gutherson rang the changes with John Smith, Kevin Coe and Lee Straughan all returning to a starting berth for what turned out to be a 5-0 St. Valentine's Day massacre over fellow strugglers Belford. In the 16th minute a beautifully-flighted Stuart Foreman pass picked out Coe and he slipped a low shot into the net. Coe added a second in the 50th minute with a perfect drifting long range chip and Straughan made it three in the 70th minute when he tapped in from close range. Straughan then smacked a shot off the bar and Armstrong smashed the rebound through a crowd of bodies for the fourth. Stuart Foreman rounded things off with five minutes to go, the tricky winger smashing a 25-yard drive into the top corner, crashing down off the stanchion and settling in the net.

Leaders Amble Vikings claimed their 14th successive win with a 4-1 win over Rothbury, Michael Tall was on target for the Coquetdale men down at the mouth of the river. And successive defeats - 3-0 at home to North Sunderland and 4-0 away to Alnmouth exposed the team's frailties. In the penultimate game of the season Rothbury crashed 5-2 away to Lowick with Michael Gutherson netting from an Andrew Stewart cross and Micky Hutchison controlling and slotting in the other.

A Stuart Foreman hat-trick on the final day of the season saw Rothbury just edge clear of the relegation zone ahead of Red Row and Belford in a vital 5-2 win over Embleton at Armstrong Park. Gordon MacKenzie hammered in from 25 yards before Foreman grabbed his first with a drive from the same distance. He added a well-taken second to make it 3-0 but Harry Armstrong pulled one back. Foreman completed his hat-trick on the hour and Michael Tall made it 5-1. John Wilkins added the visitors second.

Coquetdale League select side at Armsrtong Park opening, 1949. Courtesy Robin Murray.

1998/99
Honours: Bilclough Cup Winners

B EDLINGTON TERRIERS entered their reserve team in the Second Division of the North Northumberland League at the start of the season, and they would go on to a heartbreaker, going down on penalties in the Bilclough Cup Final under the floodlights at Shielfield Park against Rothbury.

New boss Phillip Bathgate brought in tough-tackling midfielder Richie Bathgate and prolific striker Ken Douglas, who was quickly off the mark with a hat-trick in a 7-1 opening day demolition of Red Row at Armstrong Park with a much improved team performance from the previous season. Michael Atkins also netted a treble and Stuart Foreman added the other after Alan Lilburn had given Red Row the lead following a defensive mix-up.

But the following week Spittal Rovers A took all three points with a 3-1 win at Rothbury, Stuart MacKenzie pulling one back after Rothbury had gone two down just after the break. Kevin Proudlock then hit the post and keeper Woodcock made a fantastic diving save to keep out a Douglas snap-shot before Armstrong hit on the break to complete the scoring just before the end.

Stuart Foreman and Michael Atkin scored up at Lowick as Rothbury won 2-1 and three superb saves from Belford keeper Eddie Stocks kept Belford in the game during a 1-1 draw. Gordon MacKenzie shot Rothbury in front from the penalty spot but John Duncan played in Phil Duncan to make it all-square.

In the first round of the Northumberland FA Minor Cup Lowick were put to the sword with an impressive 8-3 victory after extra time at Armstrong Park. Stuart Foreman and Lee Straughan put Rothbury 2-0 up at half time but it ended 2-2 at the end of 90 minutes. Further goals from Douglas (3), Richie Bathgate, Ian Fenwick and another from Foreman settled it.

But Rothbury were brought crashing back down to earth the following week with a 6-1 reverse at the hands of North Sunderland, a Ken Douglas goal the only bright spot on a black day in Coquetdale.

North Sunderland completed the double with a 2-0 win at the coast before Rothbury lifted their spirits as Haltwhistle Red Star were hit for six in the NFA Minor Cup second round. Richie Bathgate fired home the opener from 12 yards in the 20th minute then Douglas was sent tumbling in the box and Gordon MacKenzie lashed in the spot kick for two. Douglas put Atkin through in the 29th minute to make it three and MacKenzie wasted a good chance to add a fourth five minutes after the break when he fired a second penalty over the bar. Douglas ran through to make it 4-0 and put away a Mick Hutchison cross for five. He completed another hat-trick when he tucked away an Atkin cross.

In the Anderson Cup Rothbury drew 1-1 at home to Lowick with Dave Black giving the visitors the lead just before half time and Atkin crossing for Douglas to head a deserved leveller late on.

The good form continued with a 3-1 away win at Alnmouth. Paul Arkle's low cross was half-cleared and Stuart MacKenzie smashed it in for the opener with Atkin making it 2-0. John Bathgate fired the third in off the post with David Wilkinson grabbing a late consolation for the Seasiders.

Rothbury went out of the NFA Minor Cup in the third round with a disappointing 3-1 defeat up at Spittal Rovers A, but went through 4-2 on penalties after a 3-3 draw at Second Division Hedgeley Rovers in the Bilclough Cup.

A 5-1 thumping at Lowick finished the club's interest in the Anderson Cup as they went out 6-2 on aggregate. Rothbury were sitting fifth in the table and came away with a point in an uneventful goalless draw at Wooler before a fifteen-minute Stuart MacKenzie hat-trick and further goals from Atkin and Straughan saw off Belford 5-3 at home. The red and whites then progressed into the semi-final of the Bilclough Cup with a 7-1 mauling of Percy Seniors at Alnwick. Straughan proved a handful and hit four with Richie Bathgate and a Ken Douglas double completing the rout.

The club moved into second place in the League table with a 2-1 win over Springhill. Despite being reduced to ten men in the 18th minute when the volatile Richie Bathgate was given his marching orders. Straughan struck in the 44th and 83rd minutes to secure the three points, Steven Dixon netting for the Berwick visitors.

In the fifth meeting of the season with Lowick, Rothbury emerged victorious in a tremendous 4-1 win at Armstrong Park with the on-fire Straughan adding two more, Richie Bathgate and veteran Kevin Proudlock adding the others.

But the title charge lost momentum as Red Row gained revenge for their heavy opening day defeat, turning the tables with a 3-1 win. Ian Fenwick hit a late consolation for Rothbury.

In the Bilclough Cup semi-final Rothbury beat North Sunderland 3-2 after extra time with both teams being reduced to ten men in a hot-tempered clash. Straughan hit the opener after ten minutes when he capitalised on a defensive error and North Sunderland looked to be in real trouble when Stuart Romaines was sent off in the 55th minute for a second yellow card for persistent dissent. A Ken Douglas volley made it 2-0 in the 75th minute but late on David Wright side-stepped Keith Appleby and pulled one back. In the dying seconds Gary Irving headed in a corner to break Rothbury's hearts with an equaliser. In extra time a free kick was spilled into the path of John Bathgate who fired in the winner but late on his brother Richie saw red for the second time in a month and was sent off.

Rothbury kept up the pressure at the top of the table with a 3-0 win at Springhill with Douglas netting twice and Foreman dancing through the defence in trademark style to slide the ball home for the third.

North Sunderland gained revenge as they sent Rothbury out of the Sanderson Cup with a 2-1 at Armstrong Park in the quarter final. But Rothbury clinched the silverware in the Bilclough Cup winning a penalty shoot-out 6-5 against Second Division Bedlington Terriers reserves after the game ended all-square at 1-1 up at Shielfield Park. An early Lee Straughan header was cleared off the line but Rothbury took the lead just after half time when Michael Atkin broke clear and saw his initial shot blocked by the goalkeeper, but followed up to shoot home. With the Terriers young side playing fast, counter-attacking football Brian Murray cracked in the leveller with a powerful low shot. But ultimately the Terriers reserves would end up heart-broken as the penalties went to sudden death.

In the league Spittal Rovers A leapfrogged Rothbury with a 6-1 win at Berwick and the club dropped two points with a 2-2 draw at Shilbottle. Foreman pounced on a mistake to give Rothbury the lead in the 10th minute and Stuart MacKenzie added a second ten minutes after half time. John Smith fouled Dodds in the box, who dusted himself down to tuck away the penalty and made it 1-2, with George Brown shooting through a crowd of players to level in the 83rd minute for the Colliers. A third place finish was secured with a 3-1 win over the Colliers in the return fixture. Michael Gutherson fired in in the 3rd minute and although skipper Gordon MacKenzie missed a penalty after 20 minutes with Richie Robson saving the effort, Atkin and Straughan secured the win late on after Lee Harrison had levelled.

1999/2000
Honours: Anderson Cup Winners

To MARK fifty years at Armstrong Park, Rothbury reverted to their old style red and white striped shirts as worn by the players on August 20th 1949 when the Park was opened by Dr. Reginald Armstrong. The original shirts were reputed to have been given to the club by Sunderland AFC. The pitch was in superb condition and Rothbury did it justice, storming to their best ever NNFL start with an 8-0 thrashing of Lowick. Bruce, Coe and Darren Arkle had boosted the team, signing from Alliance neighbours Wallington, and striker Michael Gutherson played in goals with Keith Appleby unavailable. Bruce marked his return to Armstrong with FOUR goals, Paul Arkle, Darren Arkle, Foreman and Coe completing the demolition.

A Richie Bathgate penalty and a goal from Kevin Coe, playing up front, earned a point in a competitive 2-2 draw at Belford. But Rothbury were far too strong for Shilbottle in the Sanderson Cup, returning home with a 4-1 win from the Welfare Ground. Stuart Foreman struck twice with Michael Atkin and Peter Higgins netting the others. Bruce fired Rothbury in front in the opening minute of a 3-1 win over Wooler. Jeffries equalised right on half time with Rothbury winning it with goals from Coe (78) and Gutherson (81).

Silky veteran midfielder Kevin Proudlock returned to the Rothbury team after a long time out of the game but Gutherson was the star of the show with a hat-trick in a 3-0 win over Alnmouth, Bruce and Foreman causing all sorts of problems.

Micky Hutchison netted after just 30 seconds as the fantastic start continued with a 5-0 thrashing of Shilbottle CW. Goals from John Beattie, Foreman and John Bathgate made it 4-0 at the break. Coe added the fifth in the 80th minute.

After a tight goalless first half at Berwick Rangers A, Michael Gutherson headed in the opener at the far post three minutes after the break. A Michael Sherry penalty made it 1-1, but two goals in the last three minutes maintained the unbeaten league record.

Second Division Longhoughton offered stubborn resistance but Rothbury went through 2-0 in the first round of the Bilclough Cup. Foreman hit the first in the 65th minute and Gutherson doubled the advantage three minutes later.

Gutherson then hit his second hat-trick of the season in a resounding 5-0 success at Hedgeley Rovers. Bruce and Higgins added the others as Rothbury topped the table with 19 points from seven games, leaving Wooler trailing by four points in second.

Rothbury were brought crashing back down to earth in the NFA Minor Cup first round as they were thumped 7-1 at home by Wallsend United on a miserable afternoon. Stuart Mackenzie scored the only goal.

The club suffered their second cup defeat in a week as they went down 3-2 at Wooler in the first round first leg with a Guthrie penalty winning it in the 85th minute. Ian Fenwick and Foreman scored.

Bottom club Bedlington Terriers reserves were hammered 8-1 at Armstrong Park. John Bathgate hit two, as did Coe, with Bruce and Foreman also scoring. Tough-tackling full-back John Smith added a rare goal and Mick Kearney grabbed his first for the club.

Rothbury turned it around to send Wooler crashing out of the Anderson Cup with a stunning 3-0 win with goals from Richie Bathgate, Bruce and Paul Appleby in the second leg taking the Cup Kings through 5-3 on aggregate.

Rothbury crashed to their first league defeat at Spittal Rovers A at Christmas. The unbeaten Spittal side were sitting ominously in second spot just a point behind and would eventually overtake Rothbury in the title race in the new Millennium. A Harry Armstrong hat-trick put Rothbury on the back foot, John Bathgate and Bruce replying in the last five minutes as Rothbury refused to lie down.

The club just lost out in the Championship race in one of their best league seasons for years but went all the way to two Cup Finals.

Rothbury were looking to retain the Bilclough Cup but went down 1-0 to Wooler in the Final at St. James's Park, Alnwick. The Coquetdale side went into the final in confident mood, having beaten Wooler 2-1 away in the League just a week earlier, Stuart Foreman looping in a rare header for the winner, but Mick Strangeways solitary goal was enough to win the Cup for the Glendale men after a disappointing display.

Wooler dominated and in the tenth minute Barry Guthrie headed on for James Scott whose vicious half-volley through a crowd of players smacked out off the underside of the bar. Scott then blazed over from 22-yards as Wooler kept up the pressure.

Kevin Coe sent Darren Arkle clear in a sporadic break at the other end, but his low driven effort was smothered by keeper Kevin Stanwix.

Wooler came out guns blazing in the second half and in the opening minute the pacey Shepard charged through on goal and rounded keeper Keith Appleby but could only hold his head in his hands as Paul Appleby raced back to clear his rolling effort off the line. Four minutes later a deep cross evaded everyone and fell to the unmarked Strangeways who fired a low shot into the net from the edge of the box for the winner.

Influential midfielder Guthrie had a great chance to add number two six minutes later when Wooler were awarded a penalty, but Appleby flung himself to his right to parry away the powerfully struck low spot-kick.

John Bathgate almost grabbed an undeserved equaliser with two minutes to go, but Stanwix got down well to slap away his header and Rothbury's last chance, and their grip on the trophy, slipped away. League secretary Norman Laidler presented the Cup to Wooler and said: "It's fitting that the first final of 2000 should be played between two teams which have been in existence for over 100 years. Both sides are a credit to North Northumberland football."

Just three nights later Rothbury redeemed themselves by claiming the Anderson Cup silverware with a 5-2 hammering of Berwick Rangers A at Shielfield Park. Kevin Coe hit a hat-trick as the Borderers' suffered the backlash from the Bilclough Cup disappointment.

Thunder and lightning storms and persistent rain had produced a greasy surface on the pitch which became a goalkeeper's nightmare for young Gordon Asprey in the Berwick goals. Rothbury got off to an awful start and Rangers had the ball in the net in the third minute, only for a linesman's flag to chalk the effort off. The alarm bells weren't heeded and two minutes later Michael Sherry raced through on the Rothbury goal, rounded the exposed Keith Appleby and tucked away neatly into the empty net. But Rothbury levelled ten minutes later when Kevin Coe and Mark Bruce exchanged passes on the edge of the area, Coe firing in a 20-yard drive that Asprey looked to have comfortably covered, but the ball squirmed through his grasp, slipped over his shoulder and bounced over the line.

Rangers restored their lead on the half hour when a mad moment of hesitancy allowed Sherry to nip in and again round Appleby for his double. Controversy raged four minutes later when Rothbury equalised with a hotly-disputed goal. Coe's long throw-in was flicked on by Darren Arkle and John Bathgate's close-range volley through a pack of players appeared to be blocked on the line, but the linesman indicated that it went in to Berwick's despair.

Asprey was almost left red-faced again just before the break when Mick Kearney drilled in a shot from distance that skidded up and squirmed from the keeper's grasp, but he span and fell on the ball before it embarrassingly crossed the line.

Rothbury had three players booked for dissent before a match-winning substitution in the 72nd minute. Skilful winger Stuart Foreman had been controversially dropped by manager Phillip Bathgate after a lacklustre display against Wooler, and he had a point to prove. He had been on the pitch only seconds when he released the overlapping Gordon MacKenzie whose swinging cross was powerfully headed into the corner of the net by Coe. Three minutes later Foreman made it 4-2 when he had the net bulging with a spectacular overhead bicycle kick that gave Asprey no chance. Coe completed his amazing hat-trick with ten minutes to go when he netted another header from a Kearney free kick.

Sherry had a chance to net a hat-trick himself in the closing stages when his pace won him a penalty, but Appleby was again equal to the shot and blocked it to leave the young Berwick striker raising his eyebrows to heaven.

2000/01

THE FOOT AND MOUTH outbreak that would devastate farms throughout the Borders and culminate in pillars of sickening black smoke billowing into the air from piles of burning animal carcasses started at a farm near Heddon-on-the-wall and Rothbury Football Club were to prove the first sporting casualty as the club were forced to resign from the League.

The North Northumberland League First Division side made the shock announcement following a meeting of the club's committee.

The Anderson Cup holders, who were sitting comfortably in mid table until their resignation, cited Foot and Mouth as the problem.

Long-serving Secretary of Rothbury Football Club Bill Snowdon said: "A decision was made at a meeting we held on foot and mouth and the weather, and came to the conclusion we could not see us fulfilling our fixtures."

The club's Armstrong Park ground backs on to National Trust property said Mr Snowdon and discussions had taken place between the two.

He added the National Trust was unhappy with the club continuing to play on their ground with Foot and Mouth rampant.

A spokesman for the North Northumberland League said they had received Rothbury's resignation and it took effect immediately. There was nothing stopping the club from reapplying at a future date, he added. Rothbury Reserves, who play on the same ground, were to continue playing their games as they only had a few left, said Mr Snowdon, with the possibility their remaining games would be played away.

The club was in the media for happier reasons earlier in the season as Reserve team goalkeeper Matthew Barnes made headlines in the national press when he scored TWICE with clearances from his own penalty area in a game against Embleton. Big-kicking postman Matthew, then 25, launched his first 95-yard effort when Rothbury were 2-1 down. A high wind caught the ball and it bounced once before clearing the stunned opposition keeper and hitting the back of the net. But cheeky Matthew decided lightening could strike twice - and five minutes later did the same again. "The first time was a complete fluke but for the second I thought I would give it a try. I didn't dare try for a hat-trick," he said. "The lads went mad. A couple of spectators sprinted on to the pitch and jumped on me." Reserves manager Anthony Sutton said: "We were all in disbelief after the first effort so you can image our reaction when the second one went in." FA statistician David Barber could not recall a goalkeeper scoring twice in a game with clearances before - meaning Matthew had booted himself into the record books. His efforts were in vain though, as the reserves went down 7-4. "I'd done the strikers job for them – it's a shame they couldn't do my job for me," groaned Matthew, from Thropton.

Rothbury had been in reasonable form and beat Belford 4-2 at Armstrong Park, going 2-0 in front after eight minutes with goals from Kevin Coe and Jimmy Moffat.

Then in the last five minutes of the half a second goal from Moffat and a Martin Roberts goal saw Rothbury well in control at the interval.

Belford pulled a goal back through Ian Laverty five minutes into the second half and got a second through substitute Walter Dunn after 85 minutes but were left to ponder about missed chances during a game which also saw Rothbury hit the woodwork twice.

But Rothbury's attempts to retain the silverware in the Anderson Cup were dealt a blow with a shock first leg defeat at lowly Hedgeley Rovers in the First Round, where four players were dismissed in a bad-tempered affair. The first half hour was fairly even until Wayne Scott was brought down in the area and Barry Forrest netted from the spot to put Rovers in front. Both teams had a player dismissed and in the 35th minute a Gary Robinson pass found Forrest who netted his second.

Rothbury had two more players dismissed and were reduced to eight men before half time. Ten minutes into the second half Rothbury broke and pulled one back with a Paul Arkle goal while Barry Forrest was unlucky on the hour when his header hit the bar.

League leaders Lowick suffered a blow to their title aspirations when Rothbury became the first team to beat them in the league with a brilliant 3-1 win. The writing was on the wall for Lowick when Jimmy Moffatt shot Rothbury in front after only ten minutes of the contest.

The visitors were then guilty of missing a guilt edged chance of equalising when they had a penalty well saved by the home goalkeeper Keith Appleby on 27 minutes.

Things got worse for the leaders when Michael Tall netted soon after to make it 2-0 and then after 47 minutes Tall got a second to make it 3-0.

Lowick fought to get back into the game after the break but their only consolation was a Colin Anderson goal. The win left Rothbury six points behind the leaders in a mid-table position. It was a good game with Lowick not making the most of their chances while Rothbury also hit the bar and post during the game.

But soon after the Foot and Mouth crisis struck and Rothbury were forced to withdraw from the Sportsworld North Northumberland League with the very future of the 125-year-old club in doubt.

The Reserve side fulfilled their final fixtures, going down 7-1 at home to Berwick Rangers A.

Rothbury kicked off with ten men but went in front with a Michael Tall goal. Goals from Stephen Strachan and Ian Renton saw Berwick in front at half-time.

After the break Stuart Greenlees made it 3-1 after 60 minutes and further goals from Mark Hope, Philip Hogg, Chris Scott and Chris Jenkins completed the scoring for Berwick.

And they were then humiliated with a 10-1 humbling at Bedlington Terrier Res. Rothbury were 4-1 behind at the break with Michael Tall scoring the goal. The home teamed scored another six in the second half to secure the win and move up into third place. Scorers for Bedlington were Stephen Tyler (4), Jason Boyle (2) and one each for Graham Ord, Rob Eastway, Keith Rowlands and Peter Darley. They ended the campaign with three points from a 5-2 win at Alnmouth A after coming from behind to rally late on.

Two goals from Andy Metcalf saw Alnmouth ahead at half-time. Then in the 77th minute Adrian Newman netted, and Ben Fenwick after 82 minutes levelled the game. Jimmy Moffatt put Rothbury in front after 87 minutes and completed his hat-trick with two goals in injury time.

North Northumberland League neighbours Wooler battled through to the NFA Minor Cup Final and travelled to Portland Park, Ashington to take on the University of Northumbria for the silverware. Wooler found it tough going on a hard surface against their Northern Alliance opponents and after a goalless first half, the students scored twice in the second to lift the trophy.

2001/02

FORMER WORLD CUP STAR Chris Waddle stunned football when he turned out for Belford at Armstrong Park in 2002. The ex-Newcastle United, Sunderland and Marseille ace, who was capped 62 times for England and played in a World Cup semi-final against West Germany, left Rothbury's players gobsmacked when he pulled on the Belford shirt for a First Division fixture. Waddle, who was 41 at the time, is the most famous name to ever appear in the North Northumberland League.

Gateshead-born Waddle, whose career began at Tow Law Town when he worked in a sausage factory, made his appearance through Belford defender Graham Preston's brother, who was friends with the classy left-sided player from his schooldays.

Belford secretary Walter Dunn said: "Graham rang me the day before the game and said he had a good player who was available for us. I couldn't believe it when he said it was Chris Waddle. We were a bit short anyway so I obviously agreed to use him and you should have seen the player's faces when he turned up at Rothbury. He played the full game in central midfield and took the corner from which I scored our goal. We had beaten Rothbury twice before that season but they obviously raised their game when they saw Chris was playing."

Kevin Coe levelled Dunn's headed opener from the penalty spot in the 1-1 draw - and couldn't resist joking: "That's the way to put them away, Chris!" as he jogged back to line up.

Rothbury Secretary Bill Snowdon said: "Our lads couldn't believe it when Chris Waddle turned up but it probably did us more good than Belford because they had beaten us 6-0 and 1-0 earlier in the season."

North Northumberland League chairman Norman Laidler hailed Waddle's appearance as 'a tremendous feather in our cap.'

"I did it for a mate of mine - but we drew 1-1 so I made a great difference didn't I?" Waddle joked to the Evening Chronicle.

"The game at that level is so very important. It's the real lifeblood of football, which is why I've been more than happy to return to it. I have a genuine love of the game and that's why I keep on playing. That and the camaraderie that's to be found in the non-league. There's no egos and none of the in-fighting that goes on in some Premier League dressing-rooms. We all have a pint together after a game."

"I'm 43 now but I'll play football twice on most weekends this season. I always carry a pair of football boots in the back of the car just in case! The concern was getting loads of abuse from the touchline and getting kicked. But in truth you get kicked just as much in the Premier League. You play to the same rules whatever the level. It's just that ego gets in the way of some players who think grassroots football is beneath them."

Waddle went back to the Queen's Head Hotel with his new team-mates and the Rothbury players after the game. His appearance was all the more poignant as Rothbury Football Club's very future had been in doubt at the start of the season due to a player shortage after the Foot and Mouth disaster.

The club was struggling to put together a team to re-join the league and new Red and Whites boss Anthony Sutton said: "We've got pre-season friendlies organised so we'll just have to see who turns up. We're getting desperate. We don't know who's coming and who's not. There have only been seven or eight turning up for training and some of them are going away before the season starts."

Sutton made the move up from the disbanded reserve side following the departure of manager Phillip Bathgate.

Club secretary William Snowdon said: "We haven't enough players coming to run a team. Hopefully, three or four new signings might be coming from up the valley. We have 11 players signed on at present, but getting people to turn up is the trouble."

"We also have a lot of young lads going away to university now, which didn't really used to happen. In the past lads would get jobs in the village and play for the team."

Rothbury treasurer, and prolific former striker, Nick Gutherson added: "It would be a disaster if we stopped playing now. If we stopped now, it would take some starting up again. The foot and mouth has had a lot to do with it, I feel. We haven't played a game since February and a lot of the lads have got out of the habit of playing. It's all about the lads in the village getting the other lads to play."

In recent seasons Rothbury had lost powerful midfielder Darren Arkle and winger Stuart Foreman to Northern Alliance neighbours Wallington, first-choice goalkeeper Keith Appleby was linked with Wooler, several players had work commitments and long-term injuries and a sizable chunk of local talent had left the area, leaving the club with a huge selection headache.

But a number of player rallied around and they were rewarded as many jokes were cracked in the home dressing room when the name of Chris Waddle appeared on the Belford team sheet, but when the former Newcastle and England star appeared with his boots, things turned a little more serious.

Armstrong Park presented a fine playing surface for the ex-Magpie to display his skills. His ability to beat men without touching the ball with a shrug of the shoulders and his range of passing from his midfield role was a pleasure for the few assembled spectators to watch.

It was Rothbury who created the best chances in the first half with Dutchman Jan Deckers shooting wide after rounding the keeper and then hitting the bar with the Belford No.1 well beaten.

Kevin Coe and Ian Fenwick won the aerial battle at the back for Rothbury and the latter probably got greatest satisfaction from the two fine tackles he put in on Waddle to win the ball as the midfielder ran in on the Rothbury goal.

It was goalless at half time with both goalkeepers having made good saves. Belford opened the second half stronger, forcing several corners, and it was from one of these that they took the lead. Waddle's in-swinging kick was not cleared and Walter Dunn lashed the loose ball into the back of the net.

Rothbury hit back and when from a corner Kevin Coe was fouled, he took the penalty kick himself, and with Chris Waddle looking on, showed the ex- England star how penalties should be taken by crashing the ball into the back of the net.

The tough-tackling Ian Armstrong and Michael Tall had chances to win the game for Rothbury but it ended level and the points were shared. The draw left both sides in mid-table.

The season got off to a bad start with a 2-1 defeat at Spittal Rovers A in a wind-spoilt game where Dale Dixon should have put the home team in front but he missed from the spot. The game remained goalless at half-time but five minutes into the second John Bathgate put Rothbury in front. Substitute Noel Evans came on to settle the home team and with 15 minutes left Michael Wales scored to level the game and with ten minutes left Spittal were awarded a penalty and Innes Gray scored from the spot.

Berwick Rangers A were beaten 2-1 in a close even game at Armstrong Park, Rothbury taking the lead after 35 minutes with a Chris Bews goal. Berwick levelled four minutes later with a goal from Chris Falconer. Both teams had chances to take the lead but it was not until the 61st minutes that Rothbury regained the advantage with a goal from Gavin Stewart that saw them take the points.

Springhill then travelled down and took the points in a good, close game when Nicky Wilson scored from a free-kick in the fifth minute. It turned out to be the winner as both teams missed chances during the game. Rothbury came close to earning a deserved point but one shot came back off the post.

In the Anderson Cup, Rothbury were sent spinning out by the same side in a crushing 5-1 reverse. Rothbury played well during the first half and led at half-time through a 12th minute goal from Michael Tall. But a four-goal burst from Wayne Donaghue and a Nicky Wilson goal in the second half for the visitors ensured Springhill advanced.

Rothbury's indifferent form continued as they crashed to a 6-0 defeat at home to Belford. Two goals in the first 15 minutes saw Belford in front at half-time and four more after the break gave Belford an easy win. Goals scorers for Belford were Matty Collins (2), Ross Priestly (2), Jamie Emons and Tom Crethe.

Rothbury went down 2-1 at Wooler on a dry pitch in windy conditions and it was all Wooler during the first-half with McKenna and Scott having good chances. The home midfield of Terry Carr, Malthouse and Romaines pushed forward at every chance but good defending by Fenwick and Coe kept the game goalless at half-time. Wooler took the lead early in the second half after a good through ball from Jamie Carr put Malthouse into the area. As he attempted to cross he was fouled and Jamie Carr scored from the spot. Wooler continued to press and were rewarded when a through ball from Simon Romaines was crossed into the area by Garry Scott, it was knocked home at the far post by Terry Carr.

Wooler were caught out when Rothbury broke and good work between John Laidler and Ian Armstrong saw the latter net at the near post. Wooler continued to attack but couldn't extend the score before the final whistle

But Craster Rovers were seen off 2-0 at Armstrong Park. Rothbury took the lead in the 27th minute. A Paul Arkle free kick saw John Bathgate shoot and when the keeper could only parry the shot, Martin Roberts was on hand to net the rebound.

Both teams missed chances but with 60 minutes played a powerful header from Kevin Coe made it 2-0 at the final whistle. Rothbury thanked referee Alan Cairns for officiating at short notice.

Come November, Rothbury went down 3-2 at home to Bedlington Terriers Reserves as they still found points and consistency hard to come by. The Red and Whites missed chances in the early stages and were made to pay when Jason Smith put the visitors in front after 29 minutes.

They held the lead until half-time. John Bathgate equalised for Rothbury in the 61st minute but goals from Gary Scott and a second from Smith put the visitors 3-1 in front. Sub John Laidler got a second for Rothbury after 89 minutes.

They crashed out of the Bilclough Cup 8-2 on aggregate with a 3-1 defeat at Springhill. With both clubs struggling to raise a team 16 year old David Shell on his debut put Springhill in front after two minutes and it was 2-0 in the 15th minute when a good move through the middle saw David Stitt score. Good work from Nicky Wilson and Ian Hossack gave Taffy Veean the chance to make it 3-0 but just before half time John Bathgate scored for Rothbury to make it 3-1.

Rothbury recovered and Coquet rivals Amble United Reserves were put to the sword at Armstrong Park. Two goals from John Bathgate in the 19th and 25th minutes plus a 32nd minute goal from Paul Arkle put Rothbury in front before Tim Mallen pulled a goal back for the visitors after 42 minutes. Ian Armstrong made it 4-1 in the 72nd minute and Paul White netted a second for Amble after 86 minutes to make the final score 4-2 to Rothbury.

And a point was picked up away to Bedlington Terriers Reserves where neither team could manage a goal in a dour struggle played on a heavy ground. Bedlington had the majority of the chances with Rothbury's best efforts coming in the last five minutes. Lee Williams was man of the match for Bedlington with goalkeeper Lee Straughan pulling off some good saves to take the award for Rothbury.

But the club were then hammered 8-0 away to Red Row Welfare in the league. On a heavy pitch Red Row attacked from the start and took a fifth minute lead after Stu Marshall went one on one with the keeper. He got a second after 15 minutes following a move involving Shanks and K Flanaghan and just before half-time he completed his hat-trick when he got onto a through ball from Pringle.

Five minutes into the second half he got a fourth and went on to net another to make it 5-0. Red Row made three changes and added three more goals from subs David Mavin (2) and Rizard Oszinski. Lee Straughan had a busy game in goal for Rothbury while at the other end Mark Summers had little to do.

And top side Lowick piled on the misery with a 5-0 thumping. Lowick went in front after 35 minutes after an Andrew Robertson cross had been spilled by the keeper.

The attempted clearance rebounded into the Rothbury net and gave the home side the lead at half-time. Five minutes into the second half Robertson got a second when the keeper couldn't hold his shot and five minutes later a Stuart Payne cross was headed home by Craig Dixon for the third.

Mid-way through the second half Anthony Murray won the ball in his own defence, beat two players played a one two with Mark Murray and ran through to shoot home from 20 yards. The scoring was completed on 80 minutes when a Stuart Payne cross was headed home from close range by Steven Ramsey.

The relegation trapdoor was looming when Spittal Rovers A trounced Rothbury 4-1 at Armstrong Park.

After 11 minutes Cromarty gave Spittal the lead following a free-kick just outside the area and he doubled the lead from the penalty spot after 33 minutes.

John Bathgate netted just after half-time to pull a goal back for Rothbury but Cromarty completed his hat-trick with another free-kick after 56 minutes. Craig Smith scored a fourth the visitors in the 89th minute to seal the win.

But Rothbury showed fighting spirit and fought back to secure a stunning 6-2 away win at Springhill. The game was even during the opening period but after 25 minutes a Jimmy Moffatt cross saw Ian Armstrong give Rothbury the lead and five minutes before half-time John Bathgate doubled it.

In the second half Ian Armstrong made it 0-3 before an Ian Hossack through ball saw Stephen Dixon pull a goal back for Springhill. Straight from the restart Jimmy Moffat made it 1-4. A push in the area saw Ian Hossack make it 2-4 from the penalty spot but tough-tackling midfielder Ian Armstrong completed his hat-trick and John Bathgate got a second to complete the scoring for Rothbury.

A 4-1 thumping at Alnmouth underlined the team's frailties as a Brian Straughan header gave Alnmouth a fifth minute lead but Rothbury levelled through Martin Roberts after a goalmouth scramble following Kevin Coe's throw in. Former Northern League Alnwick Town striker Darren Coxford put Alnmouth back in front before half-time with a looping header over the keeper and he got a second following a Shaun Baston cross. After 75 minutes another ex-Alnwick player Craig Pentleton sent David McCann through to net from 15 yards to finish the scoring.

And Rothbury were as good as down when they put up a fight but crashed 3-2 at Craster Rovers. During the first half Gordon Saunders made a good save from John Bathgate and in the 43rd minute David Hogg curled the ball into the net from the edge of the area to give Craster a half-time lead.

In the second half Hogg was tripped in the area but stayed on his feet, referee Colin Bland waved play on, Hogg beat two defenders and scored his second goal. Alan McFaul then played a ball over the Rothbury defence and saw Andrew Hogg run onto to score with his first touch after coming on as sub.

Fifteen seconds earlier Rothbury pulled a goal back when John Bathgate was allowed to run through and net and he got his second from the penalty spot after 82 minutes when a harmless looking cross was handled in the area by Andrew Forster.

Rothbury crashed out of the NNFL top flight for the first time and looked to rebuild by signing a number of youngsters during the summer, including promising 15-year old hit-man Jackie Angus.

Rothbury had a very successful team in the Morpeth Sunday League during the late 80s and early 90s. Here skipper Mark Bruce receives a set of new shirts from Peter Reed of the Newcastle House Hotel in 1988.

2002/03

Honours: Division Two Champions.

FORMER SKIPPER Gordon MacKenzie took the managerial reigns and Rothbury went unbeaten in the League all season to ensure a swift return to the top flight. Rothbury were proving too strong for the Second Division and continued their great start with a 2-0 win at Shilbottle CW. Play was fairly even for the first 20 minutes until Rothbury took the lead following a defensive error. Shilbottle keeper Brian Brooks failed to gather the ball clearly allowing Doug Braithwaite to stab the ball home from close range to put the visitors in front.

Worse was to follow for the Colliers five minutes later when Mark Henderson slipped up whilst attempting to clear from the edge of the box allowing Stuart Foreman to win the ball and round the keeper to put Rothbury two up.

Shilbottle hit back strongly following this setback with Martin Mallaburn missing a good chance from close in and Johnny Mallaburn putting a good attempt just over the bar.

Just before the break Karl Chapman almost pulled a goal back for the Colliers as he rounded the Rothbury keeper only for this effort to be cleared off the line.

Winger Stuart Foreman was back at the club after a year out of the game recovering from a broken leg suffered to a horror tackle from a Wooler defender while playing for Wallington as the Glendale side went on to the NFA Minor Cup Final in 2001. Foreman embarked on a trademark solo run to give Rothbury a 17th minute lead against Shilbottle in the home return fixture. With 30 minutes gone Les Cairns equalised for the Colliers but two minutes later Jimmy Moffat scored to see Rothbury in front at half-time.

Fifteen-year-old striker Jackie Angus headed home from a Paul Arkle cross to make it 3-1, but in the final minute James

Mackay scored for Shilbottle to make the final score 3-2 in a game which Rothbury were the better team in the first half and the visitors in the second.

While the club was romping through the Second Division, they were brought crashing back to earth with a 8-2 home thumping at the hands of Alnmouth in the Second Round of the Bilclough Cup.

Strikes from Ben Keenan, Alan Wallace and Martin Pringle saw Alnmouth in front at half-time. Mick Chilton made 0-4 before Doug Braithwaite pulled a goal back for Rothbury. Martin Pringle added two further goals to complete his hat-trick and Dean Edwards netted to make it 1-7 and although Stuart Foreman pulled a goal back it was veteran hit-man Albert Straughan who scored the eighth goal five minutes from time to complete the scoring.

Shilbottle gained revenge for their league defeats at the hands of Rothbury to dump them from the Runciman Cup after extra time at the first hurdle. The Colliers took a 15th minute lead when an attempted clearance rebounded off a defender into his own net and although there were further chances the score remained the same at half-time. After the break Shilbottle had a lot of the play and in the 80th minute Scott McMullen missed a good chance to double the lead when he was clean through but his shot came back off the bar.

Rothbury broke and Jackie Angus scored to see the game level. In the last minute Jamie McKay had a good chance to win the game but Rothbury keeper Keith Appleby pulled off a good save to see the team's level at the end of normal time. Scott McMullen again broke and this time he netted what turned out to be the winning goal for the home team.

But Rothbury went to the semi-finals of the Robson Cup with a string of good results.

Berwick Rangers A were thumped 5-1 up at Shielfield as Jackie Angus gave Rothbury a second minute lead but Paul Hastie netted after 13 minutes to level for Berwick. Goalkeeper Keith Appleby restored the visitors lead from the penalty spot just before half time to put Rothbury in front. During the second half goals from Neil Johnson with a 25-yard effort, Paul Arkle and Martin Roberts sealed the win for Rothbury. The score-line could have been greater but the visitors had two goals disallowed and keeper Appleby missed from another penalty. The game was competitive throughout with Rothbury making the most of the chances created.

Stobswood Welfare Res were beaten 3-1 in the same competition in a good end to end game. Stuart Foreman gave Rothbury a fifth minute lead but David King levelled in the 10th minute. Chances were at a premium but in the 45th minute Stuart Foreman got his second to give Rothbury the lead.

Neither team could make any headway during the second half until an 85th minute goal from Paul Arkle sealed the win.

Rothbury continued their unbeaten run in the league with a 6-0 win at Berwick Rangers A with Paul Arkle giving Rothbury a first half lead and then striking again to double the advantage at the start of the second half. A Stuart Foreman hit-trick in the space of 20 minutes signalled that the winger was back in top form and an own goal from David Roscesky completed the scoring in a game where the home side applied plenty of pressure but just couldn't find the net.

The Wee 'Gers youngsters were trounced 3-1 in the return fixture but took a 12th minute lead when Andrew Gibson netted just before half time. Stephen Sparrow levelled for Rothbury. During the second half, goals in the 52nd and 54th minutes saw Sparrow complete his hat-trick and the scoring as Rothbury continued their unbeaten league run in a hard fought game.

The poor cup form continued with Rothbury again going out to Shilbottle after extra time in the NNFL Lancaster Laidler Cup. Shilbottle just squeezed through to the semi-finals of the competition with victory in a tight encounter at an immaculate

Armstrong Park. Play was very even early on with defences on top and few chances being created.

The Colliers went close with a Johnny Mallaburn free kick that was just off target and Martin Mallaburn should have put them ahead shortly after when he shot wide with a good chance. On the hour a snap shot from Les Cairns flew just wide while Rothbury had a couple of chances that were comfortably dealt with by Brian Brooks in the Shilbottle goal. It was no surprise when the match went into extra time and with penalties looming, the Colliers finally broke the deadlock. A ball into the box was controlled by Martin Mallaburn who played in Les Cairns to stab the ball past Keith Appleby in the Rothbury goal from close range. The Colliers comfortably played out time to record a fine victory against the runaway league leaders.

The Championship was secured when a long range free kick from Philip Arkle gave Rothbury a fifth minute lead at Springhill. On ten minutes the referee was injured and unable to continue. Later in the half a defensive mistake saw Stuart Foreman double Rothbury's lead. During the second half the young Springhill side came more into the game but Rothbury held on for the win and secured the silverware to bounce back into Division One at the first attempt.

But Rothbury just could not overcome their Shilbottle Cup hoodoo and were beaten in the semi-final of the Robson Cup as a superb hat-trick from young Scott McMullen fired the Colliers into the final with a tremendous victory over the Division Two Champions at Armstrong Park.

Shilbottle were quickly into their stride and took the lead after ten minutes when a scorching 30 yard volley from McMullen flew into the top corner of the net giving Keith Appleby in the Rothbury goal no chance. Rothbury hit back and almost drew level when a free kick from Stuart Foreman hit a post and they then allowed another good chance to slip away. The Colliers should have been two up when Wayne Gair put a free header wide of the post but did produce a second goal on 35 minutes. Rothbury conceded a free kick on the edge of their box and Scott McMullen put a brilliant strike over the wall and into the same top corner as his earlier goal.

Shilbottle effectively settled the tie on 55 minutes with another fine goal. Good interplay between Paul Lock and Les Cairns saw Karl Chapman released wide on the left and his pinpoint cross was struck home from ten yards by McMullen. It was the third occasion during the season that Shilbottle had beaten Rothbury in Cup competitions despite Coquetdalers' 100 per cent record in securing the Division Two Championship.

Rothbury's Kevin Coe and John Smith were on the scoresheet late on in a win over Embleton WR and they then beat Springhill 3-1 with the Berwick side's Gavin Bain cancelling out Martin Roberts opener. Rothbury missed a penalty before John Laidler scored twice. The red and whites completed their Division Two season unbeaten with a mid-week win over Stobswood Reserves, who finished as runners-up. Every member of the team scored during the season – including keeper Keith Appleby.

2003/04

Rothbury's return to the top flight saw Ian Richardson net the winner at home against fellow promoted side Stobswood Reserves at Armstrong Park but the going was tough and two goals from Neil McFarlane plus one each from Neil Jefferson, Paul Gough, Phil Duncan, Alan McFarlane and sub Darren Thompson saw Belford thrash Rothbury, with Ian Richardson again on target, netting a consolation in the 7-1 thumping.

Red Row then moved up to joint second in the Division when a hat-trick from Stuart Marshall, two from Shaun Black and one from Andrew Taylor saw Rothbury crash to another heavy defeat.

Only five clubs from the North Northumberland league progressed into the second round of the Northumberland FA Minor Cup, a goal from cultured centre-half Kevin Coe not enough for Rothbury at home to Blyth South Beach as they went down to a shock 2-1 defeat at Armstrong Park.

Amble took over at the top of Division One as five goals from Paul White, a hat-trick from Andrew Patterson and a Darren Riddell goal saw them overrun Rothbury with a thumping 9-0 win at Armstrong Park as the club continued to struggle to regain the form that had won them the Second Division so convincingly.

The poor run continued when a Richard Brown cross was slid home by Stephen Watson to give Craster a tenth minute lead in a 3-1 defeat at the coast. It was doubled five minutes later when Watson played in Barry Armstrong whose powerful shot went in via the goalkeeper. After 30 minutes Craster got a third when Adam Durham set up Armstrong for a half volley that gave the keeper no chance and although there were further chances for Willy Curry, Richard Brown and Barry Armstrong, Craster couldn't increase their advantage. During the second half Rothbury came more into the game and pulled a goal back when John Laidler prodded home from a free kick following a good save from keeper Kevin Carr.

Rothbury got back to winning ways with a 5-0 drubbing of Wooler at Armstrong Park. Rothbury included veterans Paul Appleby and Gordon McKenzie but it was 16-year-old John Angus who took the honours with a first half hat-trick to see the home team lead at half time.

Rothbury had the better of the play but it was the 85th minute before John Laidler added a fourth and in the 88th minute Angus grabbed his fourth to round off the scoring.

But the joy of the win was short lived as Craster won 4-0 at Armstrong Park in the first round first leg of the Anderson Cup. In an even first half the only goal came after 27 minutes when a mix-up in the Rothbury defence allowed Barry Armstrong to run through and net and give Craster the advantage. During the second half Craster were playing the ball long and causing Rothbury's defence all sorts of problems. Two goals from Richard Brown in the 56th and 87th minutes plus a Michael Watson effort in the 60th minute gave Craster an insurmountable advantage for the second leg.

Skilful young striker John Angus was back on the goal trail and he put Rothbury ahead at home to Spittal A but a second half goal from Simon Laidlaw saw the points shared.

And struggling Wooler had Jamie Jeffries on target twice as a much improved performance saw them take a point against Rothbury, who had John Angus and Michael Atkin on the score sheet in the run up to Christmas.

The club recovered in the New Year and moved up the table with a good 3-1 home win over Belford. Darren Arkle, Stuart Foreman and Michael Atkin were all on target, with Ross Thompson replying.

But bogey side Craster Rovers brought Rothbury crashing back down as two Richard Brown goals saw them lead at half-time against the red and whites, who scored through Neil Johnson. In the second half, pint-sized hit-man Michael Tall levelled but Barry Armstrong netted the winner for Craster 20 minutes from time.

There was more heartache as a James Jeffrey goal saw Wooler send Rothbury tumbling out in the Sanderson Cup. And league leaders Lowick piled on the misery as two each from Mark Murray and Mark Lockhart saw them beat Rothbury 4-0.

Rothbury, however, progressed in the Bilclough Cup as goals from John Angus and a late winner from Kevin Coe saw off the challenge of Belford, who had Darren Thompson on target.

And Amble United missed a chance to close the gap at the top of Division One when a Brad Wake goal was cancelled out by John Laidler to earn Rothbury a brilliant point at the Welfare Ground that virtually killed off the Seasiders title challenge and handed the League silverware - and promotion into the Northern Alliance Second Division - to Lowick.

For all the League disappointments in the club's return to Division One, Michael Atkin gave Rothbury a first half lead from the penalty spot and he grabbed a second just before half-time to beat Red Row 2-0 and fire Rothbury into the Bilclough Cup final against Amble United. The Seasiders exacted revenge for Rothbury shattering their Championship ambitions with a 2-0 win to take the trophy.

2004/05
Honours: Sanderson Cup winners.

TITLE FAVOURITES Red Row Welfare got their campaign off to a great start with a 4-0 win over Rothbury in windy conditions and on a hard ground. A forgettable first half was littered with mistakes and neither side created many chances. But with stern words spoken at half time, Red Row started the second half strongly and gradually outplayed Rothbury in every department.

The goals started in the 55th minute when Stu Dunn fired home a free kick and five minutes later a good cross from Scott Fulton was duly despatched by Mark Waddell for a second goal.

Wayne Simpson and Ronnie Warwick combined for the latter to net well from ten yards and Waddell added a fourth near the end of the game to complete the scoring.

Best for Red Row was Scott Fulton with Keith Appleby and Stephen Wood best for Rothbury.

The red and whites got back on track with a 3-0 win at Wooler. Rothbury started well and created and missed some good chances during a goalless first half. After 50 minutes Ian Smith gave Rothbury the lead and as they dominated the game Darren Arkle, who had returned from Northern Alliance Wallington during the summer, headed home a second. Smith grabbed a third towards the end to ensure the victory.

Rothbury battled their way to the top of the table but were brought crashing back down with a heavy 6-1 loss at Shilbottle CW. The Colliers recorded their first win of the season as a bright start saw Shilbottle take the lead after only ten minutes when a shot from Richard Brown was parried by Keith Appleby in the Rothbury goal for Ross Jackson to follow up and shoot into an empty net.

The Colliers struck again after 25 minutes when Shaun McKay headed in from a left wing corner.

Jamie Black should have put Shilbottle further ahead when he shot over the bar from a good position and the home side were made to pay when slackness in defence allowed Rothbury to pull a goal back on 40 minutes from Ian Smith.

However, Black atoned for his earlier miss by reinstating his side's two-goal advantage with a strike from close range just before the interval.

The game was settled shortly after the restart when the Colliers hit two further goals within a minute. A shot from Scott McMullen from the edge of the box managed to sneak into the net at the keeper's near post and, almost from the restart, Richard Brown broke clear to round the keeper to score the Colliers' fifth.

A further goal from Jamie Black after 75 minutes left the visitors a demoralised and well-beaten side.

Red Row Welfare overtook Rothbury at the top of the table but were stunned on a visit to Armstrong Park. The Coquetdale men were five points adrift and needed a win to stay in touch at the top.

They settled into the game immediately and duly took a fourth- minute lead when Stuart Foreman cracked in a superb left-foot strike after a mazy run had seen him evade three challenges.

Sensing their opponents' defensive frailties, Rothbury continued to press forward and were rewarded with a second after eight minutes following excellent work from Tom McPherson.

The defender intercepted a dangerous ball before striding forward and threading a perfect pass to Ian Smith who skipped around the goalkeeper and slotted the ball home from a tight angle.

The home side began to see more of the ball with Gutherson and Smith causing problems down the left. However, the score remained 2-0 at the interval.

With the league leaders realising their unbeaten record was under threat, they began to press forward in an attempt to get back into the match.

This was proving a fruitless task, with the home side's back four and keeper repelling everything.

However, Red Row were gifted a lifeline on 58 minutes when the referee awarded a dubious spot kick which was calmly converted by Warwick. The goal rocked the home side for a time as Red Row pushed for an equaliser.

Rothbury brought on Northern Alliance hot-shot Stephen Gibbard in an effort to regain their foothold on the game and in an amazing few minutes he did just that as he won a penalty with his first touch and slotted it away with his second.

Three minutes later he put the game well and truly beyond Red Row as he struck a perfectly flighted free kick into the top corner after Foreman had been brought down.

Two minutes after Gibbard's heroics, Rothbury added a fifth when Kevin Coe's free kick was expertly headed in by Darren Arkle.

There was still time for both sides to hit the woodwork as well as for goalkeeper Appleby to once again make a fine save for the home side.

Rothbury, however, were worthy winners after producing what manger Gordon MacKenzie described as being 'the best Rothbury performance for years.'

The good form continued with a 2-0 win at Spittal Rovers A to keep the club in contention at the top.

In an even first half with plenty of chances but none taken the teams were goalless at the interval. Five minutes into the second half a Chris Wood cross was netted by Michael Atkins to put Rothbury ahead and after 75 minutes, with Rothbury pressing, a Darren Arkle cross was only partly cleared by Scott Middlemiss and Ian Smith shot home to double the lead. Spittal created a few chances but had nothing to show for their efforts at the final whistle.

Rothbury gained revenge on Shilbottle CW for their Cup defeats the previous season when the advanced in the NNFL Bilclough Cup First Round with a 1-0 win.

Shilbottle paid the price for a host of missed chances as they went down by the only goal at the Welfare Ground. For Rothbury, however, the away win continued an excellent recent run of form.

The Colliers opened brightly and should have taken the lead when Ross Jackson managed to force a good cross over the bar from close range.

A fine effort from Richard Brown was well saved by Keith Appleby in the Rothbury goal and shortly after further good play from Brown was again thwarted by the Rothbury keeper.

At the other end, Shilbottle keeper Brian Brooks did well to turn a Darren Arkle free kick over the bar.

The interval arrived with the visitors having created very little but still in the game following a first half without a goal.

The visitors found their feet after the interval, passing the ball with much more confidence.

Rothbury missed a good opportunity to take the lead shortly after the restart but the effort went well wide of the target.

The Colliers again missed a good chance to take the initiative on the hour but Andy Metcalf side footed wide with the Rothbury keeper stranded.

It was Rothbury who finally broke the deadlock on 65 minutes when a short corner found its way to Darren Arkle, who in turn fed Chris Wood 20 yards from goal. He produced a fine strike from the edge of the box that found the top corner.

Play became scrappy as the game wore on, with Rothbury content to hold on to their lead and Shilbottle lacking the ability to break them down.

JCB Eindhoven were thrashed 7-1 at Armstrong Park in the First Round of the Northumberland FA Minor Cup and Belford were then taken apart in a 3-0 win that saw Rothbury cruise into the semi-final of the Sanderson Cup with a workmanlike display. The home side flew out of the blocks and when a corner was flicked on by the excellent Tom McPherson, Kevin Coe volleyed the ball into the top corner to give Rothbury a second-minute lead. Instead of building on their lead, the hosts appeared content to sit on their comfortable position. On the half hour, Coe thought he had doubled his tally when a far post header flew in only to see it ruled out for pushing, despite no protests from the Belford players.

Rothbury added two more in the second half to progress.

And Belford were again on the receiving end in the league at Armstrong Park as Rothbury recorded their sixth successive victory with another hard-working performance.

Rothbury opened the scoring as early as the first minute when a Graham Swivell free kick was headed in well by Darren Arkle. The perfect start gave Rothbury lots of confidence as they played good passing football against a physical Belford side.

Rothbury extended their lead on 19 minutes when a good move down the right saw the tricky Stuart Foreman beat two men and drill an excellent shot across the keeper and into the corner.

Instead of kicking on from their advantage, the home side allowed Belford back into the game as careless errors boosted the away team's hopes. Only excellent defending by Tom McPherson maintained the two-goal cushion as Belford began to see lots of the ball.

Just after the half hour Belford pulled a goal back after a long-range effort cannoned back off the bar and was headed in from close range by Ross Thompson.

The half time whistle was welcomed by Rothbury as they regrouped with Belford in the ascendancy.

An injury to Rothbury keeper Keith Appleby forced a change with Michael Gutherson taking the gloves and handling very well.

The home team soon rediscovered their passing game and made several good chances, which were thwarted by Belford's keeper making a fine save from Stuart Foreman.

The clinching goal finally arrived with three minutes to play when Kevin Coe played a marvellous ball through to Michael Atkin, who calmly slotted home to secure the points for the home side.

The run continued with a 5-1 home drubbing of Wooler that saw Rothbury play well and go ahead after seven minutes with a goal from 16-year-old debutant Stuart Kidd. Further goals from John Angus, after nine minutes, and Darren Arkle, after 30 minutes, put them in control at half time.

Ten minutes into the second half a powerful header from Kevin Coe added a fourth and inside the last five minutes Gary Scott netted a consolation goal from the penalty spot and sub Stuart Foreman netted a fifth for Rothbury.

But it came to an abrupt end at Berwick Harrow as Rothbury were beaten 4-2. A ball over the defence saw Aaron Punton run through and give Harrow the lead. On 15 minutes he turned provider when his pass saw Stuart Bloomfield add a second from the edge of the area.

Michael Atkin pulled a goal back for Rothbury from the penalty spot but the Harrow still led at half time. A Les Short through ball saw Punton run through, beat two defenders and net his second and on 65 minutes a quickly-taken free kick saw Jonathan Brown score a fourth for the Harrow. With a minute to go, Tom MacPherson ran through to net a second for Rothbury.

Worse was to follow with a heavy defeat and shocking performance at Amble United but Rothbury were intent on big improvements and three important points. Whilst they did achieve the latter, the performance was still short of their best in a 2-1 win over Craster. After just 11 minutes Rothbury took the lead. Winning the ball in midfield, Chris Wood played in Michael Atkin whose shot was saved, but as the ball spun up in the air Ian Smith acrobatically volleyed in for a superb goal. Just before the interval, Craster's goalkeeper produced the save of the match as he somehow diverted a tremendous 25-yarder from Wood. The second period began with the home side creating several good chances but wayward finishing kept the away side in the game. Craster began to come more into the game and centre-back Darren Arkle was working overtime for Rothbury to keep them at bay. But Ian Smith scored following good work from substitute Jackie Angus. The goal should have seen Rothbury close the game out, but instead they made hard work of it as David Punton cashed in following a slip in the home defence and put Craster back in the game. After Rothbury were denied a certain penalty kick, nerves began to fray and Craster pushed forward. However, the Rothbury back four and goalkeeper Appleby saw that Craster left pointless and the home side won.

Trailing 2-0 from the first leg, Rothbury then went out of the Anderson Cup at the Quarter Final stage with a 2-2 home draw with Amble United. The opening exchanges were cagey with neither side wanting to give anything away. Brad Wake, Amble's best player throughout, was creating problems for the home side with his clever runs and accurate passing. He came the closest to scoring for the Seasiders with a 20-yard effort that Keith Appleby did well to save. Rothbury were more than matching Amble at this point and Stuart Foreman and Stephen Wood were giving the defence plenty to contend with. After a flurry of corners Rothbury grabbed a vital first goal to half the deficit in the tie. Foreman curled in a free kick which was headed home expertly by Kevin Coe on 33 minutes. The goal gave Rothbury fresh impetus and they pressed forward looking to level the tie. With virtually the last kick of the first half Stuart Foreman had a superb effort ruled out for an apparent handball which the Amble linesman spotted. Amble began the second half brightly with Darren Riddell going close, but in general their forwards were devoid of ideas.

Rothbury travelled to a very foggy Foulden for the Bilclough Cup quarter-final against Second Division Farne FC - and with the home side packed with Portuguese factory workers, it had more of the flavour of a European tie.

Farne had strong, pacey front man Bruno Di Silva leading the line and he shocked Rothbury by hitting an early double that was enthusiastically celebrated by his team-mates, the entire team running to the corner flag and mobbing the hit-man. Stuart Foreman bent in a free kick to pull one back but Farne were leading 3-1 with just twenty minutes to play. Rothbury salvaged the game with goals from Tom MacPherson, a second for Foreman, Michael Atkin and an unfortunate own goal from a dangerous Paul Arkle centre.

Di Silva's goal scoring exploits in the NNFL Division Two saw him put pen to paper at Berwick Rangers in the summer with outstanding young Rothbury centre half MacPherson also signing for the Borderers Under19 squad during the break to become the first player from the club to sign for a League team.

But Rothbury went out to a single goal defeat to Amble United in the competition semi-final with an early Paul White goal enough to take Amble through.

Rothbury were left to rue a host of missed chances and slack marking from a corner as unmarked White poked the ball in from close range after only five minutes.

The goal rattled the home side and they almost equalised immediately as a Kevin Coe header flew inches over. Amble's keeper then produced heroics as he made three excellent saves in the space of ten minutes to deny Atkin as he palmed the ball to safety via the crossbar and then out for corners which Amble cleared and tried to use as a platform for a quick breakaway, with only their final passes halting their route to goal. The score remained 1-0 to the away side at the interval but the second period saw Rothbury again create chances at will.

First Smith saw an effort blocked by the keeper's legs before Paul Arkle volleyed inches wide following a mazy dribble.

Amble should have put the tie beyond doubt on the hour mark but a ball played across the six-yard box somehow eluded their forwards, and Rothbury breathed a collective sigh of relief as they endeavoured to grab a deserved equaliser. Michael Atkin then had an effort superbly blocked by Stephen White.

On 80 minutes Rothbury keeper Keith Appleby made a fine save from a Shaun Black penalty to keep his side in the cup.

Despite a late flurry of corners into the Amble box, their goalkeeper and defence stood firm to ensure their place in the final. Rothbury considered themselves very unfortunate to have gone out of the competition while Amble celebrated their final berth amidst considerable relief. Two fully committed teams ensured it was a vastly entertaining game involving lots of good football.

They enjoyed success in the Sanderson Cup semi-final as the Champagne was put on ice with a hard-fought 3-2 win against Craster.

It was the away side who began brightest as they showed a greater desire in the early stages. They duly took the lead on 20 minutes when a corner was nodded in by Alan Wallace.

The goal shook Rothbury and they hit Craster with a three-goal burst in 12 minutes.

The Fishermen got their revenge with a 4-2 win at the coast in the league. Ian Smith gave Rothbury a tenth-minute lead after he ran on to a through ball. After 30 minutes a cross was flicked home by Steve Barron to equalise for Craster. Two Brian Murray goals in the last five minutes of the half saw Craster ahead at half time. Rothbury were stronger after half time but Alan Wallace controlled the ball and set up Murray to complete his hattrick after 60 minutes. Rothbury pulled a goal back when a foul by keeper Towers saw Michael Atkin net from the penalty spot but Craster held on in the final 20 minutes to take the points.

And Rothbury ran out of steam as they went down 2-0 at Armstrong Park to Shilbottle in the final league game. It was the Colliers who were quickest out of the blocks and almost took the lead after a couple of minutes when a Ross Jackson header rebounded from the cross bar and the follow up was blocked on the line. Jamie Black then shot over the bar as Shilbottle continued to do most of the pressing without getting the vital breakthrough.

However, the first goal finally arrived just before the interval when a looping header from Scott McMullen crept in at the back post to give the Colliers a deserved lead at the break.

The second period was much more even although Rothbury rarely threatened to pull the goal back.

After Shilbottle's Scott McMullen had a further effort blocked on the line with the keeper beaten, the game was finally settled in the 83rd minute.

A fine crossfield pass allowed Mark Henderson to get to the bye-line and his pinpoint cross picked out Andy Metcalf to shoot home from close range.

Rothbury had a late effort ruled out for a foul on the Shilbottle keeper but this proved to be too little too late as the Colliers took the points.

In the Sanderson Cup Final Rothbury faced Berwick Harrow at St. James's Park, Alnwick and produced a fine, battling display to overcome the Division One Champions. Despite having only 12 men available, they were triumphant with a Michael Atkin double ensuring that Rothbury lifted the silverware for the eighth time.

However, the Harrow were immediately on the offensive as they confidently sprayed the ball around. Rothbury did well to keep chances for Berwick few and far between, restricting them to long-range efforts as centre backs Kevin Coe and Tom

McPherson stood their ground superbly. Against the run of play Rothbury crept ahead on 26 minutes when an excellent through ball from Foreman sent Atkin away. He held his nerve before side-stepping a defender and slotting home low inside the near post.

The goal gave Rothbury the confidence needed to mount more attacks as wingers Jackie Angus and Stuart Foreman began unsettling Berwick's back line.

After 39 minutes Kevin Coe spotted a good Atkin run and he duly played an excellent ball over the Harrow defence and Rothbury's number nine crashed the ball home.

On the stroke of half time Ian Armstrong almost made it three when his effort struck the bar before then crashing the rebound off the post.

The second half saw Berwick try to get themselves back into the game but tireless work from Armstrong and Chris Wood in midfield provided a valuable protection for Rothbury's defence.

When Berwick did break through, the Rothbury back line, along with keeper Keith Appleby, were outstanding. Appleby denied Simon Ruddick with a brilliant reflex stop with 20 minutes to play.

Berwick finally pulled a goal back when Punton tucked away a penalty with seven minutes remaining and despite increasing pressure, Rothbury never buckled and emerged worthy winners in an entertaining final.

The club finished third in the league on 27 points behind Red Row Welfare on 36 and victorious Harrow on 38.

2005/06

THE TALISMANIC Mark Bruce was back at Rothbury after many successful years in the Alliance with Wallington, including a Second Division Champions medal.

By his own admission, his knees were about gone and he was suffering back problems: but while most of the pace had left him, he had lost none of the old magic and retained his excellent first touch and control and the ability to turn defenders inside out with his electric skill and sharp football intelligence.

He was soon back on the goal trail for the Red and Whites, firing into the roof of the net in the 17th minute to give Rothbury the lead on the opening day of the season at home to Stobswood Welfare. Phil Tweddle equalised after 38 minutes to see the teams level at half time.

In the second half play was again close but a 64th minute goal from Kerry Shotton put Stobswood ahead and they survived a penalty appeal near the end to take the points.

Rothbury then went down 4-1 at Craster Rovers with Bruce again on target before a goal blitz saw them the leading scorers of the day in Division One as they netted 11 times against Wooler. Mark Bruce led the deluge with five goals, Luke Williamson netted twice and there were also goals from John Angus, Dean Upton, Graham Sivell and Andrew Stewart. Bruce missed a penalty to net his double hat-trick but rocketed to the top of the scoring charts. Wooler replied twice.

A good 3-2 win saw Rothbury progress away to Belford in the Sanderson Cup and they took revenge on Stobswood for their opening day league defeat with another 3-2 victory in the Anderson Cup.

In a good game Mark Bruce put Rothbury ahead after 23 minutes, but a Michael Hogg goal on 43 minutes saw the teams level at half-time. Bruce added his second after 48 minutes to restore the lead, but on 85 minutes David Curtis equalised. Rothbury grabbed the winner when Bruce completed his hat-trick in the 89th minute. The veteran striker also rattled the crossbar with a bending free kick during the game.

Rothbury produced an upset in the Northumberland FA Minor Cup when they sent Northern Alliance First Division side Wark tumbling out. The Tynedale side went in front with a header but Kevin Coe netted from the penalty spot to level. Wark missed a spot-kick before two late goals from Matthew Murray and young goalkeeper Henry Woodcock, playing as an emergency centre forward, saw them through 3-1.

The club was thumped 6-0 at Amble United before Berwick Harrow also hit Rothbury for six in the league when Darren Flanighan put Harrow ahead after four minutes and a thundering header from Martin Cornish doubled the lead after eight minutes.

Lee Lambert shot home from outside the area to add a third on 20 minutes. Although Aaron Punton hit the bar, there was no further score before half-time.

After half-time Aaron Punton netted twice with a penalty and a headed goal before Scott Pithe added a sixth for the Harrow.

During the half Ian Rutherford and Michael Sherry hit the Rothbury woodwork, while keeper Paul Watson had to be at his best to keep a clean sheet.

Bruce was back among the goals in a 3-2 win at home to North Sunderland in a close, even game that saw a sixth-minute goal from Stephen Rutter give North Sunderland the lead with a Bruce goal after 36 minutes seeing the teams level at half-time. After the break both teams created chances before David Spensley put Rothbury ahead on 54 minutes and Bruce netted this second on 58 minutes to extend the lead. In the 89th minute, Neil McFarlane pulled a goal back for North Sunderland.

Hopes were high in the NFA Minor Cup when Tyneside Amateur League Second Division side West Jesmond arrived at Armstrong Park for the fourth round, but Rothbury were left disappointed after the heroics of the previous round, crashing to a 4-1 defeat. They trailed at half-time to a 22nd-minute goal and went further behind when they conceded a 48th-minute penalty. Michael Gutherson pulled a goal back in the 73rd minute, but two goals in the last five minutes put the visitors through.

Alliance neighbours Wallington would embark on a fantastic run in the same competition - their best since finishing beaten finalists in 1976 as they went to the semi-finals.

Wallington were formed just a year after the Red and Whites in 1877 by workers on the Wallington Estate along with local farm labourers, and a succession of players had headed to Scots Gap to turn out for their old Coquetdale League rivals ever since.

Back in the NNFL Sanderson Cup Quarter Final Rothbury were made to sweat as they just squeezed through against struggling Wooler. The Glendale team started brightly and a foul on Aaron Scott saw Wooler awarded a penalty and Scott got up to net from the spot after 15 minutes.

Wooler dominated play but after 35 minutes a foul on Mark Bruce inside the area saw the same player hit the equaliser from the resultant penalty to keep up his challenge for the NNFL Golden Boot.

Rothbury were stronger after half-time and went ahead on 70 minutes when John Bathgate found himself one-on-one with keeper Chris Stanwix, who saved the original shot but Bathgate netted the rebound.

On 80 minutes, Wallington ace Stuart Foreman, signed on at both clubs and appearing as the Green's Northern Alliance fixture was postponed, netted a third for Rothbury but a Wooler goal from Steven Skeen after 85 minutes gave Rothbury a nervous last few minutes.

Keeper Keith Appleby saw red as Rothbury were again hammered at home by Harrow, who seemed to have the Indian sign on the Coquetdale side. Goals after nine, 20 and 30 minutes saw Harrow in front before hot-shot Bruce pulled a goal back for Rothbury after 32 minutes.

Harrow netted another before half-time and, although Rothbury rallied during the second half, two further goals after 60 and 87 minutes gave the Harrow the win and moved them to the top of Division One. Goal scorers for the Harrow were Stuart Bloomfield (two), Keith Ruddick, Michael Sherry, Scott Pithie and Jamie Stewart. Appleby was dismissed for a clash with a Harrow forward towards the end of the game.

But three valuable points were picked up at Wooler with a 5-2 win in a hard, physical game where Dickie Wilson put basement boys Wooler one up after 20 minutes.

Mark Bruce equalised five minutes later and Michael Atkin put Rothbury ahead on 38 minutes but a Rob Shepherd goal on 42 minutes saw the teams level at half-time.

Shaun Hogg restored the Rothbury lead on 48 minutes and then Mark Bruce missed a great chance to extend the lead when his penalty was well saved by keeper Chris Stanwix.

After 75 minutes Darren Arkle added a fourth for Rothbury and John Bathgate finished the scoring with a goal after 87 minutes.

Rothbury's defensive frailties were exposed once again as they conceded six up at North Sunderland, replying just once through John Bathgate as the club were left hanging perilously close to the drop zone, sitting third bottom above Craster Rovers by two points and rock-bottom Wooler by six. Shilbottle CW led the North Northumberland League for the first time in many years, and they displayed their title credentials with a 2-1 win over Champions Berwick Harrow.

But the Colliers were brought crashing back to earth when Jackie Angus, Darren Arkle and John Bathgate were on target to stun them with a 3-2 win at Armstrong Park the following week.

And Rothbury then thumped struggling Belford 6-2 away in the League as they pulled clear of the relegation danger. With Rothbury the stronger side, goals from Darren Arkle and Mark Bruce saw them ahead at half-time.

After the break, a second goal from Bruce and further strikes by John Angus, Michael Atkin and Stuart Foreman meant goals from Richard Turnbull and Walter Dunn were just a consolation.

But Rothbury then blew the chance of a Cup final appearance as they went of the Anderson Cup 3-2 on aggregate in the semi-final. After drawing 1-1 at home in the first leg they went down 2-1 at North Sunderland in the return fixture.

North Sunderland hit the woodwork after eight minutes from Gary Irving's free-kick. Rothbury had good possession but without threatening the home side's goal. Two minutes before half-time Dale Carr took a gamble from the right wing only to see his effort cleared off the line, with Steve Patterson first to react and tucking away the rebound.

The home side doubled their lead when veteran Rob Pearson scored from eight yards. Rothbury pulled a goal back through Dean Upton from a corner, but North Sunderland held on for the win.

Bad weather saw the next two games cancelled, and Wallington crashed out of the Minor Cup in the semi-final with a 4-1 defeat at Blyth Town reserves

Rothbury went out of the Bilclough Cup in the quarter-finals with a 4-2 defeat at Shilbottle. The Red and Whites hit the bar in the first half and took the lead when Kevin Coe tucked away a penalty after Mark Bruce had been brought down by the Colliers keeper. But promising young Rothbury stopper Henry Woodcock, who had been having trials with League Two side

Grimsby Town all week, saw four shots flash past his despairing dives before Coe added a second by cracking in a 20-yard free kick in the final minute.

Belford were hammered 6-3 at Armstrong Park with Rothbury moving seven points clear of the third -bottom visitors. Craster Rovers were second-bottom with 7 points and Wooler were locked in the basement with just three.

Darren Arkle struck twice, with Andrew Stewart, Craig Sutton and Chris Wood also hitting the net. Kevin Greshon plundered a hat-trick for the visitors.

And Rothbury moved into mid-table with a good 3-2 win at Stobswood Welfare the following week.

Stobswood pressed for most of the half and led at half-time through a 20th minute goal from Brad Wake. In the second half, a defensive error saw John Angus equalise after 52 minutes but two minutes later Stephen Sparrow headed home following a corner to restore Stobswood's lead. Craig Sutton slotted home from close range to equalise and, following another corner, Darren Arkle headed home the winning goal for Rothbury.

The red and whites gained revenge over Shilbottle for their Bilclough Cup defeat with a 3-1 win at Armstrong Park in the semi-final of the Sanderson Cup. Rothbury opened the scoring after 22 minutes when Jackie Angus latched onto a long ball down the middle to lob the Shilbottle keeper.

The Colliers hit back within a couple of minutes, when Andy Metcalf nipped in to get on the end of a long free-kick from Michael Saunders to level the scores. The home side went back in front shortly after the break when Angus again broke clear to shoot home from the edge of the box. Shaun Hogg settled the tie with a third goal in the final minute to send Rothbury into the final and the smiles continued as Rothbury moved into fourth spot in the league with a 5-3 win over struggling Craster Rovers at Armstrong Park.

But there was heartache in the Sanderson Cup as Rothbury were beaten on penalties at St. James's Park, Alnwick by North Sunderland, with keeper Kevin Carr rattling in the winner. In a dour game where chances were few and far between, Rothbury had the ball in the net but it was disallowed for offside and after two hours of football it was still 0-0. The penalty shoot-out went to sudden death where Carr became the Seahouses hero.

In the final game, Mark Bruce ended the season where he began it, finding the back of the net in a 5-1 defeat at home to Amble Vikings in the League.

World Cup winner Jack Charlton with Rothbury players Craig Speight and Richard Hooks opening an exhibition at Cragside in 2011.

S TUART FOREMAN netted with a clever free-kick but Rothbury were beaten 2-1 by champions Amble United in the Sanderson Cup final in 2006/07. They put that disappointment behind them a week later by lifting the Laidler Lancaster Cup in a 4-1 success over Hedgeley with Jackie Angus hitting a double and Craig Sutton and Matty Travis the others with Mark Bruce and Darren Arkle managing the side.

Sandra Foggon became the club's first female secretary when she took on the administrative work that goes hand-in-hand with running a local team, and Manager Anthony Sutton led the side to their first Championship silverware in twenty-five years as they pipped Lowick United to the title in 2009/10.

Burly Rothbury striker John 'Jackie' Angus slammed in 27 times to take the First Division Golden Boot as himself and strike partner Craig Sutton proved a real handful up top.

Boss Sutton had assembled a side with considerable experi-ence - Stuart Foreman, Tom MacPherson, Angus and Sutton all having played for Wallington in the Northern Alliance. He added a few of players from the Ashington area who had played for him as juniors at Bedlington, such as Alan Brown and Scott Rennison, who brought a bit of bite to the midfield and Rothbury enjoyed a fantastic start to the season as they kept winning game after game – including a top of the table clash with Shilbottle that saw Foreman rifle the only goal into the roof of the net at the near post four minutes into stoppage time, sparking scenes of wild celebration.

Rothbury opened the season with a 6-1 drubbing of Berwick Town with John Angus and Michael Old netting doubles while Shaun Hogg and Craig Sutton made up the Rothbury total. Hogg's goal was the pick of the bunch, cutting in from the right wing and firing left-footed into the top corner from 20 yards.

Jack Angus then struck four times as Rothbury followed this up with an 11-0 demolition of Bedlington Terriers reserves. Craig Sutton slammed in a hat-trick with Stuart Foreman, Alan Brown, Michael Ord and Scott Rennison adding the others and Angus grabbed another hat-trick with strikes from Tom MacPherson and Stuart Foreman taking the red and whites to a 5-2 win over Ashington Athletic.

Craig Sutton, Jackie Angus, Shaun Hogg, Stuart Foreman and Tom MacPherson shared the goals in a 5-2 win at Acklington Athletic and Rothbury were the width of the woodwork from dumping Northern Alliance side Newcastle Chemfica out of the NFA Minor Cup when Stuart Foreman's defence-splitting pass sent full back Richard Hooks clear, but his shot cannoned off the outside of the post and with neither side able to make the breakthrough after extra-time, Rothbury were unlucky to go out 4-3 on penalties.

Rothbury were in top form and slammed ten past Hedgeley Rovers without reply in the Bilclough Cup – Angus putting away four and Michael Old two. Craig Sutton and Shaun Hogg both got on the scoresheet before late goals from Foreman and MacPherson completed the rout.

Two late Jackie Angus goals salvaged a point in a crucial draw with title rivals Lowick United, who had raced into a 3-0 lead at Armstrong Park. Andrew Burgon and Carl Avery both scored before the break as they capitalised on mistakes in the home defence. It got worse when Burgon added his second in the 55th minute.

The dramatic comeback began soon after when Rennison fired home. Angus gave Rothbury hope in the 70th minute as he got it back to 3-2 and, with just ten minutes left, he hit his second to complete a remarkable turnaround in what would prove one of the key results of the season.

But the Coquetdalers were frozen out by unplayable pitches for six weeks over the Christmas period and could only watch on in frustration as Lowick opened up a four point gap at the top.

The sides were level again at the top by the end of January, Tom MacPherson and Stuart Foreman on target in an important win over Berwick Town, while an Andy Burgon goal was enough for Lowick at Bedlington.

In February, Angus gave Rothbury the lead against Alnwick Town reserves after 25 minutes and Alan Brown hit a goal of the season contender from fully 45-yards for number two. Alnwick pulled one back five minutes after the interval through Andrew Tait, but Rothbury held out for the win that moved them back to within a point of Lowick.

Rothbury's first defeats of the season both came in the semi-finals of the Cup competitions – in March - as they lost out at Ashington Athletic in a penalty shoot-out in the Sanderson and Alnwick Town in the Bilclough. They were also beaten by a controversial and hotly disputed penalty decision against Lowick in the last four of the Anderson.

Rothbury bounced back following their first defeat of the season on the 10th March – the penalty shoot-out at Ashington Athletic in the Sanderson Cup semis – to beat Shilbottle and make themselves the title favourites.

Shaun Hogg capitalised on a defensive blunder to give Rothbury a crucial lead in the 15th minute by tapping into the empty net but the Colliers levelled as sub Jordan Lowes crossed and Andy Metcalf nipped in front of keeper Henry Woodcock to poke in from close range. Shilbottle's Jonny Davis fired just over the bar and David Davidson curled a free kick just wide as they looked to turn the screw.

And when Rothbury were reduced to ten men by a red card in the 70th minute, it looked like they'd blown it. But very shortly after a poor clearance in the box saw Hogg bundle the ball over the line for his second goal. And Rothbury were in dreamland with ten minutes to go as Jackie Angus pounced to fire home a third. The Colliers hit back and were awarded a penalty for a trip in the box, but Woodcock pulled off a great save to keep out Metcalf's spot-kick. Shaun McKay did ram one in at the back post late on, but Rothbury held on for another three crucial points.

Ant Sutton's men followed this up with a 10-0 demolition of Berwick United reserves, with hit-man Angus putting away five, but fingernails were being gnawed as Rothbury were narrowly beaten 2-1 up at Lowick by Paul Murray's close range headed goal that crashed in off the underside of the bar past keeper Henry Woodcock. Shaun Hogg had headed a Foreman cross into the bottom corner to put Rothbury ahead but just five minutes later Lowick levelled when Anthony Murray flicked a header from a corner into the roof of the net. They bounced back to win three on the spin, beating Berwick United reserves 5-1, Ashington Athletic 2-1 and Berwick Town 2-0.

And in April the club went three points clear at the top of Division One as John Angus crashed in all four goals in a big win at Acklington Athletic, but Rothbury then went down 2-1 at Bedlington Terriers reserves in a bad-tempered game where a win would have virtually seen them crowned Champions. Jackie Angus was on target when he dinked over the keeper from Foreman's header, and although Craig Sutton rattled the bar soon after, Terriers levelled just before the break when an in-swinging corner was headed home and they grabbed the winner in the 75th minute.

Rothbury won their final fixture 1-0 at Alnwick Town reserves with an excellent counter attacking move 15 minutes from time. A ball over the top from Alan Brown was chased by Richard Hooks, who ran from within his own half to be through on goal. The Rothbury right back shot but the home side's keeper saved well only for the rebound to fall to Jackie Angus, who made no mistake and blasted the ball into the back of the net, sending the large travelling Rothbury crowd into raptures.

Lowick went into their final fixture needing a big win at Alnwick Town reserves during the midweek – and raced into a two-goal lead with Shaun Walton and Anthony Murray on target. United had to net seven times without reply to pinch the silverware on goal difference and while it seemed impossible, Rothbury had done it themselves when they'd last won the title, so it was with some trepidation that the players and officials who'd travelled to Alnwick to watch the game looked on helpless from the sidelines.

Lowick had thrashed an injury-depleted Shilbottle 6-1 in their previous game, when Rothbury had hoped the Colliers could do them a favour. But it was the youngsters of Alnwick – Rothbury's oldest football rivals – who fought back to draw 2-2 and hand the Coquetdale side the trophy, joining in with Rothbury's celebrations at the end. They'd done it. Rothbury were only beaten twice and drew one of their sixteen games to finish two points ahead of Lowick, scoring 62 goals and conceding 18. Lowick won 11 and only lost one, but drew five times with a scoring record of 52 for and 14 against.

The immensely talented captain Tom MacPherson went on to become a linchpin in the St. James's Park side's Northern League first eleven.

Pics courtesy Steven Bridgett.

Rothbury continued to bring on young players after the success with the likes of Craig Sutton, Dan Herron, Shaun Hogg, Michael Old, Gavin Dick and Ben Storey (all with Northern Alliance experience) becoming the central point of the team along with up-coming players such as Greg Woodburn, the Crane brothers, Sam Proudlock, Paul Appleby, Richard Hooks, Conner Smith and Brad Welch among others.

Rothbury were beaten by Tweedmouth Harrow in the Final of the Laidler Lancaster Cup at Shielfield Park, Berwick in season 2012/13 when Jackie Angus was controversially sent off early on for a handball.

Centre back Keith Oliver rose to head Rothbury in front at the back post from a free kick in the 35th minute but the Harrow levelled through Johnny Gill just five minutes later. Despite the numerical disadvantage, unlucky Rothbury held out and could have won the game in the final minute of normal time when

Mitchell Ramsay had a great chance and lobbed over the keeper but just cleared the bar. Michael Brown rifled in the winner in the first period of extra time with a shot from 25 yards.

Pic courtesy Daniel Crane

Diane Dick would take on the club's administration as Secretary and Rothbury enjoyed a good run in the NFA Minor Cup in 2014/15 before going out to Northern Alliance side Prudhoe YC in the fourth round. Rothbury celebrated lifting the Laidler Lancaster Cup in 2015/16 to hand managers Tony Dick and Graham Foggon their first silverware.

Youngster Thomas Hammond took just two minutes to get on the scoresheet in an exciting 4-3 win over Alnwick Town Reserves at St James's Park, Alnwick. Big, experienced striker Craig Sutton added a second but Alnwick replied through Colin Bickerton before half time. Mitchell Ramsay and the hugely promising young talent Chris Coe hit the back of the net to extend the Rothbury lead although two late goals from Jake Morrison made for a tense finish - and the Coquetdale football legacy left by the Aingers and their team-mates, now ghostly grey in old newsprint and photographs, continued; the studs sinking into the turf of a new season, the game going on.

Pic courtesy Jess Garrick

The Rothbury squad for the final was: Paul Appleby, Keith Oliver, Gavin Dick, Thomas Hammond, Lewis Reilly, Ben Storey, Ben Lamb, Ben Proudlock, Greg Woodburn, Dan Herron, Kyle Smith, Michael Old, Mitchell Ramsey, Craig Sutton, Gareth Jones and Chris Coe.

ALONG THE COQUET, Felton Football Club was formed in 1891 and were beaten 5-0 by Rothbury in their first season with F. Grieve, J. Clark, J. Mackay and R. Tait netting for the Hillmen. Felton joined the newly formed Coquetdale League along with Rothbury in 1902.

By 1911 they were in the North Northumberland and in 1912 they lifted the MacKenzie Cup and were the NNFL runners-up the following season. They joined the Coquetdale League after the Second World War and were the champions in 1946/47. The club had spells back in the North Northumberland after the Coquetdale became defunct in 1968.

At the mouth of the river, Warkworth Football Club was formed in 1888. Warkworth secured their first victory in a return match against Glanton in February 1889, winning 2-0, but the Glanton lads were a bit upset that two of the Warkworth team weren't 'natives.' A 4-1 defeat by Morpeth Harriers reserves followed soon after, but 'taking the Morpeth club's achievements into consideration, and remembering that the Warkworth Club is only its infancy, the performance was a creditable one' and by the December of 1889, the villagers had beaten Stobswood 1-0 away. An early team lined up: Common, Baston, Smiles, La Touche, Whiteford, Greenwell, Marriott, Laidler, Whinham, Green, Rowe.

Warkworth were also founder members of the Coquetdale League. By 1908 they were playing in the North Northumberland and despite turning up with just eight men at Wooler, only went down 1-0 in a match towards the end of 1907/08. After spells in and out of the League into the 1920s, were back in the North Northumberland in the 1950s.

The first Amble side appears in around 1887, playing against teams such as Broomhill and taking on North Seaton in the Smart Challenge Cup, which Rothbury also competed in. Amble soon established themselves as the premier team on the

Coquet, attracting a crowd of 1,000 at the port for a Minor Cup semi-final against Seghill in 1907.

Alnwick were the first association club formed in Northumberland in 1879, in premises in Narrowgate that was at one time the Temperance Hotel, by a Scotsman named Crammond who was working at Robertson's the cabinet makers, while Berwick Rangers were established in 1881. Longhorsley FC formed around 1912. In the mid-30s they were playing in the Morpeth & Wansbeck League with Wallington and both joined the Coquetdale after WW2.

The breakaway 'country clubs' that formed the Morpeth-based Northern Association in 1888 included Amble, Burradon, Bedlington East End, Horncliffe, Berwick Rangers, Tweedside Wanderers, Newsham, Backworth, Broomhill, Warkworth, Blyth, Seaside Rovers, Morpeth Athletic, Weetslade, Longhirst, Spittal, Belford, Stobswood, Seaton Burn and the big clubs Morpeth Harriers and Shankhouse Black Watch. Ashington joined the rebels following season, while Rothbury and Alnwick remained with the Northumberland. In January, 1889, the Northern put a representative team together to travel over the Border to play Motherwell and went down 5-0.

Redesdale neighbours Elsdon were playing a schoolboy's football game against Otterburn as early as 1869. After two hours it ended 1-1, the Otterburn lads being described as 'much superior in weight and size to their antagonists,' but this was before the association rules and Bellingham also had an early side playing the game.

The days of 'mob football' before the association game led to some trouble in Alnwick in 1850. The old men of the town described the Shrove game, which still takes place on the pastures today, as 'continuing the custom of our forefathers.'

When a policeman and the tenant of the pastures tried to stop the football game, they were hustled by the mob and pelted with sticks and sods of earth by young boys. As the tenant waded into the crowd, brandishing a stick to try and retrieve the ball, things turned ugly and he was clubbed to the ground, crying: "Murder!"

He was terrified of being thrown in the river and was carried home bleeding by his oldest son with the mob shouting offensive words and laughing when the policeman called for assistance 'in the Queen's name.'

After a threat to shoot the mob was made, the windows in the tenant's house were smashed and around fifty summons were issued in the aftermath.

The confusion over the starting date of Rothbury football club may stem from the fact that a match between Coquet and Rede was played in April 1876, at Horsley near Rochester. The Duke's piper, Mr. Green, played the teams onto the field and continued to strike up at times during the game for the large crowd that attended.

Redewater won the game 1-0, D. Hall being the scorer. John Robson, from Byrness, captain of the Rede team, played well for the hosts as did D. Hall, W. Haddon, R. Oliver, J. Telfer and A. Telfer while the Coquet's star performers were S. Charlton (captain), R. Carruthers, W. Little, J. Turnbull, M. Thompson and W. Mather.

With the goal being described as a 'touch down,' one can only assume that the game was an early and primitive one that mixed styles of both rugby and the kicking game, while the heavy thunderstorm that passed over during the match put a bit of a dampener on things. But it was from this first side that Rothbury have continued their long football tradition.

Long may it go on.

THE FIRST GAME

This part of the programme over, the Rothbury team, accompanied by a selected eleven representing the Coquetdale League marched on to the ground and played the first game of the season

Hardly had the sound of the whistle signalling the commencement of the game died away before Rothbury commenced to press, and, following a corner, R. Laidler scored the first goal on the new ground within three minutes. The Coquetdale League men retaliated and called upon the home defenders to put their best foot forward to clear their lines, but when the half-time whistle sounded Rothbury led by one goal to nil.

The second half was very evenly contested until 12 minutes from the end, when, receiving a long clearance from Barny Smith near the half-way line, Mills screwed his way through to beat Whittle a second time. The final score was two goals to nil in favour of Rothbury.

The Rothbury team was: Butters; Smith, Atkinson; J. Laidler, Carruthers, Ramsey; Aynsley, R. Laidler, Anderson, Mills and Winter.

The League team was: Whittle (Longframlington); R. Lee (Morpeth V.), F. Stamp (Wallington); Thompson (Longhirst), J. Learmonth (Longhirst), Kitchen (Felton); J. Richardson (Ashington W.E.), Dixon (St. George's), Davy (Thropton), J. Quinn (Meldon), Weddle (Widdrington).

LOVELY SURROUNDINGS

In opening the ground and naming it "Armstrong Park," after Lord Armstrong, Dr. Armstrong indicated that the Rothbury Football Club was singularly fortunate in having their ground placed amidst such lovely surroundings. It had many advantages, among which was the natural grandstand which almost surrounded the playing-pitch, while he congratulated those who had worked so hard since the curtain of last season fell so that everything would be in order for a new season.

Last season, the Rothbury team had won its first honour, and now everyone was looking forward full of anticipation to new triumphs, and he wished the club every success for the future.

Dr. Armstrong then unfurled a new flag of red and white — the club colours — bearing the words "Rothbury A.F.C."

Mr. James Glancy (president of the Northumberland F.A.), who was also present, congratulated the club and the supporters upon having a ground so admirably situated, and wished the teams every success for the future.

𝕳onours

North Northumberland Football League
Division One Champions 1935/36, 1937/38, 1974/75, 1976/77, 1984/85, 2009/10
Division Two Champions 1968/69, 2002/03
Anderson Cup Winners 1971/72, 1973/74, 1974/75, 1976/77, 1984/85, 1999/00
Sanderson Cup Winners 1972/73, 1974/75, 1975/76, 1976/77, 1985/86, 1987/88, 1991/92, 2004/05
Tate Cup Winners 1968/69
Bilclough Cup Winners 1985/86, 1991/92, 1998/99
Laidler Lancaster Cup Winners 2006/07, 2015/16
Ashington & District Subsidiary Cup **Winners** 1977/78
Coquetdale Challenge Cup **Winners** 1948/49

Rothbury FC in 2014/15 and below in 2011/12.   Pics by Steve Miller.

Then the Minor Cup Competition will be in full
swing, and Berwick Rangers will meet in the first
stage Broomhill Rovers. We are not aware of
anything exceptional in regard to the game the latter
give, and all round it is expected the home team will
have a sure win. The other ties bring out some good
teams—matches to be played on the ground of the
first-named club. The draw is:—

Amble received a bye.
Rothbury v. Cambois.
Berwick Rangers v. Broomhill Rovers.
Burradon Athletic v. East Cramlington Rovers.
Elswick Wesley v. Newburn Athletic B.
Westgate Athletic v. Newcastle Wednesday.
Heaton North End A v. Portland or Newcastle
    United.
Newburn Athletic A v Godfrey.
Hexham Excelsior v. Heaton North End B.
Walker Presbyerian v. Heaton Rovers.
Brighton v. Pelicans.
Newburn St. Michael's v. Wallsend North-Eastern.
Shade of Shielfield! We miss thee from the crowd.

1892. Rothbury in the Minor Cup draw – with Newcastle United and Berwick Rangers. The Borderers won the trophy that season/ George Best at Shielfield in 1980.

The Northumberland County side in 1897. The County's black and white stripes were eventually taken on by Newcastle United.

LONDON V. BIRMINGHAM.—The team to represent the Metropolis in this match at the Oval, on February 4, will be as follows: W. R. Moon (Old Westminsters), goal-keeper; A. M. Walters (Old Carthusians) and A. O. Davis (Swifts), backs; W. C. Bailey (Old Westminsters), C. Holden-White (Swifts), and F. E. Saunders (Swifts), half-backs; W. H. Ainger (Old Carthusians), A. C. Nixon (Casuals), E. C. Bambridge (Swifts), A. T. B. Dunn (Old Etonians), and F. M. Ingram (Swifts), forwards.

Walter Henry Ainger turning out for London in 1888. He also starred for the Metropolis against Oxford and Cambridge the following year. In 1887 he played against Preston North End for Old Carthusians in the FA Cup sixth round and in 1890 he was in a team that played against Wolverhampton Wanderers.

INTO THE NET

The goalmouth scene when W.J.J. Tait again scored the first goal for Ellington against Longframlington in the Coquetdale League Challenge Cup Final at Rothbury last Saturday. The cup was won by Ellington with a 3-0 win.

Captain G. Tait, president of the Coquetdale League, handing over the League Challenge Cup to Gott, the Ellington captain, after his team had defeated Longframlington at Rothbury last Saturday.

Coquetdale League Challenge Cup Final at Armstrong Park, 1950.

Woodburn, from neighbouring valley Redesdale, taking on Tynedale's Wall in the Hexham Hospital Cup Final at Hexham's ground in 1938.

Rothbury skipper Gordon MacKenzie receiving new strips from The Home Bakery in the early 1990s.

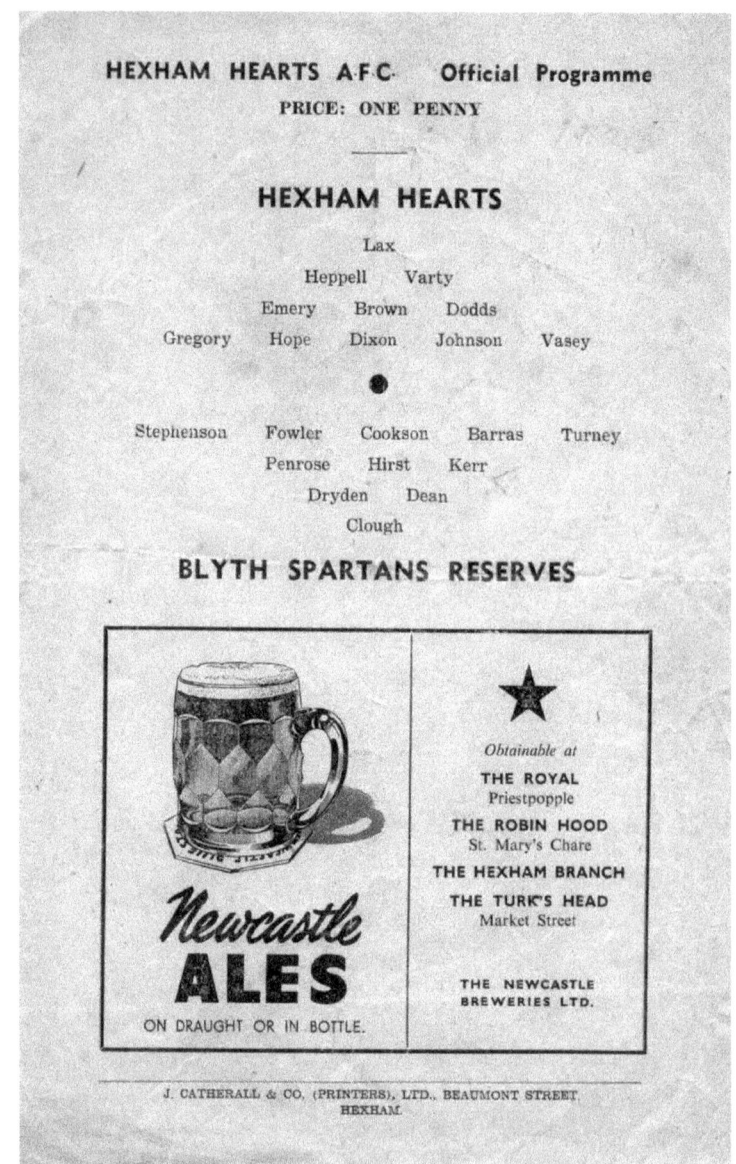

HEXHAM HEARTS A.F.C. **Official Programme**
PRICE: ONE PENNY

HEXHAM HEARTS

Lax

Heppell   Varty

Emery   Brown   Dodds

Gregory   Hope   Dixon   Johnson   Vasey

●

Stephenson   Fowler   Cookson   Barras   Turney

Penrose   Hirst   Kerr

Dryden   Dean

Clough

BLYTH SPARTANS RESERVES

Obtainable at
THE ROYAL
Priestpopple
THE ROBIN HOOD
St. Mary's Chare
THE HEXHAM BRANCH
THE TURK'S HEAD
Market Street

THE NEWCASTLE BREWERIES LTD.

Newcastle
ALES
ON DRAUGHT OR IN BOTTLE.

J. CATHERALL & CO. (PRINTERS), LTD., BEAUMONT STREET, HEXHAM.

Former Rothbury keeper Clough appearing at Hexham Hearts with Blyth Spartans Reserves in the 1950s. Hearts were one of Northumberland's top teams after WW2.

I N NORTH NORTHUMBERLAND, Wooler (Glendale) FC was formed in around 1883 and Belford started up three years later. Seahouses side North Sunderland were formed in 1890 and were very successful before the First World War, winning the MacKenzie Cup three years in succession.

Alnmouth United started up in 1901, though there were teams playing in Alnmouth from around 1897, and Craster Rovers began playing the same year. Embleton Whinstone Rovers formed around 1902.

Shilbottle, Rennington and Bamburgh were all other early sides to take up the Association game in the north of the county.

North Sunderland lifting the 1950 Sanderson Cup.

Craster were beaten finalists in the NFA Minor Cup Final in 1950. Other clubs pictured in action above include Hedgeley, Swarland, Hexham Hearts, Alnwick Town, Alndales and Alnwick Town A.

Richardson, the Alnwick Town right half, shot just outside the upright with this effort against Newbiggin C W. at St. James's Park, Alnwick, on Saturday. Other Alnwick players lying handy were Barrus (on the left) and Farrington.

OVER THE BORDER, Hearts of Liddesdale were formed in 1880 as Newcastleton Football Club. The Liddesdale teams were as often as not made up of the ancestors of the men that plundered Coquetdale during the times of the Border Troubles – the Armstrongs, Elliots, Scotts, Olivers and Davidsons.

One of the earliest ever recorded games of football took place at Bewcastle in Cumberland in May 1599 when a team of twelve of the Scots Armstrongs played a game against a dozen local English lads. When the English authorities heard about the game, they planned to take the notorious riders in a surprise attack.

The Armstrongs, however, had been tipped off about the ambush and when six of them went to the pub for a few ales afterwards they had two hundred of their mates waiting to pounce when the Warden went to spring the ambush.

William Ridley and Nicholas Welton had their throats cut, a Robson was also killed and a man named John Whitfield's guts spilled out after he was slashed in the belly. The Scots also took thirty prisoners.

Cheviot Rangers were a side from Yetholm who played in the Crookham and District League in the 1920s, reforming as Yetholm FC in 1938. Yetholm, like Rothbury, used to play a traditional Shrove game and it continues today in Duns and Jedburgh.

Hearts in action against Hawick United in 1927.

Clubs such as Jedforest, Rulewater, Hawick United, Kelso, Earlston Rhymers and Floors all had teams playing just the other side of the Cheviot hills at one time.

In 1790 Tynedale beat Redesdale 3-2 in a match played at Kielder Castle and Kielder played Liddesdale in a five-a-side game at Deadwater in 1904 with the North Tyne side lining up: R. Maxwell, J. Hedley, W. Hall, A. Robson and T. Morrow, the teams drawing 1-1 as the rivalry between the Dales was continued on a pitch well into the twentieth century.

While the Wardens and old Border laws couldn't tame the Liddesdale men for hundreds of years, football's bureaucracy finally strangled Hearts of Liddesdale in 2016 with the International Clearance Laws playing a big part.

With players registered in both the Carlisle Sunday League in England and with the Scottish club, they left the Border Amateur League and joined the Cumberland County League, but folded after a season.

Lightning Source UK Ltd.
Milton Keynes UK
UKHW021259120223
416889UK00020B/645